Contents

Internet Advertising: Links, Banners, Tiles, and More   181

Promotion and Advertising: On the Net and Off   215

Preface

Are you losing it?

Do you blink or look away, only to discover something has fallen just
a little more?

Is it slipping, silently, into places you do not know?

No, not your youth. We're talking about your reservations, client base,
orders, patrons list—your business.

Have you any doubt that the hospitality industry has come to rely on Internet marketing for a significant portion of its revenues? Don't. Sources estimate that 15 percent of those revenues will come from the Internet in 2004. That's *today*. This is serious stuff, and if you aren't part of it, you'll lose.

Hospitality businesses of all types and sizes are using Internet marketing to develop and retain business—to survive.

Why? Because they must. The guests and patrons of the world are demanding Internet information and interaction. Your guests and patrons are using the Internet to make decisions about lodging, eating, and gaming. Your job is to use all the resources at your disposal to become a competitive force on the Internet.

How? How do you build your Internet marketing arsenal? How do you ensure that your efforts will be effective? Begin here . . . with a plain language, step-by-step presentation of what you need.

Learn how to position your company, services, and goods on the Web and with your e-mail.

- Identify your Web audiences, their needs, priorities, preferences—so that you can communicate with them in meaningful ways.

- Decide what your Web site should do, what content it should have, and what it should look like—so that your Web audiences will find what they want and come back for more.
- Ensure that Web users will find you when they are looking for a business like yours.

Who? Who should bother with all this?

- Businesses that use marketing or advertising firms for their Internet marketing efforts and thus need to know what those firms should be doing for them.
- Executives and business owners who must make critical decisions about positioning their business in the marketplace.
- Marketing managers and others who are responsible for coordination and implementation of promotions, advertising, direct response marketing, client development, and other aspects of the marketing mix.
- Decision makers in national and regional chains and franchises that need to communicate a consistent and effective message to their audiences and potential audiences.
- Managers of the individual locations of chains and franchises who must compete locally.
- Owners and managers of independent lodging establishments and restaurants, no matter how small the business.
- And students who are preparing to enter the workplace ready to meet the complex marketing needs of businesses in today's hospitality industry.

USING THIS BOOK

Each part of this book opens with a list of terms and their definitions. Read through these carefully, as a preview of the terminology that is presented in subsequent pages.

The chapters begin with "The Basics" and then present more detail, explanation, and how-to in "Beyond the Basics." Various stops along the way—"Try it," "Analyze it," and others—provide ways for you to expand or reinforce your understanding or to try out a technique or tool. Don't skip them. They are not difficult or time-consuming, and they will help clarify understanding and improve skills.

A short summary and a set of review questions at the close of each chapter will remind you of where you've been and assess your mastery of concepts or tools.

The Appendix, "Resources on the Web," includes an extensive list of sites that offer tools and other assistance for positioning and for building and maintaining a Web site. Links for hospitality education programs and hospitality associations are also included.

Finally, a Glossary of the terms used in the text is provided for handy reference and review.

Students and other readers of this text will find the Prentice Hall Companion Web site very useful for review. For each chapter of the text, the Companion Web site includes five sets of questions—short answer, true/false, multiple choice, fill-in, and matching—as well as a list of chapter objectives. To access the Companion Web site, visit www.prenhall.com/cox.

ACKNOWLEDGMENTS

The authors are indebted to many friends and colleagues for various forms of assistance with this book. Educators and practitioners alike contributed to our own understanding of the hospitality industry and where it intersects with the world of Internet marketing.

We're glad that delays created by the permissions-getting process did not lead the editorial team at Prentice Hall, especially Marion Gottlieb and Vern Anthony, to give up on the project. We know it was sometimes very trying.

We once again tested the patience of spouses and families while researching and preparing the manuscript, and we are sincerely appreciative of their continuing encouragement.

Manuscript reviewers Bonnie Knutson of Michigan State University and Catherine Robb of Central Piedmont Community College offered comments for improving the text, for which we are most appreciative.

Finally, we thank everyone who offered suggestions, criticisms, or corrections. Where the text is good, it is good because of them. Still, if errors have insinuated themselves into these pages, the responsibility remains ours.

About the Authors

Barbara Cox, Ph.D., and William Koelzer, CBC, APR, write from a practical foundation in Internet marketing. Both have built and managed successful Internet marketing programs, and they continue to direct many more.

Barbara Cox earned her doctorate in education and psychology from Stanford University. Her professional life includes work as educator at college/university level, corporate trainer, course developer, and textbook author. She has directed the work of marketing departments, including strategic planning, market research, direct response marketing, and public communications. She is the principal of Cox Marketing Services and associate faculty in the Business Science Division at Saddleback College in Mission Viejo, California. She and William Koelzer are the authors of Internet Marketing in Real Estate (Prentice Hall, 2001) and Internet Marketing (Prentice Hall, 2004).

William Koelzer applies more than thirty years of marketing experience to the creation of this work. He has owned his own marketing consulting and promotional firm, Koelzer & Associates, since 1979. He was Vice President of Cochrane Chase & Co., the largest full-service advertising agency in Orange County, California. Koelzer served major clients, including Technicolor®, Carl's Jr. (TM) restaurants, Dos Equis™ beer, Armor All™, and AMF Voit®. He is the recipient of two PROTOS awards for Outstanding Achievement from the Orange County Public Relations Society of America.

To contact the authors, send e-mail to Barbara at bgcox@cox.net or to Bill at mktg4u@cox.net.

Image Credits and Acknowledgments

Carrows Restaurants; **p. 93,** Courtesy of Travel Hawaii, Hawaii Naniloa Hotel; **p. 94,** Courtesy of Hong Kong and Shanghai Hotels, Ltd., The Peninsula Group; **p. 96,** Courtesy of Fatburger; **p. 100,** Courtesy of AFC Enterprises, Inc. "Popeyes Chicken and Biscuits" logo, "Popeyes," and "Cajun Our Way" are trademarks of AFC Enterprises, Inc.; **p. 101,** ©2003, Arby's, Inc. Used with permission of Arby's, Inc.; **p. 102,** Dairy Queen®, DQ®, and related trademarks on this website are owned by American Dairy Corporation and used with permission; **pp. 105, 106,** Courtesy of Kimpton Group, and thanks to Kimpton Hotel and Restaurants; **p. 108,** Courtesy of Summit Golf; **p. 110,** Courtesy of All-Hotels, Ltd.; **pp. 113, 116, 117, 118,** Courtesy of Mandarin Oriental Hotel Group Limited; **p. 119,** Courtesy of InnFinity Hospitality (www.innfinity.com); **p. 122,** Courtesy of Hotel del Coronado; **p. 127,** Courtesy of MealsToGo; **p. 129,** Courtesy of LivePerson, Inc.; **p. 143,** Courtesy of American Hotel & Lodging Association; **pp. 149, 171, 172, 175, 176,** Reproduced with permission of Yahoo! Inc. ©2003 by Yahoo! Inc. YAHOO! and the YAHOO! logo are trademarks of Yahoo! Inc.; **pp. 150, 152,** Reproduced with permission of AltaVista Company. All rights reserved.; **p. 155,** Courtesy of Academy of Web Specialists; **p. 155,** Courtesy of Position Research; **p. 166,** Courtesy of Open Directory Project, www.dmoz.org; **p. 170,** Courtesy of DiningGuide.net, MetroGuide Operating Co., Inc.; **p. 173,** Courtesy of Restaurants.com Inc.; **p. 188,** Courtesy of RestaurantRow.com, Inc.; Courtesy of VegDining.com; **pp. 192, 193,** Courtesy of Overture Services, Inc.; **p. 195,** Courtesy of Columbine Publications, Inc.; **p. 199,** Courtesy of Travelocity; **p. 201,** Courtesy of The Real Cities Network, Knight Ridder Digital; **p. 205,** Courtesy Zagat.com. Copyright ©2002 Zagat Survey, LLC; **pp. 208, 209,** Courtesy Fortune Affiliates; **p. 211,** Courtesy of 800-Flowers.com, Inc.; **p. 227,** Courtesy Wilson Internet Services; **p. 231,** Reprinted with permission from the National Restaurant Association website, http://www.restaurant.org; **p. 242,** Courtesy of eMarketer, Inc.; **p. 245,** Courtesy PostMasterDirect; **p. 253,** Courtesy Advanced Access; **p. 290,** Courtesy of Good Cooking, Inc.; **p. 294,** Courtesy of Mrs. Smith's Bakeries.

PART ONE

Creating and Building an Internet Presence

No longer considered fad or fancy, the Internet has infiltrated our lives whether invited or not. From a quirky toy of university and government researchers, the online world has become required territory for American business. Consumers *expect* to find Web and e-mail addresses on everything from packaged goods to sports equipment, for every professional and store of every kind, for every company and organization big enough to have a business card and a telephone. Sites created for marketing and selling via the Web number in the millions (with billions of pages), some more effective than others.

Among the earliest to take advantage of the Internet's flexibility and extensive visibility were members of the travel industry. The existing airline reservation systems' databases were uniquely suited to online reservations, and it didn't take long for marketers and programmers alike to see this. The hospitality industry first began to make an appearance inside the travel and transportation sites, and it now creates some of the most appealing, functional, and informative sites on the Web. Chapter 1 introduces you to the types of business Web sites being used today, various approaches to marketing in cyberspace, and how the sites serve very different purposes.

Among the first questions we usually hear from businesses and professionals who are (at last) getting serious about Internet marketing are: (1) What should I put on my site? (2) What should my site look like? and (3) How should it be organized? (Sometimes this third question is, How should it work?) The answers to these questions take two forms. The first form is direct: We'll give you a list of items to put on your site, a "Do and Don't" list about site appearance, and some models that show how sites are organized.

The other form is "It depends." It depends on how you wish to market your business, product, or services; how you wish to be perceived; whom you want to attract; and what you want them to do after they find you. In short, it depends on your *positioning* and your *goals*. Chapter 2 addresses positioning and its implications. We'll help you decide how to differentiate your business, products, or services from others, especially on the Internet. Chapters 3, 4, and 5 discuss the key principles for site content, functioning, appearance, and organization.

The chapters in Part One are:

Chapter 1   Hospitality Businesses on the Web

Chapter 2   Standing Out From the Crowd: Positioning, Audience, and Goals

Chapter 3   More Than a Pretty Face: Web Site Content

Chapter 4   Stickiness: Online Reservations and Other Interactive Functions

Chapter 5   Look 'n' Feel: Your Site Appearance and Organization

LEARNING THE LANGUAGE

These terms are used in Part One. Familiarize yourself with them by reading the plain language definitions provided.

animated .gif.   A type of graphic that appears to move. An animated .gif combines several images, each a little different, that automatically appear one after another to give the appearance of motion, much like a motion picture.

auction.   A site that offers items for sale using a bidding process. At a predetermined time, the auction closes and the high bidder "wins" the auction and pays the seller. Many auction variations are now available, but the significant player is eBay at www.ebay.com.

audiobooks.   Files downloadable from the Internet or available on disk, that users can listen to using a computer audio program; they are similar to "books-on-tape."

autoresponder.   A function on a computer that sends an automated response to a command from a Web site or to an e-mail with a particular addressee or subject line.

B2B.   Business-to-business. B2B sites are constructed to sell business products and services to other businesses.

B2C.   Business-to-consumer. B2C sites are constructed by businesses to sell their products and services to consumers.

bulletin board.   A Web site page that displays messages submitted by users. Most bulletin boards are specific to a particular topic.

C2C.   Consumer-to-consumer. C2C sites are constructed by individuals to sell products and services to consumers. C2C selling also occurs on auction sites such as eBay.

central reservations office (CRO).
Online communication system (also called
"central reservation system") between all
hotels in a company or chain that
maintains up-to-date room pricing and availability information. Also used as an online
communication system that acts as central
interactive database among all hotels cooperating in a CRO, sometimes with a
marketing or other third-party partner.
Today's systems provide online (Internet)
booking capability. GDSs and CROs now
interact seamlessly, providing Internet users
with extensive reservation capabilities.

cgi form.   A form on a Web page that
Internet users fill in and send to the owner
of the Web site or some other designated
recipient. Often when you complete a guest
book or a survey on the Internet, you are
filling in a CGI form. CGI is an acronym for
common gateway interface.

chat room.   A Web site function that
allows a group of people to type statements
in such a way that all of the group can see
all of the statements.

community site.   A Web site featuring
content that is primarily for or about a
particular area (this term includes city,
county, regional, and state sites). The term
also refers to a Web site that is created and
maintained by a community of users, or a
group of formally linked Web sites on a
common topic.

corporate identity site.   A Web site
whose purpose is to communicate with a
company's employees and investors. A
corporate identity site promotes the
company's market position and philosophy
and provides information about its history,
size, leadership, dedications, and so forth.

**customer relationship marketing
(CRM).**   A type of marketing based on the
goal of building long-term relationships
with customers or clients. Web sites that

support CRM goals capture data on
visitors who make reservations, join clubs,
register for newsletters, and so forth. The
sites often provide features to communicate with visitors; engage them in "conversation"; demonstrate that they understand
visitors' priorities, preferences, and needs;
provide visitor-friendly ways to purchase
items; and provide means for fast or real-
time communication between customer
service or marketing representatives and
visitors.

downloadable.   Capable of being copied
from a computer connected to the Internet
to a user's computer.

e-books.   Electronic books, downloadable
from the Internet or available on disk, that
can be read using various reading devices
such as Adobe Acrobat® eBook Reader™.

.gif.   A file extension indicating a type of
compressed file for photos and other graphics
used on the Internet. These files are more
often used for graphics than photos. GIF
stands for *graphics interchange format.*

global distribution system (GDS).
Online communications system maintained
by the airlines with up-to-date flight
schedules, pricing, and seat availability.
GDSs and CROs now interact seamlessly,
providing Internet users with extensive
reservation capabilities.

home page.   The front or main page of a
Web site. A home page often acts as a
starting point and leads to other
documents stored on the site. A page that
precedes the main, navigation-oriented,
traditional home page is often called a
"splash" page.

host.   To store a customer's Web site on a
server, thus making the site available to
everyone having Web access; a computer
system that stores data, such as a Web site,
that is accessed by a user or users from a
remote location.

htm.   A file extension indicating a page prepared in hypertext markup language (html); one of the most common types of Web pages.

html.   Acronym for HyperText Markup Language, an authoring language used to create documents for viewing with an Internet browser.

interactive catalog.   A database of items with a "front end" that allows visitors to search for an item and some means of online ordering.

interactive functions.   Functions on a Web site that allow visitors to interact with the site; that is, visitors take some action (e.g., clicking on something), and the Web site performs some action in response. Usually, clicking to go to another page, although technically causing the Web site to do something, is not included in this definition because it is so common. Examples include adding items to shopping carts, using an online order form, participating in a chat room, and starting a video stream.

.jpg.   A file extension indicating a type of file for photos and other graphics used on the Internet. JPG (pronounced jay-peg) files are usually used for photos, but sometimes are used for graphics. These files are compressed so that photos appear on the user's monitor more quickly. Photos compressed as .jpg files can be reduced to about 5 percent of their normal size, but some detail is lost in the compression. JPG stands for *joint photographic experts group,* for which the compression technique is named.

link.   A connection between a location on a page and another location on the same or a different page on the Internet. When a user clicks on a link with the mouse, the location connected to the link is displayed. Text links are often underlined and often blue. Graphics can also be linked. When the mouse is pointed at a link, the mouse pointer usually changes to a different shape, depending on the user's mouse settings.

live chat or live customer service.   A Web site function that allows a user to communicate with a customer service representative or other person by typing messages back and forth. Compare with "chat room."

mall.   A Web site consisting of many individually owned sections or "store fronts" that sell products and services.

online reservations.   Ability to make air, room, automobile, and other reservations via the Internet.

portal.   A Web site that serves as a gateway to the Internet by providing a directory (or directories) of links, featured links, and a search engine or engine(s) to help visitors find what they seek (or what the owner of the portal wishes them to find). Portals offer a very broad range of choices to help visitors locate just about anything imaginable on the Web.

position, positioning.   A specific place held in the minds of the public or a specific audience (or "market segment") concerning a product or service. Positioning is similar in many ways to "reputation."

product or service information site.   A Web site that provides information on the features and benefits of particular products or services but does not help visitors purchase those products or services.

real-time reservations.   Online reservations that are requested and confirmed when the user interacts with the GDS or CRO on the Internet. (Some reservations are requested online, but the user must wait for confirmation via e-mail from the lodging or other facility. These are not "real time.")

server.   A computer or device on a network that manages that network's resources. Your Internet Service Provider (ISP) and all of the people who belong to it share the use of its servers. Basically, a server "serves" the e-mail and Web browsing needs of those who use it.

screen savers.   Programs that display animated graphics on a computer's monitor when the computer is turned on but has not been used for a period of time. Screen savers are small programs that are easily downloaded.

shopping cart.   A selecting and ordering mechanism on some sites that sell products and services. A shopping cart usually allows visitors to select items to "put in the shopping cart" or "basket" and later "check out" using a credit card or other payment mechanism.

streaming media.   Technology that transmits (streams) audio and video from a server to a user's computer. Streaming video is played on the user's computer as it is received from the server.

teleconferencing.   Voice conferencing using an Internet connection and a microphone and speakers connected to users' computers instead of telephones.

transaction-oriented site.   A Web site that provides some level of online purchasing capability so visitors can buy products or services, make reservations, and so on. Although these sites emphasize the selling of their products or services, they do not provide much visitor-friendly information or communication tools.

UMPS.   Acronym for *unique marketing positioning statement*; a concise statement intended to express the characteristics that combine to make up your position.

URL.   Acronym for *uniform resource locator*, the worldwide address of Web pages, Web images, documents, and other Web resources. Each page and image or graphic on the Internet has its own URL.

user-controlled catalogs.   Catalogs that allow users to custom design or select particular models, colors, pieces, and so forth to suit themselves.

videoconferencing.   Similar to teleconferencing via the Internet but allows transmission of video as well. Videoconferencing can be used between two people or can connect several people in different locations at one time.

vortal.   A "vertical portal," a Web site that serves as an Internet gateway to pages and sites related to a particular topic or interest.

Webcasting.   Internet broadcasting; transmission of live or prerecorded audio and video to users connected to the Internet.

Web fax, Internet fax.   A Web site function that allows visitors to send a document from their computer to another person's fax machine.

Web page.   A page of a Web site. Every Web page is identified by a unique address called a URL (uniform resource locator). Although a page is often considered to be 11 inches long, Web pages actually can be very long and take up many paper pages when printed.

Web site.   An organized, related, interconnected group of Web pages. Sites typically include a "home page," which is the first page seen by someone entering the site, and additional pages that are accessed from the home page or using internal links.

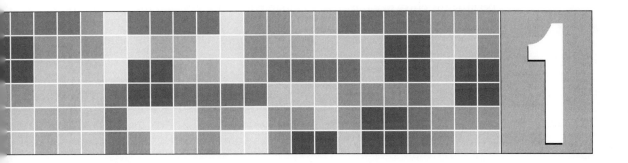

Hospitality Businesses on the Web

The Web site of The Ritz-Carlton Hotel Company, L.L.C. positions the company as a luxurious brand with meticulous service and elegant amenities. The site, redesigned in mid-2002, presents the company philosophy: "The Ritz-Carlton provides the finest personal service and facilities throughout the world." The image is clean and inviting. While serving as a gateway to individual Ritz-Carlton hotels everywhere, the home page links to its hotels' services and amenities. In addition, it points directly to company news for stockholders as well as its 22,000 employees worldwide. (Screen capture from www. ritzcarlton.com/home.asp.)

© 1998–2002. The Ritz-Carlton Hotel Company, L.L.C. All rights reserved. Reprinted with permission of the Ritz-Carlton Hotel Company, L.L.C.

Because the entry of a business into marketing on the Web is inexpensive and easily done, thousands of companies and business people add their sites to the Internet galaxy every day. Every type of business or organization imaginable has some type of Web presence. Every conceivable industry and every type of product or service is represented. From mega-billion-dollar corporations to kids selling lemons, they're there. And the competition is fierce.

How are businesses in the hospitality industry using the Internet to market their services and products? Is it different from traditional marketing? What types of lodging, dining, and gaming businesses are using the Web effectively?

Firms create Web sites to sell themselves to investors and contributors and to sell ideas, wares, and services. This chapter introduces you to the marketing approaches that businesses, including lodging, dining, and gaming establishments, use on the Internet, and begins by providing a general view of the types of businesses and the general categories of Web marketing.

THE BASICS

The tremendous variety of marketing approaches on the Internet makes a clear-cut categorization difficult. Most Web sites have multiple goals and use a number of strategies to reach them. They have unique looks and operate differently. Nonetheless, most business-oriented Web sites fit roughly (not neatly) into one of four broad groups, although the "fit" is more a matter of emphasis than strict conformity to a particular category.

Parent or corporate identity sites.   These sites, often expansions of the familiar "capability brochures," are usually built for the stakeholders—the employees and investors—in the business. They promote their market positioning and their philosophy, size, history, and other characteristics to attract and retain quality management; consistent workers; dedicated investors; and capable, knowledgeable, tough, and inspirational leadership. Parent identity sites usually link to other sites the business has developed for its brands. Cendant.com, for example, links to sites for the Ramada Inn®, Days Inn®, and Cendant's other property brands. Sometimes, a parent site provides a reservations tool that allows Web visitors to search all of its holdings for accommodations availability and make reservations through the central reservation office (CRO) database.

Parent identity sites in the food services industry work much the same as they do in lodging, with the exception of the CRO capability. El Torito Restaurants, Inc., for example, links to pages about its El Torito, Casa Gallardo, Who-Song & Larry's, and other brand-name establishments.

Web sites of chains, franchises, and memberships.   Chains, franchises, and memberships are a form of management structure. They share the feature of branding. Regardless of the type of ownership, these entities carry a "brand name" that they hope is recognizable. The Ramada Inn® chain of hotels owned by Cendant, for example, carries the brand identity. The Web sites of chains, franchises, and memberships are similar to the parent identity sites in that they work to build positioning. In this case, however, the positioning is focused on the brand. These sites usually link to pages or Web sites for their individual locations. They almost always provide real-time online reservation-making capabilities. They often have a link back to the parent identity site.

Some chain sites are also corporate identity sites. That is, they may not have parent and sister brands, but may indeed have investors as part of their audience. A good example of the extensive overlap in Web approaches that is a fact of the Internet world is the Ritz Carlton site shown at the opening of this chapter—a brand-name site that also works to inform and attract investors.

Web sites of individual locations or establishments. Web pages and Web sites that present information about a particular location or establishment usually go into much greater detail about the accommodations, services, and amenities. These sites include the individual locations of chains, franchises, and memberships, and also the thousands upon thousands of independent establishments that are not part of larger management structures. Many of them are, however, part of groups created for marketing purposes or they participate in Web associations or groups. A particular bed and breakfast, for example, may have a Web site, a page on the Bed and Breakfast Association of America Web site, and pages in several Bed and Breakfast Internet directories. These Web sites and pages may or may not have real-time online reservation system capabilities, although most of the locations that are part of larger management structures do.

Portals and vortals. A portal is a Web site or service that offers a broad array of resources and services, such as Web-based e-mail, forums, search engines, and online shopping malls. Yahoo.com, msn.com, and about.com are examples.

A vortal, derived from the phrase "vertical portal," is a site that offers the array of resources and services but focuses on a particular topic or area of interest. Among the earliest and most successful of the vortals are the travel vortals. Fairly familiar travel vortals include Orbitz.com, Travelocity.com, Expedia.com, and the travel pages of Americanexpress.com and America Online. Such sites play an important role in the advertising and accessibility of lodging establishments and some restaurants. Vortals also exist that are even more specific to lodging and food services, such as lodging.com and restaurants.com. Part Two, particularly Chapter 6, addresses portals and vortals in detail.

B2B or B2C

The types of sites listed previously focus primarily on marketing to consumers. Marketing on the Internet includes both business-to-business (B2B) and business-to-consumer (B2C) selling. In the hospitality industry, much of the B2B selling is by businesses that serve the hospitality industry, particularly restaurant suppliers and manufacturers and retailers of hotel furnishings. B2B marketing done by lodging, dining, and gaming establishments usually builds on and uses approaches similar to their B2C marketing, and often falls into a category of corporate account prospecting or group promotions to travel agencies, although this is diminishing. A hotel chain that positions itself as lodging for the convention world, for example, may target corporate accounts, but they do not use the e-marketplace sites and exchange sites that manufacturers use.

Information, Transaction, or Customer Oriented

Regardless of whether the basis of a site is a large corporation or an independent historic inn, a food conglomerate or a local deli, we can ask whether the site is information, transaction, or customer oriented. Information-oriented sites do a lot of telling. They don't ask Web visitors to make a reservation or buy something, and they don't involve the visitors with interactive functions. A transaction-oriented site focuses on facilitating a purchase, placing an order, or, more often in hospitality, making a reservation. Although customer-oriented sites provide the tools that encourage and handle a transaction, they also have functions and tools that support a long-term relationship with its visitors. These may be opt-in newsletters, Web-cams of the ocean or golf course, virtual tours of the property, no-fail recipes from the chef, lessons on wine ordering, or other ways that build a positive customer relationship. Some of these sites are supported by customer relationship management (CRM) tools that gather information about the site's visitors, clients, or patrons. The business then uses that information to tailor its site, promotions, marketing events, and other customer interactions to the needs, preferences, and priorities of its clients.

BEYOND THE BASICS

Let's look more closely at the general Web site categories and examine some of their characteristics. This will provide a framework for your own decision making about the goals, audience, and purpose for Internet marketing.

Parent or Corporate Identity Sites

Many sites exist primarily to inform and influence target audiences favorably about the site's owner. Parent identity sites typically emphasize a firm or organization's mission, size, scope, services, revenue, profitability, stock market success, industry leadership, and so forth, much as an annual financial report does. In fact, much of what you find on corporate identity sites is placed there to influence Wall Street, stockholders, and investors, and to instill a sense of pride among company employees. A corporate Web site usually enables quick access to in-depth information about the company.

A corporate identity site is a market positioning tool. Its primary goal is not the direct selling of a tangible object or a service; rather, its goal is providing information that creates or reinforces a favorable opinion about the firm in the minds of site visitors—public relations. Visit www.cendant.com. Cendant (formerly the Hospitality Franchise systems) uses several strategies to build its positioning. A band across the center of the figure lists Cendant's major hospitality holdings. These are names that many people in the general public recognize, including Days Inn®, Ramada®, Travelodge®, and others. The band changes to display lists of Cendant's major holdings in finance, real estate, vehicle, and travel distribution services. The navigation links at the top of the screen tell the story of the site's target audience: Investor Center with annual reports, financial releases, board of directors, and other information for investors and potential investors; Media Center for public relations contacts, news media, and other members of the communications world; Franchising with information for prospective hotel, real estate, and tax preparation franchisees; and Careers with Cendant, which includes information on available positions, benefits, and other data of interest to position seekers.

Other corporate parent Web sites include those for Starwood, Choice Hotels International, Carlson Companies, Inc., and Holiday Inn Worldwide, all of which have major hotel brands. Carlson Companies, Inc. (see Figure 1.1), is parent to both lodging and food service chains. The links on the left of the

FIGURE 1.1 Carlson Companies, Inc. (Screen capture from www.carlson.com.)

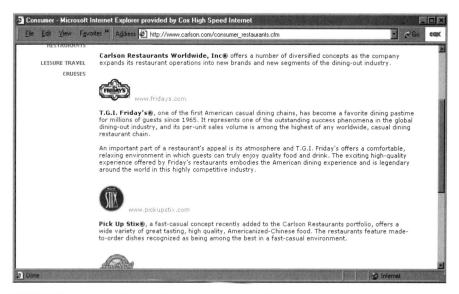

FIGURE 1.2 Carlson Companies, Inc., page describing its restaurant chains. (Screen capture from www.carlson.com/consumer_restaurants.cfm.)

home page take Web visitors to further information about the corporation. Links listed under Consumer Services take visitors to more information about Carlson's holdings in hotels, restaurants, and travel. Carlson displays the logos of its various chains along the bottom of the page. Clicking on the "restaurants" link takes visitors to a page with short descriptions of Carlson's restaurant chains and then provides links to the Web sites for the chains themselves (see Figure 1.2).

Parent company Web sites usually provide a list of locations along with the street address, phone number, and often the e-mail address of each location (office, dealer, facility, franchisee, etc.) nationwide or worldwide. Sometimes, they create a Web page or separate Web site for each location. The drop-down menu on Cendant's site contains links to the sites of its various companies. Clicking on "Wingate," for example, takes the visitor to www.wingateinns.com.

Many companies provide an interactive database for their offices to share. Often, this is based on the company's CRO. They may also use the functions of a global distribution system (GDS), a huge database and reservation system used by travel agencies, among others.

Web users expect the Web sites of parent companies to provide information on their brands or links to Web sites that give the accommodation, rate, and availability information for the entities in the company or franchise network. Figures 1.3, 1.4, and 1.5 are pages from the Benihana, Inc. Web site.

The corporate page (Figure 1.3) and the home page (Figure 1.4), which emphasizes the Benihana restaurant chain, both have a "locator" function

FIGURE 1.3 Benihana's corporate page. (Screen capture from www.benihana.com/corporate.asp.)

FIGURE 1.4 Benihana's home page. (Screen capture from www.benihana.com/default.asp.)

FIGURE 1.5   Benihana's page for its location in Golden Valley, Minnesota. (Screen capture from www.benihana.com/locator_detail.asp?id = 53.)

that allows visitors to find the nearest Benihana restaurant by displaying the page for the nearest location. Figure 1.5 directs the visitor to the restaurant location nearest to Zip code 55912 in Minnesota, for example.

Chains, Franchises, and Memberships

Similar to parent or corporate identity sites, chain or franchise sites emphasize positioning, with one primary difference—the degree to which the sites address the investor audience. Also, where parent sites link to the chains, the chains link to the individual locations.

The Web presence of most chains, franchises, and memberships in the lodging business amounts to much more than a brochure posted online. To be competitive in today's Web arena, the sites must offer a high degree of functionality, providing the interactive tools that are central to the Web's great selling power. For lodging chains, the site's main functionality is the real-time online reservation capability (see Chapter 5 for more detail). Users are encouraged to check availability for a given location and date from the chain's primary Web site. For example, the Web site for the Radisson hotels shown in Figure 1.6 immediately greets visitors with an invitation to enter a city name and check-in/check-out dates to determine availability and make a reservation.

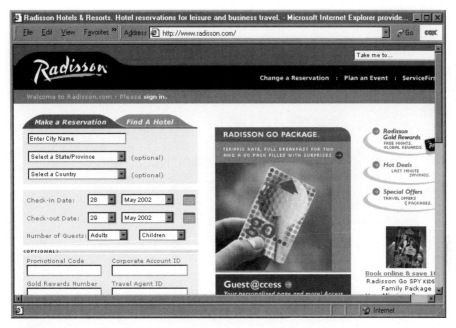

FIGURE 1.6 Radisson. (Screen capture from www.radisson.com.)

Competition on the Web

The availability of information and instant reservation making on the Web has put price pressure on the lodging industry. In May 2002, Cendant joined Starwood and Six Continents in guaranteeing "best available rate."

Cendant Hotels Guarantee Best Web Rates

Tuesday, May 28, 2002, 3:18:24 PM

PARSIPPANY, NJ—Following a trend started by Starwood and Six Continents, Cendant Corp.'s hotel group will introduce a best available rate guarantee in June on all of its branded Web sites.

Beginning June 17 under the guarantee, if customers find lower published rates for any Days Inn, Super 8, Ramada, Travelodge, Howard Johnson, Knights Inn, Villager, Wingate Inn and AmeriHost Inn hotel in the United States and Canada through any other online travel site, they will receive the lower rate plus an additional 10% discount.

"As the world's largest hotel franchisor, we are committed to ensuring our customers' trust and confidence in our brands," said Steve Rudnitsky, chairman/CEO of the hotel group. "With the best available rate guarantee, our customers will get the best deals as well as quick, convenient service through our branded web sites."

Source: www.hotelbusiness.com/links/archive/archive_view.asp?e-mail_friend = Y&ID = 15486.

FIGURE 1.7   Taco Bell. (Screen capture from www.tacobell.com.)

Let's look at an example in the food services industry. Figure 1.7 shows the home page for Taco Bell. Although Taco Bell does not yet enable users to buy tacos online, the site actively works to involve visitors. It includes nutritional information for all items on its menu, a restaurant location finder, and some animated cartoon clips for entertainment. Click on the "New 7-Layer Nachos, 99 cents" link and you'll see without question that this site is working hard to sell Taco Bell.

Analyze it

1. Visit the Web sites for Triconglobal (www.triconglobal.com) and Hilton Hotels (www.hiltonworldwide.com). What aspects of these sites tell you they are "corporate identity" sites? How do they treat their individual hotels? Who are their primary audiences? How are they alike or different?

2. Visit the Web sites for Taco Bell (www.tacobell.com) and Tim and Wendy's Planula Bed and Breakfast (www.planula.com.au). Are these corporate identity sites? Are they more oriented to providing information or conducting online transactions? Explain your answer and give examples.

Web Sites of Individual Locations or Establishments

Web pages and Web sites for a particular location or establishment usually provide much greater detail about the establishment and its accommodations, services, amenities, or menu. These sites include the individual locations of chains, franchises, and memberships, and the many independent establishments that are not part of larger management structures. As stated earlier, many of them are part of marketing groups or they participate in Web associations or groups. The lodging Web sites may or may not have real-time online reservation system capabilities, and although most restaurants display their menu, few have the need for an online reservation function.

Deceptively simple at first appearance, the Charles Hotel site (see Figure 1.8) is rich with content and functions for Web visitors. For those who may already know the Charles and are focused on getting there or making reservations, the links across the top right go straight to the heart of the matter. The links at the left are for those who want to learn about the Charles, its accommodations, services, amenities, and history.

An establishment does not have to be a multimillion-dollar operation to have key information on the Web. The Web is host to a multitude of bed and breakfast directories and associations that often provide reasonably priced listings and pages on their Web sites, including links to separate Web sites for the individual members.

Notice in Figure 1.9, for example, that the Brooks Street Bed & Breakfast is listed in the Taos Association of Bed & Breakfast Inns®, New Mexico Bed and Breakfast Association®, and the Professional Association of Innkeepers International®, among others.

FIGURE 1.8 The Charles Hotel. (Screen capture from www.charleshotel.com.)

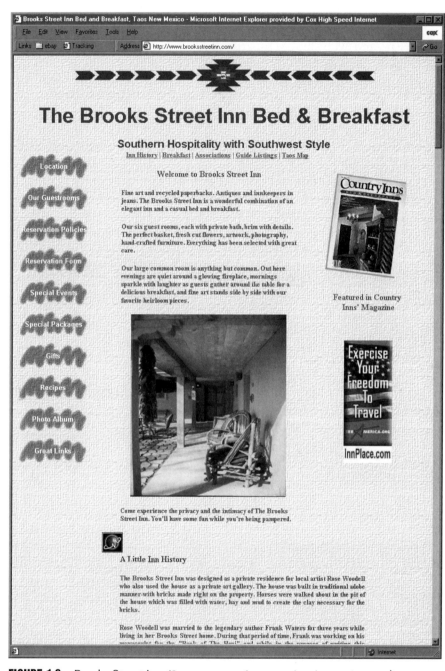

FIGURE 1.9 Brooks Street Inn. (Screen capture from www.brooksstreetinn.com.)

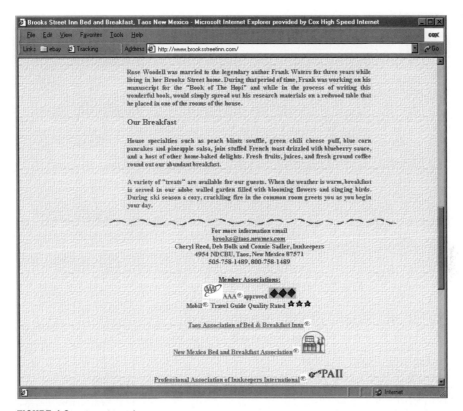

FIGURE 1.9   Continued.

Portals and Vortals

Portals, such as Yahoo.com, msn.com, netscape.com, with their search engines, directories, and other points of access to the world of the Internet, are very popular among millions of Web users, especially novices who are learning their way around the Web. Portals, except for their search engines (which are mostly objective), dictate the content that Web visitors are able to find. They help new users become acquainted with what is on the Web, however, they only display the portion of the Internet that they, not the users, deem most important. Portals do this, in many cases, because they generate income by including links to advertisers' sites or to their own properties or partnerships.

Vertical portals, or vortals, focus on a particular topic or business or interest. They are the specialists, with news, articles, guidance, updates, and specialty directories. Travel vortals were among the earliest to appear on the Web, and they have continued to proliferate—often successfully. What gave them great appeal from the beginning was their real-time online reservation capability. The early emphasis on airline reservations has extended to other

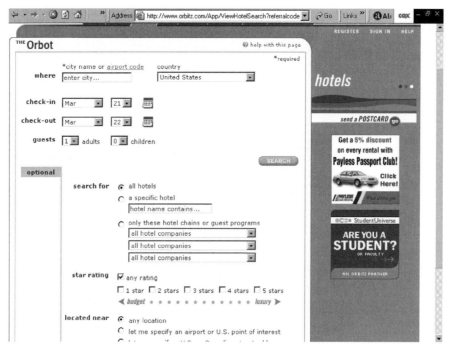

FIGURE 1.10   Orbitz.com. (Screen capture from www.orbitz.com.)

transportation reservations as well as lodging. Among the best-known travel vortals are Orbitz (see Figure 1.10), Travelocity (see Figure 1.11), Expedia.com, and the travel sections of America Online.

Among the most useful of the hospitality industry vortals are those for the industry's associations. International, national, regional, state, and other associations of hotels, inns, bed and breakfasts, restaurants, and casinos can be found in some abundance on the Web. Not all association sites, of course, are vortals, but many are, and their numbers are increasing. See Figures 1.12 through 1.15 for examples.

The National Restaurant Association (Figure 1.12) is the leading industry group in its field. Its Web site is a *vortal*, a *gateway* to restaurants and restaurant industry information, nationally. Additionally, each state has its own association, many of which meet the definition of a vortal (see Figure 1.13).

Some vortals act as virtual communities for the restaurant industry, such as OnTheRail.com (see Figure 1.14). About themselves, OnTheRail.com says, "The site has grown into a thriving community for professionals in all areas of the restaurant industry. The membership has grown, and the newsgroups and bulletin boards are very active. OnTheRail has become a valuable resource online for anyone who wants to know more about the industry and those who want to find a place online that speaks their language." The site contains its own B2B section at www.ontherail.com/site/links/b2b.asp.

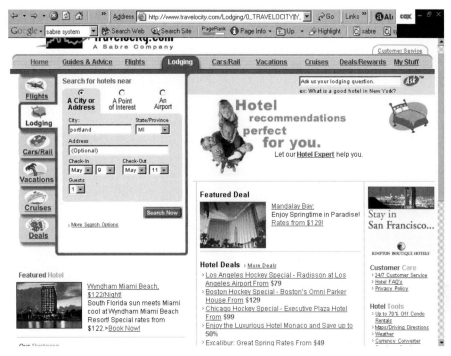

FIGURE 1.11   Travelocity.com. (Screen capture from www.travelocity.com.)

FIGURE 1.12   National Restaurant Association. (Screen capture from www.restaurant.org.)

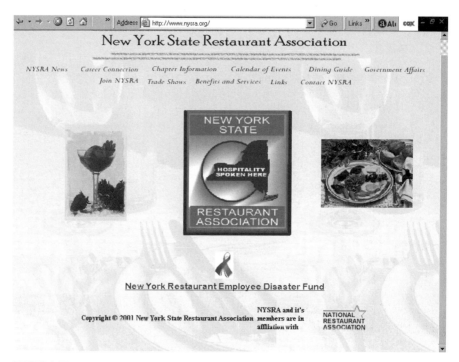

FIGURE 1.13 New York State Restaurant Association. (Screen capture from www.nysra.org.)

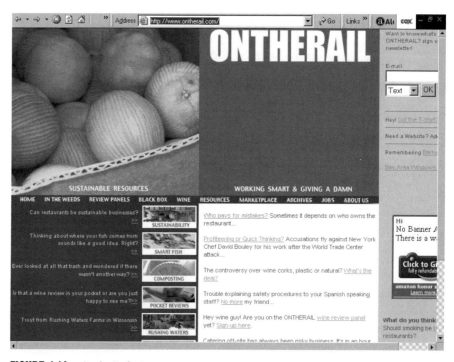

FIGURE 1.14 OntheRail. (Screen capture from www.ontherail.com.)

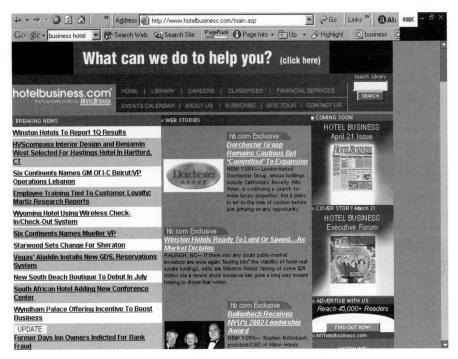

FIGURE 1.15   Hotelbusiness.com. (Screen capture from www.hotelbusiness.com/main.asp.)

Vortals may include directories of restaurants, bars, hotels, and casinos; for example, the National Bar and Restaurant Directory site at www. americanbars.com.

Strictly speaking, the distinction between a vortal and a directory tends to be that vortals provide links to news, information, guidance, and other helpful resources, whereas directories link only (or primarily) to the pages or Web sites of the establishments that have registered (sometimes for free, sometimes not) with the directory.

HotelBusiness.com is a B2B vortal that provides late-breaking news and analysis for "nearly 45,000 decision makers including owners, general managers, management company and financial executives—the individuals involved in making decisions for all aspects of hotel ownership and operations."

Chapter 6 provides detailed information about portals, vortals, directories, and how to use them to ensure that your hospitality Web site has the best chance of being found by Web users.

B2B or B2C

B2C sites are the most familiar to the Web-using public. These sites, in almost every possible industry, market goods and services to consumers. Many stores—

department, variety, book, car, fabric, music, electronic, clothing, food, hardware—that you know from experience also have Web sites to sell you merchandise. Other B2C sites have no "bricks-and-mortar" facilities; they sell exclusively over the Internet. Not all B2C sites provide online ordering—some market goods and services that consumers then order via telephone or through an agent. Examples of B2C sites include Amazon.com and Barnes&noble.com (books and other), Bloomingdales.com and Nordstrom.com (department stores), Pontiac.com and Lincoln.com (vehicles), Staples.com and Officemax. com (office supplies), and a host of others.

In the hospitality industry, virtually any site that asks consumers for patronage is a B2C site. Thus, sites such as Hilton.com, Carlsjr.com, Mcdonalds.com, Ihop.com, Lindy's Restaurant in St. Thomas (www.stthomas.com/mafolie/lindys-index.html), Econolodge.com, andMotel6.com are all B2C sites, engaged in marketing goods and services to consumers.

Despite the economic downturn at the beginning of 2001, a generally gloomy outlook for the dot-world at that time, and the post-September 11, 2001 market environment, Jupiter Research (www.ecommercetimes.com/perl/story/6515.html) predicts that companies around the globe will increase their spending on B2B e-marketplaces (exchanges, auctions, etc.) from US $2.6 billion in 2000 to $137.2 billion by 2005. Goldman Sachs' estimates are more aggressive: worldwide B2B spending will reach $4,500 billion by 2005—out of total online commerce spending of $60 trillion by that year. Furthermore, Goldman Sachs expects that 80 percent of B2B commerce worldwide will be conducted online over the next 20 years ("B2B: Just How Big is the Opportunity?" Goldman Sachs Global Equity Research [May 9, 2000], www.gs.com/hightech/research/b2b-opp.pdf).

According to ActivMedia Research ("B-to-B Companies Go Online as a Matter of Survival: Value Found in Relationship Building, Not Profitability," ActivMedia Research [August 15, 2000], www.activmediaresearch.com/magic/pr081500.html), "Most B-to-B web sites are established for a dual purpose—to both [sic] sell products and services, either directly or indirectly (98%), and to provide information (73%). The primary means for creating a sale for 77% of sites is by stimulating customers to make an offline contact. Most B-to-B sites also provide pre-sale support and purchasing information (62%) and generate leads for staff to follow-up (60%) as ways to make a sale through their website."

The same article claims the following B2B site function proportions: 33 percent of B2B sites market, but do not sell, products online; 25 percent of B2B sites offer professional services; and 15 percent sell products at the site to business end-users. Buying organizations have unique procedures they follow when making complex decisions.

In the hospitality arena, such sites include lodging and food industry sites aimed at business and corporate accounts as well as those businesses that serve the industry. BigTray (see Figure 1.16), for example, is one of many B2B firms providing equipment and supplies to restaurants nationwide.

FIGURE 1.16 BigTray. (Screen capture from www.bigtray.com.)

BigTray, and firms like it, make it easy for restaurants to place orders in a number of ways: "Our Website allows you to purchase all your E&S online, 24 hours a day, from your home or work place. Or if you prefer, simply call us at 1–800–BIGTRAY (1–800–244–8729) to place your order with one of our specialists. From outside the United States, please call 415–863–3614. Our Reorder feature allows you to easily replenish frequently bought items."

The drop-down menu on the left side of the screen capture from International Hotel Supply (see Figure 1.17) shows that this B2B hotel supply firm offers a huge array of products for hotels.

The Eastin Hotel, located between Petaling Jaya and Kuala Lumpur, positions itself almost exclusively as a "business hotel" (Figure 1.18). Oddly, more hotels positioning themselves as "business hotels" seem to be springing up in countries other than the United States. Business hotels typically feature on-site secretarial services, automated office equipment, Rent-an-Office, workstations or boardrooms, and videoconferencing facilities (Figure 1.19).

Information, Transaction, or Customer Oriented

As with most things on the Internet, tremendous variation exists from site to site. Information-oriented sites are basically focused on *telling*, much like brochures and pamphlets. They give little reason or opportunity for Web

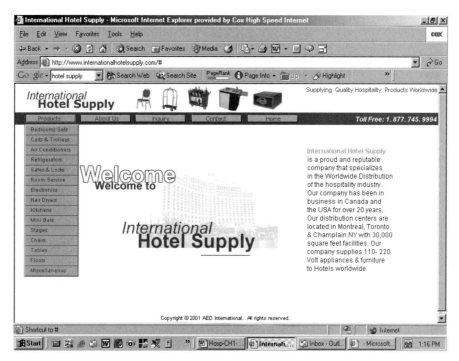

FIGURE 1.17   International Hotel Supply. (Screen capture from www.internationalhotelsupply.com.)

FIGURE 1.18   Eastin Hotel. (Screen capture from www.eastin.com.)

FIGURE 1.19   Board or teleconferencing room at the Eastin Hotel, Malaysia, a business hotel. (Screen capture from www.eastin.com/business_facilities.html.)

visitors to ask questions, initiate discussions, order gifts, or make reservations online.

Information-oriented Web sites reflect a product focus, but usually do not communicate urgency or establish an information exchange with site visitors. Restaurants that do not accept reservations or handle any online orders for pickup or delivery commonly create this type of site or page with limited interactivity. Likewise, lodging facilities that do not participate in a large reservation database tend to create information pages, often as part of a travel directory or a local community directory.

Customer-oriented sites typically feature many interactive elements, including online chat with a company representative, newsletters, voting in a poll, providing an opportunity to give feedback to improve the site, or using a chat room with other site visitors. Free e-mail, a guest book for leaving comments, free Web site offers, and free reports and updates (sent by e-mail) are popular elements. Hospitality sites with high interactivity ask users to complete an online profile—and then greet each visitor by name with new information related to that visitor's interests when he or she returns. Experienced Web users look for sites with online lodging reservations, including options for hotel amenities, such as dining reservations or spa appointments. Local restaurants, such as delis, cafes, pizza places, and others, can offer online reservations as well as online menu orders for later pickup or delivery. (Various Web site functions are discussed in greater detail in Chapter 5.)

The customer-oriented site is the best model for many hospitality firms that want to conduct e-business. Although a site in this category is usually

Analyze it

Visit and explore three of the sites listed below. Write a statement about what each site does to make friends with its Web visitors and keep them coming back. Which site do you think is most effective at doing this? Why?

www.carmelasrestaurant.com

www.gamblingnewsletter.com

www.hotel-discounted.com/newsletter.asp

www.hotelresource.com

www.johnnyjet.com

www.venetian.com

a selling site (transaction-oriented), it goes beyond the sales pitch to be-friend a prospect, client, guest, patron, or other customer in a powerfully appealing way. Such sites combine the best of information-oriented and transaction-oriented Web sites with an appreciation of customers and desire to establish a long-term relationship with them.

Customer-oriented sites work to educate visitors, providing ample information and sometimes links to information on other sites. These CRM-oriented sites typically offer many ways for visitors to communicate with the "proprietors" of the site and vice versa. Why? Because there is a happy immediacy in doing so, reminiscent of the service that people used to give and get in the small town hardware store. These sites stand apart from the anonymity of many Web applications and seek to engage the visitor in an on-site activity. Online banking was among the earliest and most successful Web-based services. Not only can users get information about bank office hours and locations, types of accounts, rates, terms, and other bank products, but they can also access their account information; transfer funds; pay bills; plan a reinvestment, retirement, or home loan refinance; and communicate with the bank. The technologies and approaches used for these functions have been expanded and adapted for use by other types of businesses such as clothing, automobile, cosmetics—and hospitality.

Summary

Table 1.1 summarizes the chief characteristics of hospitality Web pages and sites. The distinctions made in the table and in the chapter text are not clear-cut because the open architecture of the Internet results in significant

TABLE 1.1	Lodging and dining Web site description summary.			
Site "Owner"	Main Goals	Audience	Features	Examples
Corporate/parent	Positioning, build recognition and awareness	Investors	Company news, annual reports, company description, history, statistics, links to brand companies	Choice Starwood Six Continents Cendant
Lodging chains, franchises, memberships	Positioning, increase reservations chainwide, build wide recognition and awareness	Investors, potential franchisees, potential guests, corporate and group travel coordinators, travel agencies and other third parties	Company description, real-time online reservations, information to support segmentation (price category, business v. leisure, etc.), lodging locator, links to locations (and to parent if applicable)	Radisson Ramada Days Inn Best Western (membership)
Restaurant chains, franchises, memberships	Positioning, build recognition and awareness	Investors, potential franchisees, potential patrons	Company description, information to support segmentation (price category, theme, style), restaurant finder, links to locations (and to parent if applicable)	El Torito Carlson
Lodging locations	Positioning, get property-specific reservations, build general and local recognition and awareness	Potential guests, corporate and group travel coordinators, travel agencies and other third parties	Property, amenities, services description, real-time online reservations, information to support segmentation (price category, business v. leisure, etc.)	Radisson Minneapolis Ritz Carlton Bali Motel 6 Phoenix
Restaurant locations (chain or independent)	Positioning, build general and local recognition and awareness, build local business	Potential patrons, banquet/catering coordinators	Menu, specific location/directions, services description, information to support segmentation (price category, theme, style)	Marie Callendar's Kansas City; Scott's Seafood San Francisco; Wendy's Hamburgers 10th St.; Jim and Carrie Sue's Family Diner; Rainbow Room
Independent hotel, motel, inn, bed and breakfast, etc.	Positioning, get reservations, build general and local recognition and awareness	Potential guests, corporate and group travel coordinators, travel agencies and other third parties	Property, amenities, services description, real-time online reservations, reservations by e-mail, fax, or phone, information to support segmentation (price category, business v. leisure, etc.)	Rex's Montana Dude Ranch Victoria's Bed and Breakfast Golden Door MGM Grand Hotel

overlap and merging of the classification schemes. Nonetheless, the information provided here will help you consider various Web characteristics as starting points for hospitality Internet marketing.

In addition to the scheme shown in Table 1.1, this chapter introduced you to portals and vortals, the distinction between B2C and B2B marketing on the Web, and the qualitative ruler that looks at Web sites as information, transaction, or customer oriented.

Review Questions

1. Who are the most common audiences for a corporate or parent identity Web site?
2. What do hotel Web sites usually have that restaurant Web sites do not?
3. What information do Web sites for individual locations or establishments often include that sites for chains or brands do not?
4. What is typical about a transaction-oriented Web site?
5. What distinguishes a customer-oriented site from other sites?
6. Name four interactive elements that a Web site can offer visitors.
7. Why is it that portals and vortals may not always provide "objective" data?
8. What is a vortal and how does it differ from a portal?
9. What purpose might there be for a business to construct a vortal?
10. What is B2B?

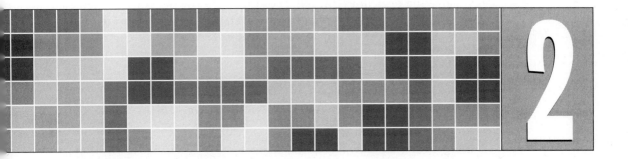

Standing Out from the Crowd

Positioning, Audience, and Goals

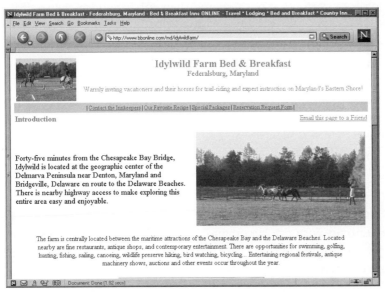

Bed and Breakfast for people who travel with their horses . . . (Screen capture from www.bbonline.com/md/ idylwildfarm.)

Basic marketing principles involving positioning, knowing target audiences, and establishing goals are as important in Web marketing as they are in "traditional" marketing. Planning effective Internet marketing strategies requires certain key decisions about your market positioning, audience or audiences, and goals. This chapter will help you with these decisions.

THE BASICS

Defining Your Position

Whether your interest is Internet marketing for the lodging, dining, or gaming markets or a combination thereof, you have a story to tell about your operation that sets you apart from your competitors. The details of that story may seem elusive at first, but the difference is there. Your marketing will become fully effective only when you discover that distinctiveness and communicate it.

To stand out from colleagues and competitors, you must have a market position—a *unique* market position. You must be perceived as being different from others, as being somehow special. What do you do best? In what ways do you excel? Think of ways in which you are different from other choices in your area, or at least different from what they claim to be. Of course, these special characteristics should be both positive and valuable to patrons.

Your business may have already claimed and established a market position—in which case, your Internet marketing will build on that position. Some businesses may have a market position or "reputation" that they aren't aware of or using well. Their products, services, pricing, location, appearance, or other factors have defined who they are in the customers' minds. In this case, the job is to clarify that position and then enhance it (or change it if it isn't positive), making sure that the position on the Internet enhances the overall position and marketing goals of the company. Here are a few examples:

The hotel with the easiest airport access, the lowest rates in town, or the most luxurious lobby.

The bed and breakfast for people who love horses, or with the most romantic suites or great Swedish breakfasts.

The inn where you spend your days in quiet contemplation.

The motel for large families.

The diner that transports you back to the 1950s.

The hot dog specialists.

The finest Basque cuisine.

The restaurant with the largest and most sophisticated wine selection.

The café that serves the heartiest homemade soups or the best lemon pie in town.

The fastest take-out service.

The casino with the best evening entertainment, the loosest slots, or plenty of amusements for the whole family.

Are you any of these: the most experienced, caring, or knowledgeable about something; the busiest, oldest, friendliest, hardest working, most elegant, homiest; or something else that differentiates you from other establishments? (Use the checklist on pages 47–49 to help you decide your position.)

Defining Your Target Audience

By virtue of the medium we're discussing, the Internet, the characteristic most common to the majority of your audience is that they have access to the Internet—at home, work, school, the library, a cybercafe, or through a friend or relative. Much of this group falls in a middle- to upper-income range. But your target audience has other distinguishing characteristics. How well you understand this audience affects the outcome of your marketing, as well as dictates or influences some of the characteristics of your business.

Some of the important characteristics are long familiar to marketers in the hospitality industry. Most lodging entities know, for example, whether their appeal is to business people traveling for work, families on vacation, couples wanting a quiet get-away retreat, or travelers who expect only the most luxurious accommodations. How well you stand out from other establishments that cater to those same groups may depend on how well you can define those groups and then do things to attract them. (See pages 47–49 for help defining your target audience.)

Defining Your Internet Marketing Goals

The goals you set for your Internet marketing affect the content and design of your site(s) and pages. Following are some examples of Internet marketing goals, particularly goals for Web sites.

1. Generate interest and trials.
2. Increase online reservations.
3. Increase the loyalty of each guest.
4. Provide information on rates and services to save staff time.

Goals also should be set for Web site performance. These are usually related to the number of visitors a site has per day or hour, how many inquiries or reservations are submitted, how many people sign up for a newsletter or information, or how many people send e-mail inquiries using the site.

The most common mistakes that new-to-the-Web businesses make with their Web sites are:

Assuming that Web users will find the site on their own, just because it is there.

Not establishing clear goals for the site.

Not providing a clear message or direction for visitors.

Not allowing sufficient budget for promoting the Web site.

Not providing sufficient opportunity for visitors to interact with the site and the business that it represents.

Remember that these goals should enhance or build on and be consistent with the overall marketing goals of your service, product, or company.

BEYOND THE BASICS

Positioning: What Is it? Why Is it Important?

Say "Holiday Inn®" and people hear "family."

Say "Waldorf®" and people hear "luxury."

Say "Four Seasons®" and people hear "elegant, expensive, and elite."

Positioning on the Internet and in marketing in general refers to how you (your company, products, or services) are perceived by customers, often in relation to your competitors. It is exactly that—a *perception* that people form. It is a ranking of you and others like you. In early literature on positioning, Ries and Trout discuss the proposition that "a company must create a 'position' in the prospect's mind." They continue, "A position that takes into consideration not only a company's own strengths and weaknesses, but those of its competitors as well.... To cope with our overcommunicated society, people have learned to rank products on mental ladders. In the rent-a-car field, for example, most people put Hertz on the top rung, Avis on the second rung, and National on the third. Before you can position anything, you must know where it is on the product ladder in the mind" (Ries, A. & Trout, J., *Positioning: The Battle for Your Mind*, London: McGraw-Hill, 1986).

Phillip Kotler, long known for marketing theory and education, defines positioning this way: "A product's position is the way the product is defined by consumers on important attributes—the place the product occupies in consumers' minds relative to competing products." Kotler outlines the steps required for successful positioning as: "identifying a set of possible competitive advantages upon which to build a position, selecting the right competitive advantages, and effectively communicating and delivering the chosen position to a carefully selected target market" (Kotler, P., Bowen, J., & Makens, J., *Marketing for Hospitality and Tourism*, New Jersey: Prentice Hall, 2002). Positioning is long term and overarching. It drives or underlies promotions, advertising, and other market communications.

Positioning is not something that you can touch. Positioning can be fragile and may require continuous tweaking. Your particular positioning refers to the position of your company, products, or services in the minds of others. For practical business purposes, it is how people rank your products, your firm, or your services on a graduated good/bad perception scale against similar choices.

The marketing firm Osseum (www.osseum.com) says the following about market positioning:

> There are no bad attributes as long as you don't try to fool the consumer. If you position yourselves as a premium brand and set your retail accordingly but you have poor art and production values, the consumer will smell a rat. If you can't afford to be a premium brand then don't. Celebrate the frugality of your production values. Undercut your competition's pricing and position yourself as the value brand. Become the consumer's advocate for sensible products at sensible prices. Force your competition to lower their margins to compete.
>
> If you don't define your product or service, a competitor will do it for you. By saying, "Have it your way," Burger King implied McDonalds didn't. Burger King influenced McDonald's positioning and turned the two letters, "Mc" into a new prefix synonymous with bland, generic, mass-produced products. Positioning is your competitive strategy. What's the one thing you do best? What's unique about your product or service? Identify your strongest strength and use it to position your product but be aware of your weaknesses too. (www.osseum.com/business_solutions/marketing/)

Standing Out from the Crowd: How Do You Distinguish Yourself?

By the very nature of positioning, you must distinguish yourself as "something"—ideally, as something special. What can it be for you? What can you tell people about your firm, products, or services that *differentiates* them from others in the minds of your Web site visitors?

Many firms on the Web today are not projecting any specific or distinct positioning whatsoever. Their sites' pages say and show basically the same things—a company logo, product photos, a list of services, a list of cities served, a general statement about "willingness to give 100%," or a profound belief in real customer service. Site reviewers for Web directories like Yahoo! categorize these sites as "Lookie Me" sites; that is, sites that appear to be most concerned with the company's ego. These sites could be called "epitaphs for living companies," and reviewers rank them lower than sites that demonstrate a sincere concern for the interests and priorities of their visitors.

Your site must focus on creating and reinforcing a particular identity, ability, characteristic, feature, benefit, or service—a *position* in the minds of current and potential guests and patrons. Emphasize a single theme, and then let functions, related points, information, graphics, and links to additional pages and sites support the position. Note that you must have a *particular* position, one that separates you from other companies and Web sites that operate in your field (your competitors).

The following list provides some examples of market position statements, taglines, or themes that make some lodging, dining, or gaming facilities stand out. Circle or highlight any that sound like you.

Luxury Hotel

The Detroit Businessperson's First Choice

Tourists' #1 Choice in Maui

The Hotel with the Staff that Makes You Smile

Your Home Away from Home

Traveling Families Are Our Favorites!

Exciting. Distinctive. Hilton. (Hilton Hotel Corp.)

The Lodge with Outdoor Living

Oldtown Denver's Largest Hotel

On the Riverwalk in San Antonio

Bed and Breakfast

Beachfront Breakfasts with Every Room

First in Family Lodging

The Mountainside Retreat

Fine Dining

Fine Dining at Fair Prices

As Home Cooked as You'll Ever Find

Home Cooking the Way You Like it

Understated Elegance, Exquisite Cuisine

Where You Dock Your Boat and Dine

Quick Service

Have It Your Way

Cooked in Seconds to Your Order

In and Out in Under a Minute

Gaming

More Fun and Excitement

All Day All Night High Stakes Games

Sophisticated Players Choice

No Strangers Allowed

Segments Aren't Positions

Traditional or conventional marketing lore segments businesses by various characteristics. The segments are no less valid in Web marketing. They help define a particular business, and that definition underlies some positioning . . . but it isn't enough. Often, positioning helps a business stand out from other businesses in the same segment. Bed and breakfasts, for example, may constitute a segment. "The bed and breakfast where you wake to the shepherd's call" is a positioning statement that separates that particular establishment from other bed and breakfasts.

The following list includes some of the segmenting in the hospitality industry according to overall ownership or operations structure, activity or use, location, markets, price, and to a certain extent, ratings.

Hospitality

Ownership/Operations
parent of various brands
chain, franchise, or membership
individual location or establishment

Lodging

Activity or Use
convention
dude ranch
casino
health spa
extended stay
bed and breakfast
resort
transient

Location
airport
highway
waterside/mountain/desert/city/historical/themepark

Markets
business
groups
leisure

Segments Aren't Positions (continued)

Price
deluxe (above 150)
mid-range (65–145)
budget (below 65)

Ratings
5-, 4-, 3-star

Food Services

Price
fine dining
family meals
quick serve
standard table
buffet
food court
banquet
catering

Ratings
3-, 4-, 5-star (or diamond or other)

Service Type
fine dining

Specialty, Theme, or Other

International, ethnic, regional, or other specialty

Theater, magic, opera, sports TV, or other entertainment

*Casino hotels are an exception to the pricing categories. Because their profits are based primarily on gaming, they work to fill their rooms with prospective players and often reduce rates to do so.

Examples from the Web

The following figures show a few examples of Web pages that work effectively to position their businesses.

Figure 2.1 shows the webpage for an inn that has positioned itself with an historical theme ... history and the Vikings. The tagline reads "Nordic Inn, Medieval Brew & Bed." The secondary headline says "Where History comes alive," to communicate a sense of entertainment. Other information follows to support the message about the fun of lodging and dining at the

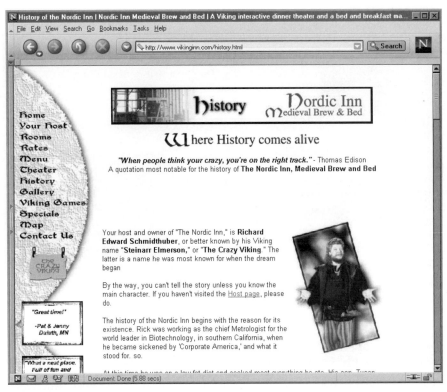

FIGURE 2.1   Nordic Inn, Medieval Brew & Bed. (Screen capture from www.vikinginn.com/history.html.)

Nordic Inn. The positioning is distinctive—there aren't any other inns claiming this position in the same geographic area.

The positioning for The Barn Bed & Breakfast (see Figure 2.2) is far different from that of the Nordic Inn. The tagline reads "A unique farm experience is waiting for you!" and the images of the big red barn say it's all about country. The text reinforces the general or overall position of The Barn Bed & Breakfast as a country inn:

> *Stroll or bicycle down country lanes, observe adjacent fields of grain, cattle peacefully grazing, a wide variety of wildlife activity, pick mulberries and wild plums in season. Witness space-age technology contrasted by antique tractors working the fields. Bring your own horse to ride, or hike on a guided tour to see where Lewis & Clark traveled and bald eagles still soar, along the mighty Missouri River. Camp, picnic, swim, or fish along the Missouri or one of the area's small ponds. Visit a fur trading post built in the 1850s, a one-room schoolhouse.*

FIGURE 2.2   The Barn Bed & Breakfast. (Screen capture from www.bbonline.com/sd/thebarn/.)

Branding

"Branding," a well-established marketing concept, became a huge concern for Internet marketers after the Web became a viable advertising medium about 1998. Thousands of firms began "banner wars," filling Web pages with small banner and tile ads (see Chapter 7) in the effort to "brand" their firm through repeated impressions at the expense of competitors. They strived to create brand identity and a resultant share of the market.

The idea was that if you placed millions of tiny billboards on the Web to increase name recognition or brand awareness, you would make people remember your product or service or Web site and then do business with you.

Successful branding demands synergy from advertising, public relations, sales promotion, customer service, direct mail, newsletters, volume discounts, co-op programs, word of mouth, event sponsorship, point of sale (POS) visibility, hospitality suites, and other available communications tactics. Combinations of these methods deliver a consistent message about a company or its products and services. Delivering that consistent message is especially important on the Web where things happen fast and brands can be established or swept aside overnight, at least with Web users.

If you are a small firm that provides local services, you may never become a national name, a brand name recognized in millions of households. You must, however, work to establish clear positioning in your target area.

Branding

According to Brand.com (www.brand.com),

Brand is the proprietary visual, emotional, rational, and cultural image that you associate with a company or a product. When you think Volvo, you might think safety. When you think Nike, you might think of Michael Jordan or "Just Do It." When you think IBM, you might think "Big Blue." The fact that you remember the brand name and have positive associations with that brand makes your product selection easier and enhances the value and satisfaction you get from the product.

While Brand X cola or even Pepsi-Cola may win blind taste tests over Coca Cola, the fact is that more people buy Coke than any other cola and, most importantly, they enjoy the experience of buying and drinking Coca Cola. The fond memories of childhood and refreshment that people have when they drink Coke is often more important than a little bit better cola taste. It is this emotional relationship with brands that make them so powerful.

About *brand identity*, Brand.com says

Brand identity includes brand names, logos, positioning, brand associations, and brand personality. A good brand name gives a good first impression and evokes positive associations with the brand. A positioning statement tells, in one sentence, what business the company is in, what benefits it provides, and why it is better than the competition. Brand personality adds emotion, culture, and myth to the brand identity by the use of a famous spokesperson (Bill Cosby for Jello), a character (the Pink Panther), an animal (the Merrill Lynch bull), or an image (You're in good hands with Allstate).

Brand associations are the attributes that customers think of when they hear or see the brand name. McDonald's television commercials are a series of one brand association after another, starting with the yellow arches in the lower right corner of the screen and following with associations of Big Mac, Ronald McDonald, happy kids, Happy Meal, consistent food quality, etc.

Advertising legend David Ogilvy said years ago that a brand was "the intangible sum of a product's attributes: its name, packaging, and price, its history, its reputation, and the way it's advertised."

Put whatever your company stands for behind your brand and carve out your chosen position in the marketplace. How will you know when you are getting close? You'll know when someone mentions your product or firm and immediately someone else says, "Oh yes, they're the company that . . . "

And what they say next dictates not only the "online" future of your firm, but the degree of its overall success at branding as well.

The elegant style and eye-pleasing watery graphics of the Halekulani's Web site communicate its position at a glance. Its opening graphics show its pool's famous mosaic orchid, and the soft taupe floating script

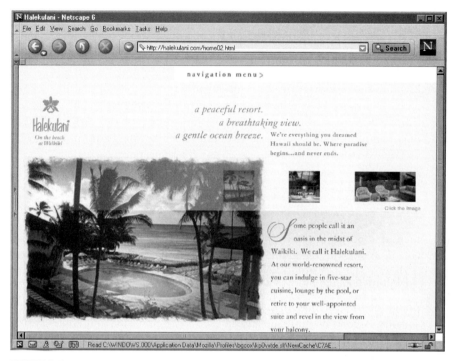

FIGURE 2.3   The Halekulani. (Screen capture from www.halekulani.com/home02.html.)

reinforces the image. The entry rests at the navigation page, shown in Figure 2.3, where it says, "a peaceful resort. a breathtaking view. a gentle ocean breeze. We're everything you dreamed Hawaii should be. Where paradise begins . . . and never ends."

Positioning continues throughout the various pages of the Halekulani site. Figure 2.4, for example, shows the invitation to enjoy a gift of rich dark or milk chocolates—which links to "Learn more about our Pastry Chef" and positioning of the hotel's culinary offerings as well.

Scott's Seafood Restaurants (see Figure 2.5) positions itself as "The best place to dine in the East Bay." It does this with its tagline, graphics that tell visitors about the restaurant's ambience and fine cuisine quality, and by prominently displaying its 5-star awards.

One purpose of Krispy Kreme's corporate Web site (Figure 2.6) is to sell more franchises. To this end, the company does a good job of creating desire among Web site visitors to purchase a franchise in one of the smaller U.S. markets. Krispy Kreme does this, in Figure 2.7, by pointing out that ALL of the franchises in the bigger market cities have been sold (ergo, they must

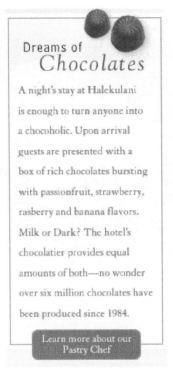

FIGURE 2.4   Dreams of Chocolates, Halekulani.com. (Screen capture from www.halekulani.com/ about/introabout.asp.)

already be highly positioned in the minds of prospects as well as consumers, otherwise they could not be so successful).

Notice how two famous casinos chose entirely different home pages to cause you to hold them in a certain *position* in your mind. Harrah's (Figure 2.8) shows you golden money (chips), lots of it, and a woman who may have just won a jackpot. The site implies, "Easy money for you to win and lots of fun here."

As an added reinforcement of this theme, if you run your cursor over the coins, they collectively produce a sound similar to the one that a slot machine makes when you hit a winning combination. This site appeals to the weekend getaway gambler, the slot machine player—middle America.

Contrast Harrah's home page with that of Caesar's Palace at www. caesarspalace.com, with its Corinthian columns, fine statuary, and fountains. Its focus on "the Empire" speaks "class and culture." This becomes appealing to its primary audience—the longer-stay, upscale visitor who is likely to be a high roller, playing baccarat, roulette, and high-stakes poker. To a parent, Caesar's looks like a safe place to take the whole family for a stay!

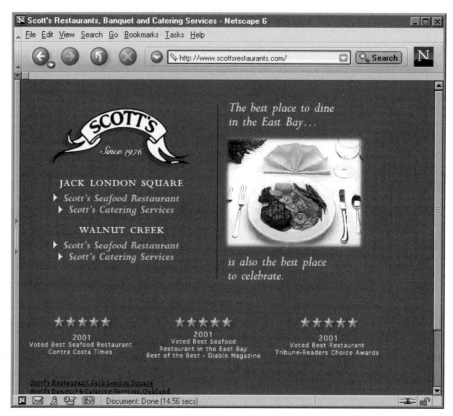

FIGURE 2.5 Scott's Seafood Restaurants (Screen capture from www.scottsrestaurants.com.)

FIGURE 2.6 Krispy Kreme Doughnut Shops. (Screen capture from www.krispykreme.com.)

THANK YOU FOR YOUR INTEREST IN A KRISPY KREME DOUGHNUT CORPORATION FRANCHISE.

As you may be aware, we have granted development rights for all of the major metropolitan markets within the United States. These markets are currently under development and stores will be opening soon. There are no additional franchise opportunities in any major metropolitan market. Regarding future development and franchise opportunities, Krispy Kreme is in the process of finalizing our smaller market strategy. Smaller markets are those markets with populations of less than 150,000. Krispy Kreme plans to develop the balance of the United States with stores in every market and we expect to make an announcement in the near future regarding our expansion into smaller markets.

FIGURE 2.7   Krispy Kreme. (Screen capture from www.krispykreme.com/us.html.)

FIGURE 2.8   Harrahs.com. (Screen capture from www.harrahs.com/index2.html.)

Identifying Your Position

How do you know what position to establish and capture through your Web site? Ask yourself several questions:

What do we do best?

Where do or can we excel?

What positions haven't other businesses in our field already taken?

Whom do we want to attract?

What do we want to accomplish?

Select something in which you excel. The concept of where you excel might be related to price, audience ("We cater to Kids!"), category or segment (business, luxury, leisure, etc.), or some other dimension. The careful delineation of goals (that is, your anticipated accomplishments), is especially important because it must be a realistic assessment of what you can achieve.

Use the checklist in Figure 2.9 to help you think about the position you might want to claim. Place a check next to the items that best fit you; your work; your company, product, or service. Thousands of descriptions can be created or considered, of course, so don't be limited by the few examples provided here.

Identifying Competitors' Positions

Don't overlook what your direct competitors are saying about themselves. Why? Mostly to avoid trying to occupy a position that someone else has already claimed. Also, looking at competitors' positions may give you related ideas or refinements to use for your own position. Examine both the implicit messages (imagery, such as ad photos shot in upscale locales, using celebrity spokespeople who stand for something, etc.) and explicit positioning (what they say about themselves in print, radio, TV, online). Look for subliminal messages too.

Analyze it

For each of the following, which phrase or statement do you think has the most effective positioning? Why?

1. Hotel: "200 rooms on the Colorado River" or "Rated Laughlin's #1 Waterway Hotel"

2. Restaurant: "Continental cuisine, comfortable setting" or "Detroit's biggest menu fits fussy families"

3. Casino: "400 slots with great odds for you" or "Independent studies show our odds pay best"

PART 1:   What do we do well? What are we? Where do we excel?

❑ Advising patrons about which service or time of year best fits their specific needs.

❑ Explaining how to use each service so that patrons really "get" it.

❑ Helping guests decide on the right price and the right time to visit us.

❑ Helping guests expand their business (offering seminars, business center).

❑ Helping guests with a certain type of problem.

❑ Serving large groups. Serving small groups.

❑ Providing unusual or creative services to help those entertaining guests.

❑ Understanding specific needs and priorities of our guests or patrons.

❑ Meeting individualized needs with personal attention.

❑ Allowing guests access to computers for business purposes.

❑ Helping guests with their selections, rooms, meals, or other needs.

❑ Providing terrific concierge services.

❑ We have the most diverse menu in the city.

❑ We provide free limousine service from downtown to our hotel.

❑ We are superb at serving large travel incentive groups.

❑ We excel at serving the religious groups who come to the area to visit the shrine.

❑ Most of our staff members are Muslim; we cater to Muslim guests.

❑ Our online reservation-making system is the easiest to use.

❑ No one makes better desserts than we do.

❑ Every customer at our scuba diving floating hotel gets a free underwater camera and gift bag.

❑ We provide impeccable service to small groups of top executives.

❑ Our chefs were all trained at Le Cordon Bleu in Paris.

❑ We have won top awards this year in our industry.

❑ _____.

Now develop a position statement or "tagline" that fits your business.

FIGURE 2.9   Checklist: Identifying a market position.

PART 2:   What is my hotel or restaurant like?

Check the boxes next to the terms that most accurately describe you or your business.

- ❑   luxurious and utmost quality
- ❑   efficient and timely
- ❑   casually elegant
- ❑   upscale, but "beachy"
- ❑   a family-operated B&B
- ❑   casual
- ❑   formal
- ❑   respectful
- ❑   experienced
- ❑   fun
- ❑   busy
- ❑   friendly
- ❑   _____
- ❑   _____

**PART 3:   What is our product or service like?
What are its features and benefits?**

Check the boxes next to the terms that most accurately describe you or your business.

- ❑   fast check-in and check-out
- ❑   large rooms for family comfort
- ❑   safe side street for pedestrian safety
- ❑   walk to the beach to save time
- ❑   centrally located for local shopping
- ❑   biggest (smallest, fastest, crispiest, hottest, thickest, lightest, etc.)
- ❑   most "like at home" for stress-free comfort
- ❑   food is served within four minutes of ordering
- ❑   food is consistent from visit to visit (You know what you'll get)

FIGURE 2.9   Checklist: Identifying a market position *(continued)*

❑   TexMex barbecue—best in the West

❑   fine dining in an elegant atmosphere

❑   gourmet health food

❑   the pizza with the crispy crust

❑   diverse menu

❑   _____

FIGURE 2.9   Checklist: Identifying a market position *(continued)*

Unique Market Position Statement

A lodging, dining, or gaming facility should be perceived as unique or distinctive when compared to similar products so that the target Web audience values and remembers it. After deciding on a position, communicate it by creating and using a memorable "tagline" or "signature statement." We call this statement or phrase a *unique market position statement* (UMPS). Note that a tagline is just a short, pithy statement that reflects or communicates some key aspect of a product's or company's position—it isn't the position itself.

Martha J. Woodbury discusses the idea of using a unique selling position in "The Competition Killer" (www.nicheswork.com/usp.html). Although she speaks specifically about marketing real estate, the principles Woodbury outlines apply to any business: "You should include your [positioning] statement on everything you print, every talk you give, every article you write for the newspaper, every ad you place, every property sign or rider, in your voice mail message, on your Web site, your business cards, your fax cover sheet, your checks. . . everything you say and do."

Woodbury believes that an effective statement is one that communicates the unique services you provide, empathizes with your prospects' pain or desires, and provides a "guarantee." She prefers that you do this using 20 words or less in a phrase that is "unique, specific, and believable—but outrageous enough that your prospect will read it, stop in their tracks and say, 'Really? How do they do that?'"

She continues, "Connect emotionally with your prospects through fear of loss, greed, ego, desire, pain, frustration, to be better off than the Joneses, save more, make more, have more, spend less, get better service, etc."

How do you translate your marketing position into a UMPS or a "tagline"? Start with the checklist in Figure 2.9 and a dollop of imagination. Did you check "centrally located for local shopping"? Then consider taglines like "When you shop 'til you drop, drop here." Did you check "Providing terrific concierge services"? Consider "The ABC Hotel—We Know You're Special." Did you mark "diverse menu"? Try "If we don't have it, you probably wouldn't want it."

Try it

Write a tagline for each of the following. The name is provided, along with something important about the business.

1. Meyers Family Restaurants. Meyers is a family-style restaurant specializing in homemade soups and pies.

2. Rudy's. Rudy's is a 5-star restaurant located on the San Francisco Bay with a view of San Francisco.

3. Tommy Jean's. Tommy Jean's is a 1950s style drive-in burgers and malts restaurant, complete with carhops on skates.

4. The Morning Glory Hotel. The Morning Glory Hotel is a 5-diamond hotel located in a large city. It caters to the "arts" crowd.

5. The Slim Line Ranch. The Slim Line is a ranch-style inn located in the Midwest, far from any city, that markets to dieters.

6. The Happen Inn. The Happen Inn is an economy family motel located near the highway. The nearest town with other lodging is 120 miles away.

Put your tagline with your company, product, or service name: "Georgia's Pie Shop—We Serve Peaches of Pies!" or "The Sand Bar Lodge—Your Window onto the Sea."

Your Audience(s)

Your audiences, or target markets, are directly related to your positioning, and your Web marketing must address and serve these groups above all others. Such a focus brings more qualified, receptive visitors to your Web site and saves you money and time by avoiding audiences that are less receptive to your message.

Who are these audiences? Yes, of course, they are buyers and information seekers who use the Internet. Just as important, they are the people who will respond to your positioning. If you position yourself as the "Elegant restaurant with limousine service to major area hotels," then your primary Web audience includes people who stay at upscale local hotels.

Planning and developing your Internet marketing requires a little more information than this, however. You must put your understanding of who these people are—their needs and wants, backgrounds, lifestyles, and what motivates them—to work for you. That's why writing a target audience description is an important step in your planning process.

Note that your site may have secondary audiences. These are not the patrons of your establishment; rather, they are the people who *refer* patrons.

For example, let's say that yours is a hotel that caters to professional, or at least highly skilled, golfers. Your primary audience may be defined as the golfers themselves; secondary audiences include pro shops, sporting goods dealers, sport clothing distributors, and so on.

If your hotel is a starting point for many bicycle rides that have thousands of riders who raise millions of dollars annually for charity, after the individual riders, your secondary markets might include bicycle shops, online bicycling sites, and medical industry firms that relate to a recipient field such as breast cancer research. You might also find your audience among outdoor enthusiasts, exercise sites, gymnasiums, or YMCA and YWCA locations.

To clarify your thinking about your target Internet audiences, primary and secondary, draft a description for each of them. Why bother to write a description when you know these people so well? Writing an audience description focuses your attention on the specific characteristics of the group. You improve your ability to create effective marketing statements, think of more helpful tools to place on your Web site, clarify your understanding of what motivates each audience, and maintain focus.

What do you put in an audience description? Based on your own experience with your customers or the clients you wish to attract, write out a description of their markets, industries, lifestyle, education, approximate income, types of careers, leisure activities, and reading habits. Sometimes, this information is called audience "psychographics." Following are a few examples of audience descriptions.

Sample audience description 1: Audience of an upscale B&B on a cliff overlooking a yacht harbor on the Pacific coast

Our target audience is a retired couple, age 60 to 75, who are active, healthy (both physically and financially), and discriminating enough to know that our $200 to $400 per night rates for rooms and suites are a real value. They own their own home, drive here in their own luxury car, dine at a fine restaurant every night while here, and may breakfast in our dining room 75 percent of their stay. They are typically Californians driving from the north, who find and select us due to our high rating in AAA, Exxon/Mobil, Fodor's, or other travel guides. Most guests are physically fit and enjoy walking and working out, which makes our exercise room a selling point for them. About 10 percent of our guests travel with another couple, either friends or relatives. Few of our guests bring children.

Sample audience description 2: Audience of an upscale (for the area) restaurant that features Italian cuisine

Our target patron's average age is 47–65 years old, married, about 30 pounds overweight, retired or semi-retired with good retirement income or is at the height of his career. He owns a four-year-old upscale car or SUV and dines out at least four times weekly. Money for dinner is not a major concern, but he does demand quality food and appealing presentation, plus a good selection of wines. Special emphasis is placed on breads, and he tips generously when the food and service please him.

Sample audience description 3: Audience of college town cybercafe

Our target audience plays video and online games passionately, ranges in age from 18 through 24, is quite savvy about computers and the Internet, and uses our computers for games and e-mails to friends and family at home. Our patrons prefer hamburgers, fries, shakes, pizzas, and big sandwiches. They live with their parents when not at school, and are budget conscious, although 70 percent are subsidized by their parents. About half have their own car at school. They tend to be above-average students and take college seriously. In the past, advertising with cost-saving coupons in the school newspaper and on school bulletin boards has been an effective way to reach this target audience.

Sample audience description 4: Audience of a horse ranch bed and breakfast, presented in a "list" format

- *Family:* #1 Married couple with two or three children; #2 Retired couple
- *Home:* Lives in semi-rural area with space and zoning for one to four horses
- *Education:* Some college or college graduate
- *Career/employment/income:* Sales, teaching, management; combined annual income range of $100,000–$150,000
- *Age:* 36–50
- *Home size:* 2,000 to 2,800 sq. ft.; 4 or 5 bedrooms
- *Home entertaining:* Casual, patio, barbecue
- *Activities:* Mostly family oriented: horse training, riding events, school events, sports
- *Cars:* At least one van or 5-passenger pickup or SUV (not new)
- *Shopping:* Standard and discount malls, tackle shops, Western stores
- *Magazines:* News, horse, home improvement, gardening, country
- *TV:* Watch family programming, cable sports, animal, and kid channels
- *Pets:* Probably several dogs or cats in addition to the horse(s)

After reading these descriptions, you should feel that you know a little more about each audience. You have enough information to be able to ask a new guest a few questions to begin communication and the relationship-building process, and you have enough information to plan some of your Web site content.

Try it

Write a target audience description for one of your business's target audiences. Use either a paragraph or list format. To get started, imagine that a close friend has just said to you, "Describe the people who are your guests or patrons." If possible, give a short name description of the audience you describe, such as "Wall Street lunch crowd," "after-work-hours young singles," or "value-conscious DINKS (dual income, no kids)."

Web Marketing Goals: What Do You Want Your Site to Do for You?

Your marketing goals for your Web site must be specifically related to the goals (or some of the goals) listed in your company's comprehensive written general marketing plan. A company that has a Web site with goals that are incompatible with the overall corporate goals is misguided.

A Web site's *own* individual mission, scope, goals, objectives, tactics, policies, and procedures can, however, be structured to perform services and reach audiences that reflect, support, and enhance other company communications or specific aspects or parts of those communications without being identical to them. For example, a restaurant/bar that caters to steak-loving adults may use a really "hip" Web site to draw in a 20- and 30-something young dinner crowd for drinks and dancing in a "club setting" *after* the dinner hour.

Part of planning your Internet marketing must include determining what your Web site should offer its visitors and what you want your site to do for you. What will position the site in a particular way in the visitor's mind? What are your goals for your site? Why are you building this site? What is your practical business goal?

Goals are specific to your type of business. The Web site goals for a firm that sells antique jewelry are far different from those of a firm selling farm tractors through a nationwide dealership network. Likewise, the Web goals for a Waldorf Astoria differ from those of a hotel that serves a convention center. The goals for your hospitality Web site must become extensions of your business plan and your marketing plan. Studying those documents will give you leads on setting your Web site goals.

Following are some reasons hospitality businesses give for setting up their Web site and its individual pages:

- Getting new guests
- Expanding our visitor base
- Retaining current guests

- Getting referrals from current guests
- Initiating frequent contact with guests
- Getting newsletter subscribers
- Providing driving directions and maps to the facility
- Giving incentives such as frequent diner or frequent guest bonuses
- Publicizing art shows, auctions, performances, or seminars held at our location
- Announcing entertainers in main and secondary showrooms

Sometimes, goals are defined in the context of more information about a business; for example:

1. Our inn is losing sales to competitors because they have a site and we don't. We don't care if our site is great or not. We just need one to compete. **Goal:** Minimal presence. Probably not a customer relationship marketing site.

2. When people see our print ads for our "changes-every-day" menu, they phone and e-mail us questions about the day's menu. The Web site makes doing that easier. We post the menus for the week. The site also tells them about us and gives location and reservation information too. **Goal:** Answer the most common questions that are generated by our print ads to save considerable time on the part of our customer service staff. Probably a hospitality service information site.

3. We are a small 50-room hotel in Nebraska, situated with 10 other hotels on the freeway 6 miles outside of town. Our site tells our audience why they will like our extra-large rooms for their families. The site describes many extra services that we offer, especially for children, that none of the nearby hotels offer. **Goal:** Compete successfully with hotels that offer services that are more limited; get travelers to choose *them*. Not enough interactivity to qualify as a customer relationship marketing site.

4. Our exclusive inn specializes in selling gift products costing more than $5,000. Our site portrays our gift store as the "prestige gift boutique." People who want to buy such items often select us over others in our market niche, and we want to keep it that way. **Goal:** Maintain a position, or even leadership, in upscale gifts. Could be any of the four types of sites described in Chapter 1.

5. Our hilltop restaurant offers a vista view of the valley during the day and, at night, a glimmering "city lights" perspective—all this in a rustic 1849 theme of gold mining. We are a perfect venue for weddings with our huge outdoor patio and interior greatroom featuring Bose sound systems and AV equipment for showing photos and videos.

Goal: Capture area wedding business and families enjoying view dining. Is mainly an information site, much like a brochure.

6. Our casino has six restaurants, all of differing great cuisines, wide menus, and reasonable price ranges. We are a great choice for families on a week's vacation because we have something for everyone food-wise. Much of our Web site talks about menu items and the key dining enjoyments at each venue. **Goal:** Gain long-term stays by families due to family food choices. The site is information only and could be made stronger by offering recipes of some of their most popular dishes.

These, of course, are just examples. There are thousands of specific reasons that companies have for creating a Web presence. Now, it's your turn. Write a statement of your Web site marketing goal(s).

Try it

Describe your business briefly. List three goals for a Web site for your hospitality business.

Summary

Web sites that successfully market a company, product, or service have been built on careful, conscious *positioning*. They target specific, well-understood *audiences*, and they are designed to achieve specific, and where possible, measurable *goals*.

Review Questions

1. Why should your business distinguish itself from competitors?
2. What are some ways in which your business is different from competitors?
3. In what ways are your facilities or services different from those of competitors?
4. How are your competitors trying to position themselves in the marketplace?
5. How do competitors portray their services or menu offerings as different or better?
6. How does your positioning relate to your target audiences?
7. How do you go about defining your target audiences?

8. List three common goals of most Web sites.

9. List three common Web site mistakes.

10. How important is it to budget adequately for Web site promotion?

11. What is branding?

12. What is a "lookie-me" Web site?

13. What does a UMPS do?

14. Why are secondary target audiences important?

15. List your firm's secondary target audiences in order of importance.

16. How can your Web site attract secondary target audiences?

Review Activities

1. Write three positioning statements for the following products or services:

    a. A beach-front B&B in southern California overlooking a pier.

    b. A small casino on the outskirts of Reno. It pays the best odds in town.

    c. The finest traditional Italian restaurant in a desert town of 50,000 people.

    d. A pizza emporium serving the widest selection of gourmet pizzas in the state.

    e. The newest, finest airport hotel at LAX—free shuttles every 10 minutes!

2. Imagine you're in an elevator and you have 30 seconds to answer the question, "What business are you in?" What do you say?

3. Your company has asked you to create a bumper sticker that will communicate how your offering is special. Develop two bumper stickers—one that positions the company, one for one of its services.

4. Your Web site needs a title. Write the title using no more than 11 words.

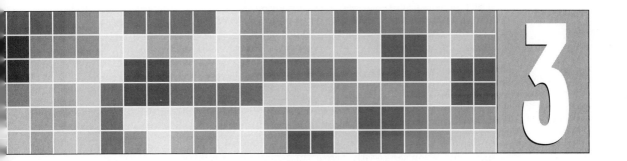

More Than a Pretty Face

Web Site Content

Tumbleweed's Web site illustrates several ways to use content that communicate positioning and increase the likelihood of repeat visits. Visitors know from its title—Tumbleweed® Southwest Grill—what this restaurant is all about. The information on "cowboy cuisine," locations, the legend of TexMex, kid stuff, coupons, employment, and investor relations provides plenty of material for visitors to explore at the moment or on a return visit. (Screen capture from www.tumbleweedrestaurant.com.)

Is Tumbleweed's a fun place? Click on the "Big Deals!!" link. Tumbleweed's celebrates Mondays with margarita specials, Wild West Wednesdays with "All-You-Can-Eat baby back ribs or chicken with plenty of fixins. And leave yer hat and spurs on, it's what city folk call 'atmosphere.'" Homefire Sundays let you "chow down on as many 10 oz. USDA Choice Sirloin steaks and potatoes as you can handle." And more . . .

The content and design of a hospitality Web site must do work. This means that content has to communicate the branding or unique market position statement (UMPS) *immediately*. As soon as a page displays on visitors' monitors, they should *know* that this site has the information, products, or Web functions they seek—otherwise they may not stay long.

When a home page compels visitors from a target audience to think, "This is the place!" they will be much more likely to explore the site. If the content is *useful* to them, as well as interesting, informative, and, in many cases, fun, they'll stick around for a while—and make reservations, order pizza, or send an e-mail to ask about banquet facilities.

This chapter helps you identify the content that will be most effective for your market position, audience, and goals.

THE BASICS

The types and sizes of businesses using the Internet for marketing are extremely diverse, and their Web sites may also be very different. Some Web sites are devoted entirely to a single product or service. Others are created specifically to provide follow-up on direct mail or telephone marketing or television, radio, or other media advertising. Some market the services of an individual location; others market the services or products of a parent company with many locations and thousands of employees.

Nonetheless, most Web sites do share some common features, including information on the location(s), the services or products available, the people, and how to contact the company. Increasingly, lodging sites provide ways for Web visitors to make reservations. Some restaurants provide ways for people to place delivery or take-out orders or provide information about a planned banquet or other event. Depending on the business type and the size of its Web site, there may be information on how to apply for a position with the company, company news, job openings, and links to other sites with related information.

Having all of these parts does not guarantee an effective Web site, however. A site could, for example, claim a particular position, for example, "most guest friendly," and then fail to support that position with easy ways for customers to find driving directions or menu choices or equipment availability. Or it might provide an online order form "for fast and easy reservations" that is so lengthy and complicated that visitors take one look at the information requested—and leave.

The content of your Web site will, as we said earlier, depend on your positioning, audience, and goals. From this perspective, regardless of the market position of a business, product, or service, the site must include content that fulfills the following requirements.

The Site Should Communicate the Market Positioning or Branding

Regardless of the size, look, complexity, or sophistication of a site, no visitor should ever leave it without knowing the intended market positioning. A company's UMPS (see Chapter 2), or that of its product or service, should be prominent and clear. Use a tagline with the company or product name to help visitors recognize the intended market position immediately. A few (very few) companies are branded so strongly that they need no more than their name to communicate their position; for example, Waldorf-Astoria and St. Regis (exclusive, attentive, elite), McDonald's (fast, consistent, kid-friendly), and Golden Nugget (mid-range gaming establishment). The names convey their image quickly, clearly, and consistently to huge numbers of people.

The Site Should Prove or Support the Market Positioning

Merely stating that this is a company (hotel, inn, restaurant, drive-thru, casino, etc.) that is or does something special is not enough. Support the overall market positioning with information about the company and its people, products, and services. Include content, both written and visual, that clearly demonstrates that a particular product is the fastest, friendliest, healthiest, or whatever else characterizes its market position.

The Site Should Give Visitors Useful Information Related to the Business, Products, or Services

This may include content that informs and educates visitors; gives them reliable resources they need or will need; helps them solve problems or make decisions related to lodging, meals, or entertainment; or entertains them. You should know from experience or from market research what your guests or patrons need or want. The Web site should help meet those needs.

The Site Should Provide Content that is Interesting to the Target Audience

Interesting content, most likely related to your market position, will attract them, hold their attention, and bring them back for repeat visits. Is yours an authentic *trattoria* Italian restaurant? Then, consider adding content or links to other sites with Italian cuisine content, such as recipes, choosing wines to go with Italian dishes, making Italian breads, or fork etiquette when eating pasta. Are you a small inn positioned as the "health spa inn that pampers you"? Then, pages with content on the benefits of meditation or mud baths or fresh air might be of interest. Does your restaurant sell its own private-label bottled salad dressing? What content would you add?

The Site Should Enable and Encourage Visitors to Take Action

Site visiters should be encouraged to ask questions, place orders, make comments, and contact you. Web sites that sell products or services direct to purchasers should include various easy-to-understand ways for Web visitors to purchase online and offline. If an important Web site objective is to increase lodging or dining reservations, the visitor should be able to guarantee or pay for the reservation online and then receive an instant confirmation either on-screen for printing or via email.

Most Web visitors like to communicate using their computers. If the only way they can reach you is by telephone, chances are they'll go elsewhere. You must provide ways for them to communicate with you. A link that opens a visitor's e-mail program with a blank, pre-addressed message is still the most common device that Internet visitors use to send questions and comments to Web site owners. Place a "contact us" link on *every* page. Explore other ways for visitors to communicate—online forms to complete, a guest book for leaving comments, bulletin boards, and even scheduled live chats. You never know when, during a tour of your site, a visitor will be struck with an uncontrollable desire to contact you, so make it easy—from everywhere on your site. (Chapter 5 discusses some of the more advanced functions for visitor communication.)

BEYOND THE BASICS
More About Communicating Market Positioning or Branding

Any visitor entering your site should know immediately what market positioning you are claiming or striving for. Your company's UMPS should be prominent and clear on the home page, and that positioning should be reinforced on subsequent pages. Such a statement, whether in text, graphics, or both, works to establish, reinforce, or build market positioning or brand identity.

A direct way to communicate a position "at a glance" is by using a tagline, headline, or visual element at the top of the page. This element or combination of elements should communicate what the company, business, product, or service means for the Web site visitor. The entry page for Six Continent Hotels, for example, indicates the Six Continent's flexibility and range with its headline: "Any location. Any reason. Any budget." (The positioning could be the overall positioning or it could be some marketing position that is developed specifically for the Web that is consistent with the "bigger picture.") The text reads: "Whether you're on business or on vacation, or whether you want luxury or the best value, we have a hotel for you. Book a hotel right here with any of our brands across the globe for all of your travel needs." Furthermore, by displaying the emblems of its various properties prominently on the page, Six Continents Hotels provides support—evidence—for its claim.

On the Tumbleweed's Web site (see chapter opening), the overall appearance, link labels, and welcome (Howdy Pardner) tell visitors that this is a friendly, casual, Western-theme restaurant where they won't find pretentiousness or snootiness . . . just fun and good food.

What is the positioning for the MGM Grand (www.mgmgrand.com)? The City of Entertainment! Visitors know immediately that the MGM Grand is a high energy, high profile, immense property with everything you'd find in a city, especially entertainment.

More About Site Content That Supports Your Market Positioning

By themselves, positioning statements may not be convincing, especially if the product, service, or business being presented is not already well known. One of the jobs of Web site content is to provide support for the position being claimed within its market segment.

As with most things about the Internet, how Web sites support some claimed position varies widely. To some degree, however, similarities can be found among some groups of sites.

In Chapter 2, we discussed ways to segment the hospitality market. One way to begin to determine what content is needed or wanted is to examine some similar types of content for those segments. The Web site must communicate both the segment being targeted and the position being claimed or supported.

Analyze it

Compare the screen captures on the following pages, related to four restaurants that serve seafood. What positioning is each claiming for its product? How does each communicate that position? (Figures 3.1, 3.2, 3.3, 3.4.)

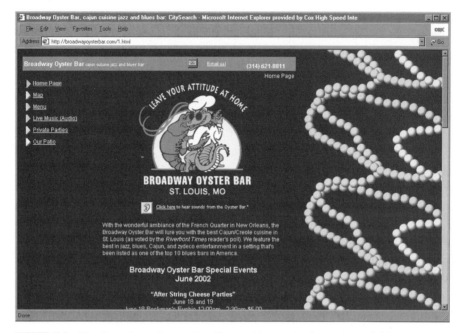

FIGURE 3.1   The Broadway Oyster Bar. "Leave Your Attitude at Home." (Screen capture from http://broadwayoysterbar.com/1.html.)

FIGURE 3.2   Neptune's Palace. (Screen capture from www.pier39restaurants.com/neptunes.htm.)

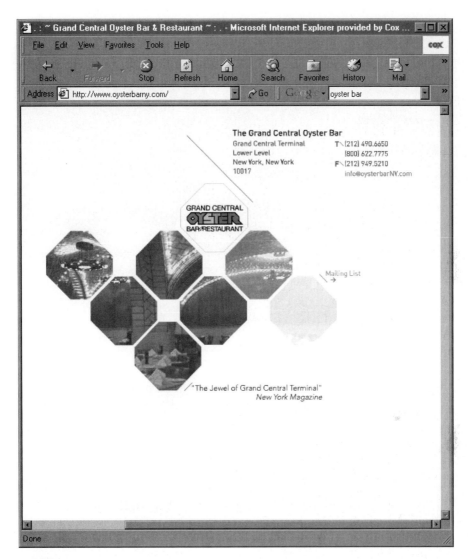

FIGURE 3.3   The Grand Central Oyster Bar. (Screen capture from www.oysterbar.com.)

The following is a list of the most common content types or categories for sites related to lodging, food services, and gaming:

- Online reservations
- The property or establishment, including a map or directions
- The place (setting)
- The services and amenities
- Products or menu
- The people

FIGURE 3.4   Red Lobster. (Screen capture from www.redlobster.com.)

- Testimonials or reviews
- History
- Gaming
- Information for job seekers
- The brand (with links to individual properties)
- Parent corporation information (with links to brands and locations), including investor or company news and media relations

Online Reservations

Whether large or small; corporate, brand, or independent; plain or fancy, lodging establishments must have a way for Web visitors to make reservations. This could be a corporatewide proprietary system, participation in one or several travel reservation systems, or something as simple as reservations by e-mail, but a driving force in Web marketing for lodging is the reservation capability.

Some restaurants may also want to avail themselves of a reservation option. If yours is a successful upscale establishment for which reservations are made far in advance, consider adding a floor plan that allows patrons to reserve a particular table as well. (This topic is discussed in greater detail in Chapter 5).

The Property or Establishment

Web visitors expect to find some basic information about a property or establishment, including its general characteristics, size, pricing, style, and valued features. This may be as brief as a few words. More often, however, it includes descriptions or photos of the accommodations, a main entrance, or courtyard or an environmental shot inside a restaurant. Often, this content is addressed in various internal sections of the site.

The establishment's address should be somewhere on the home page; a clear map and directions can be on a separate page. If yours is a one-page site or a single page that is part of a larger site, the map and directions will be on that page.

If the establishment is part of a brand line, marketed by a large company, or has a parent corporation, links to the line, umbrella, or parent company Web site can also help position the product. An example of this is a Best Western Inn in a particular city having a link to the Best Western umbrella site that leads to all of the Best Western properties in the chain.

Find, for example, the page for the Kronborg Inn in Solvang, California, which has a link (the logo in the upper left-hand corner) to the umbrella site for Best Western Inns.

The Place

Many establishments draw guests because of their geographic location or environment. This is especially true of resorts, convention and airport hotels, and some urban business centers. Web marketing for such establishments benefits from capitalizing on the location with text and photos. Businesses located in little-known areas—a bed and breakfast in an out-of-the-way valley or a dude ranch in the Arizona desert, for example—may have to educate Web visitors about the area, as well as inform them about the accommodations.

The Casa Tropicana Bed and Breakfast (Figure 3.5) in San Clemente, California, displays photos and information about its beach location. The site also provides links to information on area attractions and entertainment, such as Catalina day trips, Mission San Juan Capistrano, fishing charters, Dana Point Harbor, and local shopping.

Services and Amenities

What about services? Services can be shown on the Internet in ways similar to the brochures you find in banks, doctors' offices, print shops, or other service providers—but with a great deal more content and sophistication. How do providers of similar services distinguish themselves? Generally speaking, the answer lies in the quality and range of the services they provide. It also lies in how well the establishment communicates that it prides itself on those services. If, for example, your services are limited to

FIGURE 3.5   Casa Tropicana. (Screen capture from www.casatropicana.com/images/ 19.jpg.)

registration, housekeeping, and check-out, communicate how well you do those things. Demonstrate that these activities are important to you.

The "Amenities" page for the MGM Grand, as we saw it late in 2003 (http://mgmgrand.com/pages/amenities.asp) displayed an impressive array (see the box below). Only other large, upscale complexes could provide some of these services. Some, however, are commonly found in other segments of the lodging industry, such as "beverage and ice service" on every floor.

Down the left side of the MGM Grand Amenities page, you will see links to various amenities—Grand Spa, Grand Pool Complex, Wedding Chapel, golf, and shopping. Of course, few establishments have all of the amenities of the MGM Grand. The point is to be sure to list, describe, and point out the benefits of the ones you do have.

Does your restaurant provide take-out or delivery service? Catering? Banquet services? Help with wine selection? Does your quick-serve business have longer hours or drive-through service (or to-your-car delivery)?

You may take some of your services for granted because they are common in your market segment. Daily housekeeping, an ice machine (that works), non-smoking rooms or floors, or direct-dial telephone service may seem unworthy of mention. But using such taglines as "Fresh towels every day," "Convenient ice service," "Rooms with clean, fresh air for non-smokers," and "Phone home direct!" could make a Web marketing difference.

Be sure to label the link to your services in a way that tells Web visitors what information is lurking there. The Mayan Palace, Puerto Vallarta, Mexico (www.mayanpalace.com/puertovallarta/puertovallarta.html), lists

Only the Best at MGM Grand

MGM Grand in Las Vegas offers a number of exciting amenities and services, including a Youth Activity Center for kids, an arcade, tour packages, a golf desk, a wedding chapel, and two full-service business centers, to name a few.

MGM Grand also provides a complete line of services to cater to the guest's every need. These services include:

- 24-hour room service
- Multi-lingual staff
- Beverage and ice service on every floor
- Free covered parking for 12,000 cars
- Complimentary valet parking
- Rollaway beds and cribs
- One-stop shopping reservation/ticketing services
- Foreign currency exchange
- Safe deposit boxes
- Laundry/valet/dry cleaning
- Car rental
- Tour information
- Business center
- Voice-mail messaging
- Facilities for disabled guests
- Airport registration and hotel check-in

This last service is the first of its kind opened by a hotel at any U.S. airport: Guests of MGM Grand can check in/register and receive their room keys while they wait for their luggage at McCarran Airport. Other services available at the airport registration facility include restaurant reservations and the opportunity to purchase show tickets for MGM MIRAGE properties in Las Vegas.

many high-value services on an internal page—but the link to the page says "Facilities." Maybe Web visitors seeking a place with bicycle rentals, 24-hour taxi service, laundry and dry cleaning, car rental, travel agency, medical service, or safety deposit boxes will find the page, maybe not.

Many food service establishments post a menu on their Web site or page, sometimes with images of the dishes or of their patrons relishing their dining experience. An online menu can be especially helpful to prospective patrons who are in the process of making a dining decision.

Consider enhancing the information, going beyond the list of items to tell Web users about the nutritional content of your meals, the availability of certain seasonal foods, the lobster flown in daily, or the latest creation of your chef. Wherever appropriate for your menu, add details about heart-healthy choices, specials for kids or seniors, or the quality of your ingredients.

Businesses with various products to sell, either online or off, create store-fronts and catalogs on the Internet. The Web provides the perfect technol-ogy for catalog presentation and searching. Companies selling their own products exclusively and those retailing the products of many other com-panies are both easily found on the Net.

Catalog sites can be simple listings and descriptions of the items or com-plex searchable sites. The Ritz-Carlton, for example, lets Web visitors order products online from their gift shops (see Figure 3.6). If you have a gift shop that sells items with your logo, make the items available for sale on your site. The MGM Grand sells logo products online, which serves a dual pur-pose—the sale of logo-bearing products produces profit and the products become mobile billboards for the hotel. Do you sell your secret barbecue sauce, salad dressing, pasta, or seasonings? If you have the capability of man-aging the inventory and shipping, then add these to your site's offerings.

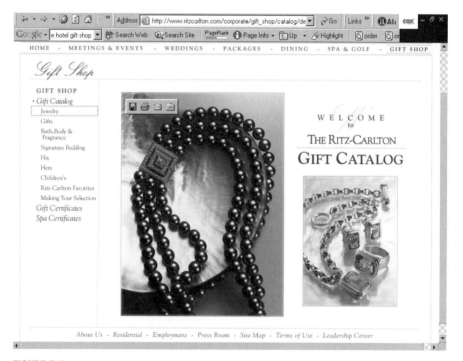

FIGURE 3.6   The Ritz-Carlton Gift Catalog. (Screen capture from www.ritzcarlton.com/corporate/gift_shop/catalog/default.asp.) Copyright© 1998–2002, The Ritz-Carlton Hotel Company, LLC. Reprinted with permission of the Ritz-Carlton Hotel Company, L.L.C.

The People

Increasingly, we see what we think is a positive addition to business Web sites—information about the people who own, operate, and work for the business. Like the pages on the company's history, its accomplishments and news or stories about the people who make it happen work to make a computer technology phenomenon more human. The approach is built on the philosophy that most people still want to deal with people. In addition, when people can send inquiries or other messages to a named individual, their confidence that the message will actually be read is significantly increased.

Use the site to introduce the owners or top management. The executives of a firm are important assets for customers, shareholders, other investors, and even employees. Don't have them dominate the site; rather, just have a home page link to "Executives," "Management Team," or something similar. Restaurants may include links to the chef's biography; hotels may include links to exhibit or convention coordinators, A/V specialists, and so forth. Include a photo and brief biography of each executive, emphasizing the aspects of their experience that are most pertinent to the business. Try to get quotes from them related to their history or their belief in the company. Avoid posting a complete (and often impersonal) business resume.

Visit Starwood (www.starwood.com), and note that it makes its management team public by first giving their names and titles and a link to further information. Clicking on the individual's name takes you to a photo and capsule biography. Offering information about executives in this manner says "We are proud of our capable management team," which is reassuring to Web site visitors—especially investors.

Tell Web visitors about your regional managers, local managers, salespeople, customer service representatives, your chef, hair designer, and other employees. Firms with branch offices, dealers, or manufacturer's representatives around the country often add photos and introductions for the managers of these operations too. Why? Because this is a way to increase the local connection with buyers or clients. Information about people can increase the comfort level of Web visitors with the business. No longer is it just an electronic brochure—it is a personal tool to build relationships.

Some small businesses (e.g., a local restaurant with about 20 employees) post a personal webpage for each employee. Each person's responsibilities are listed, along with a photo taken while working. This helps local customers get to know the people in the business and tends to increase employee loyalty. Do you name an employee of the month? Be sure to add the announcement to the Web site. Del Taco places its people stories in its "Employment" section (Figure 3.7).

One caveat: *Be sensitive to and respect the desires of individuals who do not wish to have information about them placed on the Internet!*

FIGURE 3.7   Del Taco employment page. (Screen capture from www.deltaco.com, framed from "Employment" link.)

Testimonials or Reviews

Hundreds of sites exist today into which consumers may enter testimonials about various hotels or restaurants. One of the leading sites where consumers may rate almost anything is Epinions at www.epinions.com.

Testimonials can be an important part of building credibility for a product or service, especially for businesses that are one among many clone-like competitors or for sites that sell readily available items. Historic Cary House Hotel in northern California's gold country provides a link on its home page to testimonials. Clicking on the link (see the link menu on left side of the home page in Figure 3.8) takes visitors to an entire page of testimonials (Figure 3.9). The testimonials page bears a statement, at both the top and bottom, inviting each visitor to leave a testimonial. The statement says, "Have you ever stayed at the Cary House? Give us your testimonial." The link opens a new e-mail box for sending the narrative testimonial.

Note that getting the testimonials by e-mail or common gateway interface (CGI) form allows the site owner to be selective about which comments to display and to edit or delete any truly offensive testimonials. (If you ever have a comments or suggestions section of an intranet for your employees, however, you will be wise to include negative messages if they are attributed to

FIGURE 3.8   Cary House Hotel. (Screen capture from www.caryhouse.com.)

the author. Editing or deleting these causes you to lose the trust of employees and they will cease using the comments or suggestion section.)

Has your restaurant received a positive review in the press recently? Perhaps on a restaurant review site such as Epinions.com? Be sure to add the review or a link to it to your Web site. Have celebrities eaten at your place? Did you take your picture with them? Be sure to put these on the Web site too. It's a good idea to ask their permission to post the photo on the Web, even if they agree to the photo in the first place.

History

Sometimes, the history of the business or establishment engages the personal interest of the Web visitor, enhances credibility, and supports positioning. This has been a natural for country inns and Victorian or colonial (or just old) bed and breakfasts. Other businesses have benefited from the approach as well. For example, Carl Karcher Enterprises, Inc. (owner of the Carl's Jr., Hardee's, and Taco Bueno quick-service food outlets), has an "About Us" page with three links that lead to financial info, press releases, and Carl's Jr. history. Carl Karcher Enterprises (CKE) tells an entrepreneurial "super-story" on its history page (Figure 3.10), along with a decade-by-decade illustrated look at CKE milestones—a great rags-to-riches story from the 1940s.

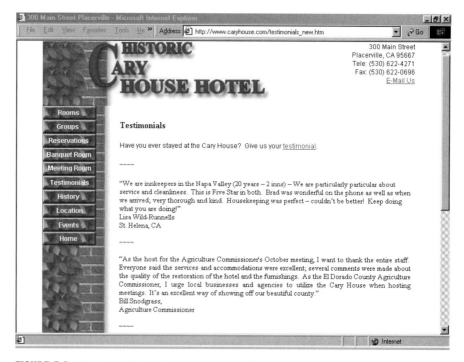

FIGURE 3.9   Testimonials on CaryHouse.com. (Screen capture from www.caryhouse. com/testimonial.html.)

Having left the family farm in Ohio, Carl moved to California with dreams of someday starting his own business. Carl and Margaret borrowed $311 on their Plymouth, added $15 of their own to buy the hotdog cart, and started their own business on July 17, 1941.

A few carts later. . . Carl and Margaret moved to Anaheim and opened their first full-service restaurant, Carl's Drive-In Barbecue, which opened on January 16, 1945. Carl always enjoyed his work and always attempted to treat his customers as if they were in his own home. He believed that hard work and dedication would make him successful at whatever he tried to accomplish. . . and it did! In 1946, Carl introduced hamburgers to the menu for the first time.

Carl's Jr. has had that story retold thousands of times by the media, gaining the firm hundreds of thousands of dollars worth of free media space over the years.

Another good example is the story told by Del Taco (Figure 3.11). So, if you have a terrific story to tell about how your business got started, or if your establishment has an illustrious, infamous, or intriguing past, tell it every chance you get! Do it especially on your Web site's "History" page.

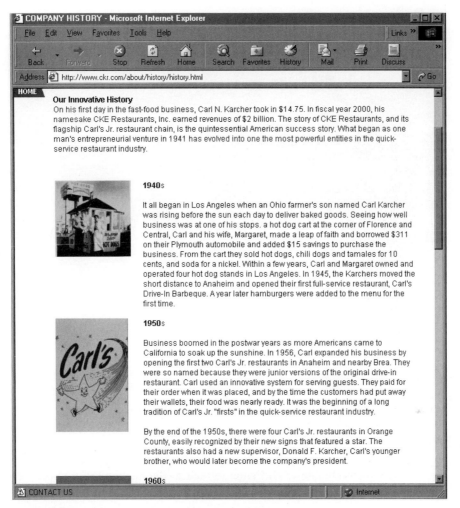

FIGURE 3.10   Carl Karcher Enterprises, Inc. (Screen capture from www.ckr.com/about/ history/history.html.)

Gaming

One of the best places to find ideas for valuable content related to gaming is through the library resources of the University of Las Vegas, particularly its section called the International Casino Promotional and Public Relations Archive (www.library.unlv.edu/speccol/grc/ICPPRA.html). About the archive, the library says:

> The International Casino Promotional and Public Relations Archive houses promotional and public relations material from casinos throughout

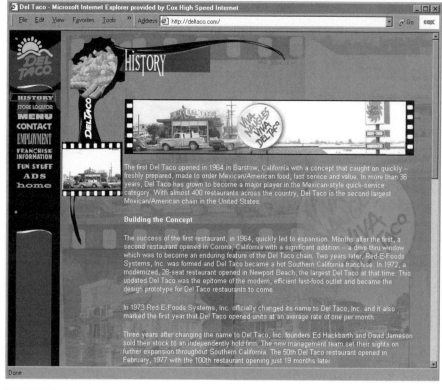

FIGURE 3.11   Del Taco's history page. (Screen capture from www.deltaco.com/
content_history.html in main frame.)

the world. Most casino public relations departments have chosen to add
the Gaming Studies Research Center to their media mailing lists and promotional lists. Typical materials received include press releases, entertainment schedules and information, publicity photographs, informational
brochures, and player newsletters and promotional mailings.

The International Casino Promotional and Public Relations Archive is
a valuable resource for both industry professionals and academic scholars.
Public relations executives will be able to consult the world's largest database of casino promotional materials. They will be able to explore what
other properties are doing throughout the English-speaking world. Academic researchers will be able to get a unique look at the business and culture of the gaming world. Because the files will be continuously
maintained, they will provide a resource for years to come.

Another valuable resource for generating ideas for gaming site content
and how to promote it can be found in the Gaming Studies Collection
(GSC) of the University of Las Vegas, located only minutes from "the Strip,"
home to many of the most famous Las Vegas hotels (see the source line for

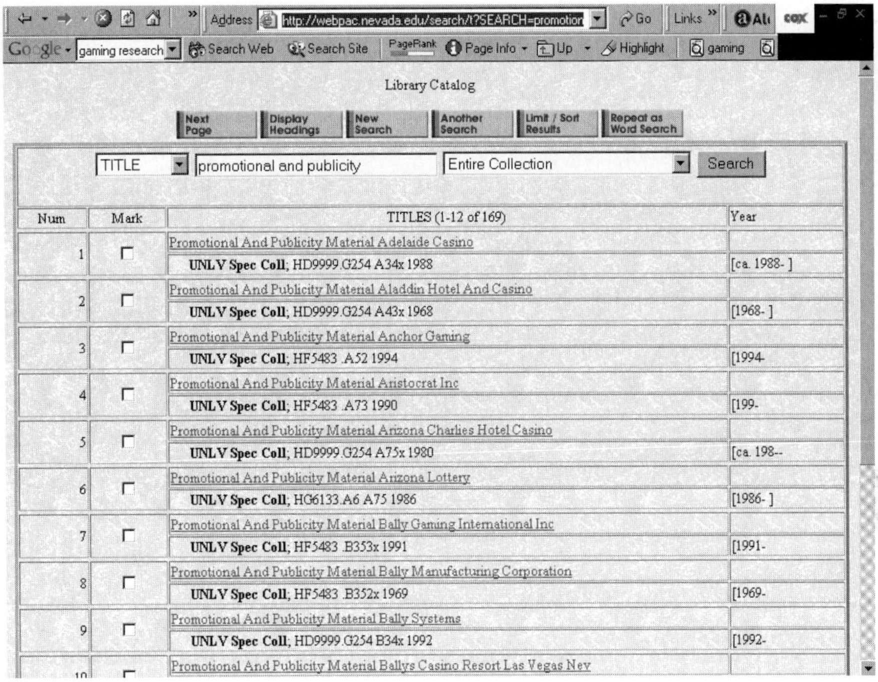

FIGURE 3.12   Gaming promotion articles. (Screen capture from http://webpac.nevada. edu/search/t?SEARCH=promotional+and+publicity.)

Figure 3.12 for the URL). The GSC collects and maintains "press releases, newspaper clippings, newsletters, and other types of promotional material from over 150 casinos, regulatory agencies, and other organizations." Use these resources to gain insight into Web site content and related promotions that you could use for your establishment.

Responsible gaming content often includes cautions about excessive or compulsive gambling. The MGM Grand Hotel and Casino does an excellent job of cautioning site visitors against getting "hooked" (see Figure 3.13).

One of the best ways to get people to try gaming is to teach them how the games are played. MGM Grand lets visitors get a taste of gaming by playing for fun. When you click on "Play Games" on a major MGM Grand Webpage, you are sent to the partner of MGM/Mirage for online gaming, WagerWorks.com, at www.WagerWorks.com.

The MGM/WagerWorks site lets people register for free (while gaining considerable contact information during the registration process), then learn how to game by playing for "points" that can be redeemed for prizes. The idea is that as people gain skill and enjoyment from playing the free games, they may well switch over to playing games for real money later.

As you might imagine, gaming conjures all forms of demons for some people, so you must be especially sensitive about what kind of content you

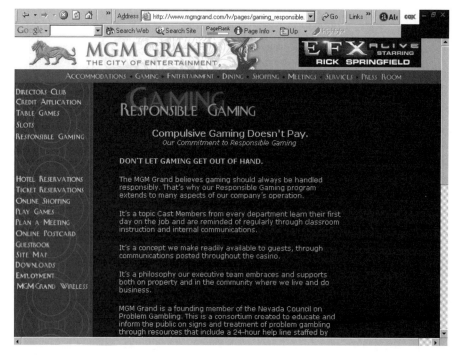

FIGURE 3.13 MGM Grand Web page about responsible gaming. (Screen capture from www.mgmgrand.com/lv/pages/gaming_responsible.asp.)

put on your online gaming site. The same caution applies to a Web site that solely serves a bricks-and-mortar casino. Use common sense and be sure to ask your Web site designers for many interim drafts and storyboard layouts of any site they make for you. Have those plans reviewed by your attorney, as well as tested by focus groups and other market research approaches. Web designers are not casino operators. They have to be guided when developing appropriate content for a casino-related Web site.

Information for Job Seekers

Information for job seekers appears on all types of sites—corporate, brand, and individual locations and establishments. Don't overlook this opportunity to connect with individuals who are seeking employment in the hospitality industry. The Internet provides a means for them to come to you with very little recruiting effort on your part.

Large hotels can employ thousands of workers. And hospitality employment bases typically exhibit a high turnover rate, sometimes as high as 50 percent a year or more. Today, the Internet is being used more and more by job seekers. Therefore, be sure to consider listing your firm's job openings on your Web site when you are adding content.

Parent Corporation Information (with links to the brands and locations)

Parent corporation sites often include information for investors such as news releases and annual reports. They also link to their various brands. For example, the emblems displayed on the Six Continents Hotels site link to the site for each brand—Inter Continental, Holiday Inn, and so forth.

Another example is Starwood, the parent firm of Sheraton, which emphasizes bargains and low price destinations on its umbrella site for its Sheraton, Westin, and Four Points properties. Links on this umbrella page take visitors to the webpages for each hotel brand, which, in turn, link to the webpages for individual hotels. Links also lead to Starwood's upscale property (the St. Regis), its "Luxury Collection" of 70 exceptional properties in more than 25 countries, and its quality W Hotels.

Corporate sites often include two categories of information that are not usually found on brand sites and even less frequently on sites of individual establishments: information for investors and for the media. Company news, changes in management, acquisitions, earnings reports, annual meeting announcements or reports, and other investor-related information can be a critical focus of those sites whose audience includes its investors and other stakeholders. Likewise, corporate sites often present information for the media about contacting your communications officer(s), being on your press release list, or who to call for more information about recent events or developments in your company.

More About Providing Content of High Interest to Your Target Audience

Arresting content and engaging functions make a site "sticky," a term that closely relates to how much time visitors spend at a site and how often they return. A few hours on the Internet spent exploring some business-related sites will provide ample examples of content that enhances the richness of a site, engages visitors' interest so that they spend time there, and earns repeat visits. Much of the information is not location, service, company, or product specific—it does not have to be. The content should, however, have an obvious relationship to the site's subject matter. Quizzes, surveys, diets, exercises, recipes, and tips are all designed to engage visitors and keep them coming back.

Table 3.1 shows examples of content that might be included on an upscale Italian restaurant's site and the site of a country inn that offers yoga classes.

Internal Pages or Outside Links?

Most large businesses prefer to have sticky content right on their own site rather than linking to other sites (which sweeps visitors away, perhaps never

TABLE 3.1 Content examples.	
Italian Restaurant	**Yoga Inn**
Positioning headline and subheads	Positioning headline and subheads
Positioning text	Positioning text
Photos of delectable Italian dishes	Data on what Yoga is; how it helps you
Menu items in the restaurant	Benefits of staying at the Inn to learn Yoga
Genuine Italian main entrée recipes	
Testimonials from happy patrons	Background of instructors
Background of chef(s)	Biography of owners
Biography of owner(s)	Philosophy of the Inn/Yoga instructor
History of restaurant	Testimonials from patrons
World's greatest recipes for:	History of Yoga links
Spaghetti sauces	Photos of: young/old students enjoying Yoga,
Italian home-baked bread	Yoga instructor in front of attentive class,
Tiramisu	children learning Yoga
Ices	
Desserts	Streaming video from a Yoga class
	Streaming voice message from Yoga instructor
Local Italian-American clubs	
Links to Italian suit stores	Amenities of the Inn
"Travel to Italy" sites	360-degree views of each category of room
	Room rates
Links to sites of Italian auto history	Unique aspects of the Inn
Ferrari	
Maserati	Things to do in the nearby area
Lamborghini	Special pricing for combo lodging/Yoga
Laforza	
	Food, dining, local area sightseeing

to return). However, this notion may be changing in favor of a different attitude called "give the visitor what they want and they'll return for more."

Most smaller businesses, especially those with fewer resources and limited budgets, can increase visitor loyalty by posting a page of useful links that users can bookmark and then visit often as a mini-portal. Early in the Web's history, people thought that offering outside links was foolish

Analyze it

1. What related content would you include for a site featuring a beachfront bed and breakfast in Malibu, California, where many celebrities have their private residences?
2. What related content would you include for a restaurant that sits on the roof of a high-rise overlooking south Miami Beach?
3. What related content would you include for a site of a casino in the desert half way between Los Angeles and Palm Springs?
4. What related content would you include for the site of a surburban coffee house that competes with a Starbucks?

because it took people out of a site. But the thousands of sites that succeed because of their many outside links have disproved that belief. So, outside links aren't all bad—but linking to a *competitor, or to a site that ultimately leads to one*, is *not* a good idea.

Most industries have one or more national (or state, county, or large city) professional or industry associations that maintain Web sites with valuable articles, data, news, and other postings. Some offer excellent tutorials on doing business in their industry.

The hospitality industry benefits from various associations, both national and state. Among the food services and lodging associations are the following examples:

National

National Restaurant Association, www.restaurant.org

National Bar and Restaurant Management Assn., www. bar-restaurant.com

American Hotel and Lodging Assn., www.ahma.com

State

California Restaurant Association, www.calrest.org

Florida Restaurant Association, www.flra.com

New Mexico Restaurant Association, www.nmrestaurants.org

North Carolina Restaurant Association, www.ncra.org

Central Ohio Restaurant Association, www.cora.citysearch.com

Colorado Hotel and Lodging Association, www.coloradolodging.com

Pennsylvania Tourism & Lodging Association, www.patravel.org

As an interesting departure from what most firms do, your links can be divided between business- or industry-related links and links to information that virtually any consumer can use. Why both industry and consumer? Because although your visitors may be potential patrons or guests, they are also human beings with the same basic information needs as anyone else. Creating several pages of general consumer links can enhance a site's stickiness.

Examples of Consumer Information Links

Art	News
Autos	Parenting
Business – Finance	Pets
Careers	Seniors
Cooking – Recipes – Wine	Shopping
Education – Reference	US Government
Entertainment – Fun	Travel – Airlines – Tickets
Health – Diet – Fitness	Maps – Zip Codes
Home & Garden	Weather

Each link could lead directly to a site offering the information described by the link or to a page of many related links. For example, the link to "Business – Finance" might lead to a single site such as Yahoo's! investing page at http://finance.yahoo.com/?u or to a page with other links.

Tip   **Finding Sites to Recommend**

Make a list of all of the topics that you would like to offer as links. If your business is in a popular fishing area, maybe you'd offer a link called "growing earthworms." To find sites to serve as a link called "growing earthworms," use a search engine, such as www.google.com, and search for "growing earthworms." What you find are pages and pages of links to sites dealing with growing earthworms. Compare a few and pick one that seems to have the best content. (And it is this same criteria that other firms will apply when deciding whether to link to *you*!)

More About Enabling and Encouraging Visitors to Contact You

One of the easiest components to add to a Web page is a link to an e-mail address. An e-mail link or group of links should appear on every page of a site. (See Chapters 9 through 11 for more detail on communicating by e-mail.)

Forms that allow visitors to enter information and "submit" it to the site owner are also easy to create and easy to use—most of them are called CGI forms. Simple surveys, guest books, comment forms, and trouble reports are usually CGI forms. More sophisticated types of interactions are discussed in the following chapter.

Placing telephone numbers and physical addresses on a site's pages continues to be important, especially for local establishments.

Summary

Review the following 10 "guidelines" for Web site content:

1. Content must communicate and support the company, product, or services market positioning or branding.

2. Content must be relevant, useful, and interesting to the target audience.

3. Content must be written and presented in language easily understood by the target audience.

4. Content must help achieve the goals established for the site.

5. Provide ways for visitors to communicate with marketing, sales, or customer service representatives using many easily found locations on the site.

6. Ask for the business. The "ask" is one of the first things taught to sales representatives and one of the most forgotten components of Web sites. Be sure that "Begin reservation process here," "Click here to order," "Call today for more information," "Please comment," and other ways of asking visitors to take action or connect with salespeople are clearly visible.

7. Provide sufficient useful content to bring visitors back for more. The corollary to this is to avoid having so much content that a visitor can become overwhelmed. Good organization (see Chapter 4) helps a lot.

8. Content must be up-to-date. Update a site by adding to it or changing it on a regular basis.

9. Avoid seas of small type. Most Web visitors absorb information in "bites" from headers and graphics. Put long articles, specifications, and reports on separate pages or as files that users can download to read later.

10. Spelling, grammar, and punctuation do count! Badly written material will quickly convince a visitor that the site represents an unprofessional or sloppy business.

Review Questions

1. What are some features that are common to many business Web sites?

2. Name a few hospitality companies whose branding is so strong that they probably do not need a tagline to communicate it.

3. Is it more important to talk about a firm's annual sales or about the visitors' interests?

4. What is the main function of the headline of a Web site?

5. What types of information should you expect to find on a corporate Web site?

6. What characteristics does including a company's 60-year history communicate to visitors?

7. What does including information about a firm's employees add to a Web site?

8. How can testimonials help a Web site's effectiveness?

9. What does a site's "stickiness" refer to?

10. What factors help make a site more "sticky"?

11. What types of content would you consider adding to the site of a small, independent vegetarian restaurant?

12. Why are some webmasters opposed to having links to outside sites?

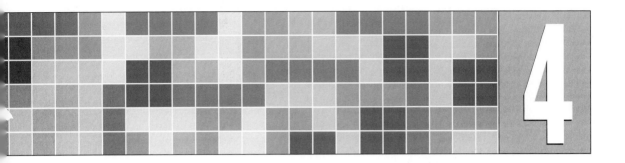

Look and Feel

Site Appearance and Organization

The look of the 5 & Diner's Web page reflects and communicates the feel of a '50s diner. Hamburger, fries, and a malt were the essentials. The red and black logo and checkerboard design are familiar to everyone born in 1952 or earlier. And those menu buttons are the platters that played continuously, selected, of course, via the jukeboxes that sat with the salt, pepper, and ketchup on every table. Sha-boom, sha-boom.

(Screen capture from www.azeats.com/5andDiner/.)

In previous chapters, you identified a distinctive market position, targeted audiences, established Web site goals, and created or found mountains of interesting information for specific Web audiences. Now, it's time to put it all together in an attractive and logical (or at least easy-to-navigate) format. How do you decide what will be attractive to visitors? How do you ensure that they will be able to find the information they want quickly and easily? Answer these questions and you'll have all of the pieces for directing your Web site design and construction.

THE BASICS

Appearance

What should a Web site look like for maximum marketing impact? What will appeal most to specific audiences? What color or style or size of typeface will best reinforce long-term positioning or a short-term promotion? Five general criteria are key to using the appearance of a site to help accomplish its goals. A Web site should reflect the positioning and be distinct, consistent, clear, and interesting.

Reflect the positioning.   The appearance—the colors, graphics, fonts, and other visual elements—of a site should be appropriate for the long-term market positioning of the services, products, or firm. The graphics and style should reinforce the intended perceptions.

For example, does the site market a luxury hotel? If so, the look must be elegant and sophisticated. If a hotel features game rooms, play houses, and a kiddie park to attract families with young children, its site should use bright colors, graphics that are clean and simple, and a typeface that makes the visitor know the site is related to kids. If a country inn is positioned as a romantic getaway, neon orange and green flashing banners will probably not communicate the right message.

Distinct.   A site's appearance should help it stand out from the competitors' sites. Do competitors' sites display their headline directly at the top center of the home page, their logo on the top right, and links to interior pages along the bottom edge? Do they always have a white background and one small photo?

Yes, we exaggerate, but after a while, many sites begin to look achingly familiar. Strive to have your site be memorable. Distinctiveness is a key consideration when planning a site: What different (yet appropriate) things can be done to a site to make it more noticeable and memorable to visitors?

Consistent.   Your visitors should always know which site they are visiting. This does not mean that every page should look exactly like every other page. It does mean that each page has some recognizable element that is the same—the same navigation bar, a small logo, a colored line across the top, or a distinctive typeface.

Clear.   If a Web site is confusing to read or navigate, visitors will leave it quickly, without learning what it has to offer. They'll find a competitor's site, one that is easier to navigate. Make sure that each page of your site is:

- Easy to read
- Clear about where to click
- Not too busy or crowded with too much information, graphics, animations, links, and other elements
- Not distracting from the main goal or focus of that page

Interesting.   Regardless of how prized a menu might be, if it is presented on the Web as a typed list of salads and entrees, it won't entice visitors to enter and browse. Use color and images to generate interest. Photos, for example, that communicate ambience and food presentation do much more to stimulate an interest in dining at a fine restaurant than a plain text description of location and hours.

And to all of these, we add that whatever the appearance of the site, the graphics *must* display quickly. No matter how wonderful those images might be, slow-loading pages will drive away those treasured visitors.

Organization

Visitors to a Web site do not start on page 1 and work their way through to page 45. Web pages are linked together, and each page has links, or "short-cuts," to other sections or pages, or even other Web sites.

Think of a site's organization as an "org chart," like one depicting a company's reporting structure. Then, realize that each box must link to some of the side boxes and to some of the boxes two levels down or up, not just the boxes directly above and below. Ensuring that visitors can find their way from one part of a site to another quickly and easily requires clear organization and directions.

Following are three general guidelines to apply to the organization of your site.

1. Provide clear navigation from the start.   A home page must provide the navigational links to help visitors start to explore the site's information and use its tools. This might be a navigation bar, a list of text links, a search box, or a simple "click here to enter" link.

2. Be directive and precise.   A Web site must clearly point the way to information, benefits, and actions for visitors. Simple, straightforward navigational tools, such as statements (e.g., click here, make reservations, reserve rental car, concierge services, banquet room information), buttons, or navigation bars should help visitors find their way. Label each link with a distinctive and easy-to-understand name that indicates what awaits the visitor who clicks there. Avoid vague, unmodified terms like "resources" or "information."

3. Use only a few layers.   Effective sites must be easy to navigate and re-navigate. Visitors should be able to remember where things are. The Web design that is complex, with many layers and crossing connections, soon confuses and frustrates users trying to find their way. Help users get to the desired information with as few clicks as possible, preferably fewer than four. Group pages logically. Use subindex pages to link to various pages of each group, rather than trying to link to all of the pages from the home page.

BEYOND THE BASICS

Appearance

Some people think of a Web site's home page as being similar to the front of a printed sales brochure. We have all heard that the purpose of a sales brochure's front page is to intrigue you enough to open the brochure and read more. But when a Web site's home page is well designed, it does much more than a brochure cover ever could.

A Web site's home page should capture the interest, so often fleeting, of people who primarily and impatiently seek information, education, and entertainment. Within a few seconds, the page must deliver something the visitor is looking for in a way that glues fickle mouse pointers to the site. The page must grab the visitor's mind immediately. It should get that "Okay! This is the place!" reaction. The site's appearance and organization are critical to getting this recognition.

Chuck E. Cheese knows how to relate to children on its Web site, as well as in its restaurants. In Figure 4.1, notice the headline directed to children (fun) and parents (well-balanced), the subtle impact of the exclamation point, the appeal of the cartoon characters, and a child's feeling of success and achievement in capturing one of the free coupons that can be downloaded from the site. The site uses bright yellow and orange colors to attract visitors.

You want to make a good first impression, one that communicates professionalism and helpfulness and is warm and inviting. Upon meeting a dining patron at your haute cuisine restaurant, you wouldn't display your own baby pictures or photos of your bathroom or your overfilled garage, or photos of you at age 10 on a Ferris wheel. If you did, your credibility as a serious restauranteur would soon slip into questionable territory. Yet, these are similar to some of the elements proudly displayed on the home pages of many smaller sites to first-time visitors.

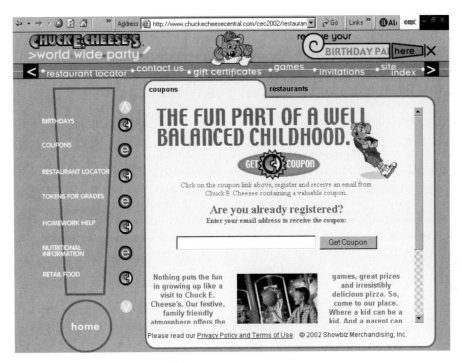

FIGURE 4.1   Chuck E. Cheese. (Screen capture from www.chuckecheesecentral.com/cec2002/restaurants/coupons.html.)

In this section, you will learn the basic criteria of appropriate Web site appearance and how these criteria can be met in various ways.

The Front Door

The entry to a Web site must look *inviting and interesting,* two attributes that you have to *experience.* If the home page looks inviting, it is. Web designers sometimes refer to this aspect of a site as its "look and feel." How do features work to make a page look inviting? Most of them help make it easier for visitors to know what they have found. Visitors are not left wondering if this site might have the information they seek. They aren't left without help finding their way through a maze of linked pages. It's a little like placing "this way to the petting zoo" markers along a path in an unfamiliar park. Some features that can lead to a desirable "look and feel" include:

- Good use of white (open) space to separate graphical and textual elements, avoiding a cluttered look.
- A clearly visible headline that instantly tells what the site is about and communicates purpose and positioning. Let them know what they've found right away.

- Clearly labeled, conveniently placed links to help visitors enter the site. Don't make visitors scrutinize the details of a page to find their way.
- Subheads or button links that offer additional categories or features.
- Smaller, rather than larger, graphics for fast downloading. Don't keep visitors waiting for slow-loading pictures—they might leave.

Use care when including special displays such as those requiring uncommon plug-ins or the need for Shockwave™, Flash, RealPlayer™, QuickTime™ Movie, or similar programs. Although these are becoming more common and user-friendlier, some older browser versions do not support them. Using features that require users to download and install plug-ins may be placing obstacles between your Web site and the users you wish to reach. Use technology that is readily available to everyone in your intended audience, even if they use older browsers. Site developers sometimes include the impressive displays from a separate link so that visitors with older programs can avoid going to a page they can't see and be irritated with you as a result.

Tip	Use Caution with "Splash" Pages

Dramatic and captivating "splash" pages currently introduce many large sites and those sites belonging to designers who are delighted to play with creating them. These pages appear before a site's home page and often feature impressive animation and sound. High-end (expensive) corporate sites often have *spectacular* splash pages. Visit www.cocacola.com for an outstanding example. The one for the Halekulani Hotel is also done very well (see www.halekulani.com).

Splash pages, however, can be slow to load, especially for users with older equipment. Also, search engines cannot find much to index on such pages (see Chapter 6 for more details on search engines). If being found by search engines is an important goal (it still is to many small to medium business Web sites), adding a splash page, which engines have difficulty adding to their index or directory, is not helpful. Web sites should first be designed for function, then for looks—this means that the smaller businesses might reap more value for their Internet budgets by spending it on top-quality content and overall appeal, saving the costly animations for later.

Appearance Can Change

Many new Web creation tools allow designers to create sites that change. Some of the changes are graphics that display at random, or in some predetermined rotation sequence, each time the page is accessed. This encourages visitors to return to the site to see what's new or what is different. Other sites place "cookies" (small pieces of code) on a visitor's Web browser so that they can recognize a repeat visitor and give that visitor different images or text on subsequent visits. A reservations site, for example, might greet customers with a personalized statement such as "Welcome back, George Smith," and then display a "recommended weekend getaway" based on George's previous searches, reservations, or a profile that he created previously. This type of personalization can be an especially powerful marketing tool and the cost for such features is declining.

Download Time

Most Web users will not wait for a slow or "fat" home page to download. Here's a *very rough* rule of thumb: a page downloads at about a half-second per kb at typical modem dial-up speeds, especially during peak Internet usage times. Using this rule, a 30 kb webpage takes 15 seconds to complete its loading; a 60 kb home page takes a half minute. Text items load almost instantly into a visitor's browser, so placing the positioning headline and subheads at the top of a page in text format helps ensure that those key elements are displayed immediately. Doing this keeps a viewer interested in reading text while the remainder of the page loads.

Check Your Site's Download and Bandwidth Speeds

Some designers who routinely work with broadband high-speed Internet access forget that some consumers' home computers do not yet have such fast access. These designers may create stunning pages that people never see because the pages take too long to load. Sites that can help you check the loading speed of a page or site include WebSiteGarage.com (www.Web sitegarage.com), which offers a free, multi-featured diagnostic center called 2Wire (www.2wire.com), whose bandwidth meter can determine the maximum throughput from your site to the 2Wire Web site; and Microsoft's bandwidth testing page at http://computingcentral.msn.com/internet/speedtest. asp. Another bandwidth testing site is located at www.pcpitstop.com/ internet/bandwidth.asp, where you can also perform other tests for download, upload, ping test, satellite ping test, trace root, and more.

Keep Image Files Small

The critical factors in download time are the images and special programs on a Web page and sometimes, the speed or amount of traffic on the server hosting the site. How fast an image loads is related to the size of the image— the image's *file size*. Two images can have the same apparent dimensions but display on a visitor's monitor at very different speeds. Generally, the larger the file size, the longer the loading time. Images with higher resolutions and with more colors have a larger file size and take longer to display. Most files with music or animations also take longer to load, so use these features, tempting as they might seem, guardedly.

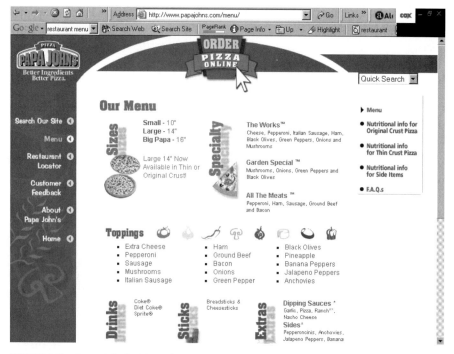

FIGURE 4.2   Papa John's Pizza. (Screen capture from www.papajohns.com/menu/.)

Figure 4.2 shows the Web site for Papa John's Pizza. The page uses open space, headlines, links, and small images, all of which help keep display time to a minimum.

Dress Code

Effectively using a site's appearance is key to accomplishing your site goals. Following are some suggestions to help you implement each of the five guidelines discussed briefly at the beginning of this chapter.

1. Reflect Your Positioning

Is your long-term market position related to a specific type of industry segment? Do you specialize in selling wholesale to businesses, retail to consumers, retail to other firms, or offering bargains to anyone who can buy? Figure 4.3 shows the home page of Olive Garden's Web site. There is little question that the Olive Garden restaurant chain positions itself as a family-friendly Italian restaurant.

Just in case a visitor might miss the point about Olive Garden being an Italian restaurant, the home page displays alternative text (also called alt tag or mouseover tag) when the mouse pointer rests on the picture

FIGURE 4.3 The Olive Garden. (Screen capture from www.olivegarden.com/homedefault. asp?busid=default.)

(see Figure 4.4). Note, too, how the home page offers interactivity—a newsletter and recipes are intended to keep consumers coming back and engaged with the Web site, as well as to reinforce the company's position in the minds of consumers.

Compare Figures 4.5 and 4.6 and notice how the positioning value gained from a site's look and feel can differ. (Chapter 1 has more examples of communicating market positioning.)

There's no question that the Brick Pit positions itself as a barbecue restaurant. Further positioning of itself as a quality BBQ restaurant is achieved by citing some of its awards and media accolades.

Whereas the Brick Pit wants to be known solely for its BBQ offerings, Carrows, a nationwide restaurant chain, displays a broad menu of popular items such as "mile high" sandwiches, chicken dishes, and children's choices (Figure 4.6).

2. Distinct

The Web page or site appearance should distinguish it from competitors.

The Hawaii Naniloa Hotel page (see Figure 4.7), located on a family vacation site, says that it caters primarily to families. The large headline

FIGURE 4.4 Mouseover tag. (Screen capture from www.olivegarden.com/homedefault.asp?busid=default.)

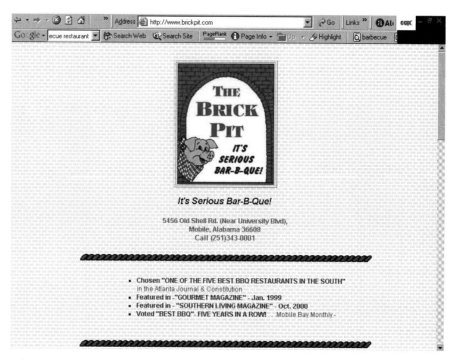

FIGURE 4.5 The Brick Pit. (Screen capture from www.brickpit.com.)

FIGURE 4.6 Carrows. (Screen capture from www.carrows.com.)

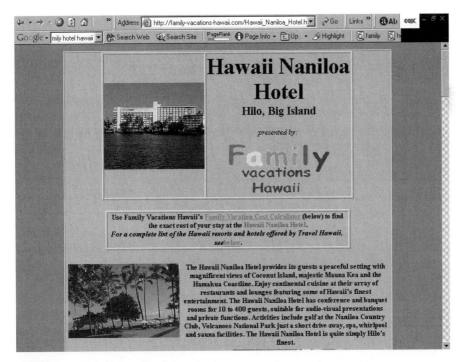

FIGURE 4.7 Hawaii Naniloa Hotel. (Screen capture from http://family-vacations-hawaii.com/Hawaii_Naniloa_Hotel.html.)

"Family vacations," the text, the use of primary colors, and the pricing work together to emphasize its family orientation. On this particular page, the hotel is positioning itself well as a hotel *for families.*

Most large hotels and hotel chains have the advantage of larger budgets and advertising agency assistance. Making their Web sites reflect their positioning and stand out from others may not be difficult because they

Analyze it

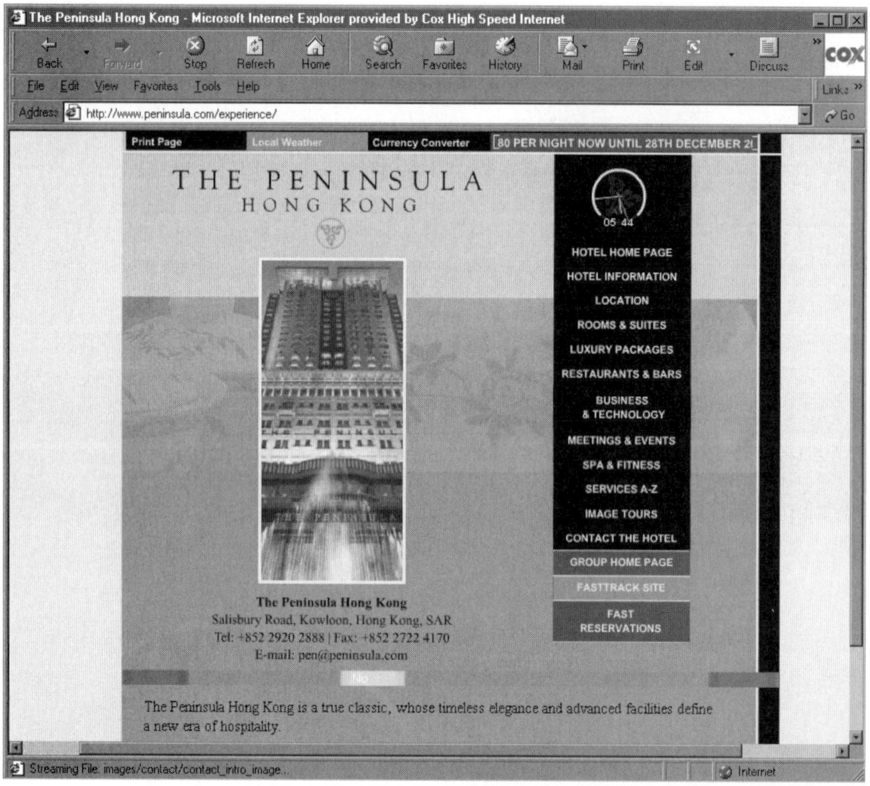

FIGURE 4.8   The Peninsula Hong Kong. (Screen capture from www.peninsula.com/experience.)

List the elements of the home page for the Peninsula in Hong Kong (see Figure 4.8) that tell you its overall market positioning. Be specific. List five adjectives or phrases to describe the look and feel of the site. For example, is the site: casual, formal, fun, boring, sedate, bright, serious, cute, elegant, sporty, official, clever, gloomy, funny, mysterious, plain, chock full, splashy, fancy, heavy, or smooth? Think of other terms or phrases that describe the site.

can build on their print and other media advertising. Independent hotels, inns, lodges, motels, and bed and breakfasts may have a little more work ahead of them, but they can still make their Web sites stand out from the competition. One way is to purchase a site from a company that uses "customizable templates." The companies that build and maintain template-based sites are improving continuously and now offer many more variations than previously available. Furthermore, in some cases, by talking with the Web site developer or paying a little extra, a company can add its own custom graphics or photos to a template site to help distinguish it from others.

3. Consistent

A Web site must have some consistency of appearance from page to page, in part, because making the site "hold together" is a good design principle. But consistency also helps to ensure that visitors always know whose site they are using and who has provided all of the useful or entertaining information and tools.

Consistency does not require every site page to look like every other page. It does mean, however, that the site should have some recognizable element that is the same on each page—a small logo, photo, a blue line (or whatever works best with the site's "color palette") across the top (or side), a distinctive typeface, and so on.

The continuity element should be visible on the portion of the page that is displayed when the visitor first loads the page; that is, not where it cannot be seen without scrolling. (Borrowing from an old newspaper term, this is often called presenting the important information "above the fold.")

Fatburger, a hamburger chain that gained fame by supposedly being patronized by many celebrities, positions itself as "The Last Great Hamburger Stand" on its home page (Figure 4.9). Click on "Nearest Location "on the left-side menu board and you're taken to a page where you can find Fatburgers in your area code. Note how the color scheme, framed menu, and framed slogan line, "The Last Great Hamburger Stand," has been carried over to the new internal Fatburger page (Figure 4.10) Seeing these repeated design elements, visitors cannot help but know that they are still in the Fatburger site (and no doubt growing hungry).

Many sites use a menu or navigation bar, either vertical (usually down the left) or horizontal (usually across the top), that is the same on each page. This not only helps with user navigation, but also shows the visitors that they are still viewing the same site. "Framed" sites also help achieve a desired level of consistency, although a controversy about using frames arises every now and again. Frames are discussed in the "Organization" section of this chapter.

FIGURE 4.9   Fatburger. (Screen capture from www.fatburger.com.)

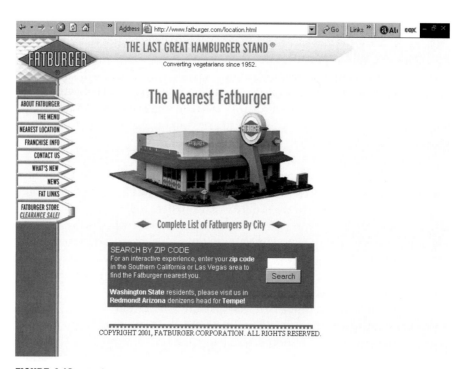

FIGURE 4.10   Fatburger interior page. (Screen capture from www.fatburger.com/location.html.)

4. Clear

A Web site must be easy to read and to navigate; otherwise, visitors will tire of it and leave, maybe never to return. The following are some guidelines.

(a) Easy to read. An average size typeface with plenty of leading (white space) so the type and graphics are not crowded makes reading easier. The typeface size should make emphasis clear. Readers will focus on a heading or phrase that stands out.

When text consists of a sentence or more, or if a small size is used to save space, use a "serif" font; that is, one with added bits to the letters. (A "sans serif" font lacks the extra bits on the letters; see Figure 4.11.) Why? because a serif font is easier to read. All the extra bits give the brain more cues for faster recognition of letters and words.

Tip	Use Uppercase and Lowercase

AVOID THE OVERUSE OF UPPERCASE (CAPITAL) LETTERS. INFORMATION PRESENTED IN ALL CAPITAL LETTERS IS ACTUALLY HARDER TO READ (FEWER VISUAL CUES FOR YOUR BRAIN TO DISTINGUISH) THAN TEXT USING BOTH UPPER- AND LOWERCASE LETTERS.

Avoid the overuse of all capital letters. Information presented in all capital letters is actually harder to read (fewer visual cues for your brain to distinguish) than text using both upper and lowercase letters. Furthermore, when everything is capitalized, the most important information loses its emphasis. Instead of using capital letters for emphasis, use italics, bold, and color.

To be sure that a phrase, tagline, or header is seen consistently from user to user, browser to browser, use an image. Browser settings, usually those of Netscape Navigator or Microsoft's Internet Explorer, control much of the appearance of regular text. A page designer might specify Avante Garde 14-point bold, but if the visitor's browser cannot find or recognize that type, it will substitute something else, such as Helvetica 12-point. For regular headers, this may not matter much. But if the type size or style is somehow part of your positioning image or relates to a font used in your trademarked graphics or logo, it could matter a great deal.

Present text in fairly short paragraphs or bulleted lists. Both strategies make your text easier for the visitor to read and comprehend. Keep line length to not more than 5 or 6 inches. Text that runs *all of the way* across the screen from left to right may be difficult for some people to read.

Far easier to read is text that is presented in
a line length that approximates the width of
a newspaper or magazine column, which we
have all grown accustomed to reading.

Serif	Sans serif
These letters are easier for readers to distinguish and recognize because each letter has some thicker parts or "feet" or other features that help with the reading process. Times New Roman, Garamond, and Palatino are common examples of serif fonts. The font being used in this box is Times New Roman.	These letters are somewhat more difficult for readers to distinguish and recognize because the letters have so few distinguishing features. They are plain. Sans serif fonts are best used for headers or short pieces of text. Helvetica, Arial, and Avante Garde are common examples of sans serif fonts. The font being used for the text in this box is Arial.
These letters are easier for readers to distinguish and recognize because each letter has some thicker parts or "feet" or other features that help with the reading process. Times New Roman, Garamond, and Palatino are common examples of serif fonts. The font being used in this box is Palatino.	These letters are somewhat more difficult for readers to distinguish and recognize because the letters have so few distinguishing features. They are plain. Sans serif fonts are best used for headers or short pieces of text. Helvetica, Arial, and Avante Garde are common examples of sans serif fonts. The font being used for the text in this box is Helvetica.

FIGURE 4.11   Samples of serif vs. sans serif type.

Use caution when placing text on a colored background. That lime green text on a marine blue background may look great using your browser on your computer, but your visitor's monitor might display this in colors so similar to each other that reading the text is made difficult. Pages using a colored background must have text that is presented in a highly contrasting color and a typeface large or bold enough to ensure readability.

(b) Clear about where to click. Pages that promise to deliver key information or benefits but fail to make the links easy to see only frustrate the visitors. The navigation bar, buttons, and text that link to other pages must be obvious and worded clearly. On Sophie Kay's Web site (www.sophiekay.com), there is no mystery about where to click for what. Uncluttered space sets off the few links, and the single environmental photo speaks worlds about her occupation.

(c) Not too busy or crowded.   Avoid crowding too much information and too many graphics, animations, links, and other elements on a page. Crowded elements distract attention from the main goal or focus of the page. A page that overwhelms the visitor with too much stuff is just as much

Tip	Make All Elements Useful
One rule of thumb that is worth following is to make sure that everything on your site is "doing work"—giving your target audiences information and solutions, building market position, or providing ways for visitors to communicate.	

a problem as a boring one. Crowded pages can actually bury the key messages they are trying to communicate.

Keep pages open and clean. Avoid gratuitous animations or other elements on the page just because your Webmaster says he or she can create "this really, really incredible special effect right on the home page."

5. Interesting

What's the most boring site design you can think of? A page with paragraph after paragraph of text, without images, mouseovers, links, borders, backgrounds, color, heads, or subheads. In the early years of the Internet, this is exactly what most pages looked like. For the most part, they were academic or government articles and reports. The Internet is a very different world today, and the expectations of Internet users have changed considerably. Web sites that do not take advantage of appropriate design tools are a waste of time and money.

The Internet is a colorful place. Virtually no one using the Internet has a monochrome monitor any longer. Colors develop emphasis and interest. Colors can help a site's clarity by delineating various areas of a page or making some features, links, or text more obvious. Include graphics and photos that tell the visitor more about the products, company, and market positioning.

Can you guess what kind of specialty food the restaurant chain Popeye's (see Figure 4.12) sells? It takes only a quick glance at Popeye's home page to know it's a great place to find a variety of chicken dishes. That's what you want your site to do—make a statement of what it is all about in a matter of seconds using its headlines and images.

FIGURE 4.12   Popeye's. (Screen capture from www.popeyes.com.)

A site's colors, graphics, fonts, and other visual elements should reflect and enhance the unique market position—the way visitors perceive the company, product, or service. Color can convey weight, warmth, coldness, mood, and personality. A Web site advertising a circus-theme family restaurant generally will not contain large amounts of black. Black and navy blue are heavy colors. Because you don't want to convey that your floating balloons are heavy, you use light and cheery colors, such as sky-blue and "happy" yellow.

Yellows and light reddish-blues are "warm"; thus they are often used on travel sites promoting warm destinations. Conversely, they may not be appropriate on a state police site. But use care: yellow may also convey envy, sickness, cowardly behavior, and backstabbing.

Red and orange are also warm colors—they strike emotional chords. Red tends to be a favorite color of fast-paced, action-oriented, devil-may-care people, which may explain why red cars get more traffic tickets than other cars.

Arby's home page (Figure 4.13) uses red, sand, and orange colors. If you visit the Arby's site, you'll see that the menu buttons on its home page are a warm muted red, the logo is a bright red, and the photo of sandwiches contains mostly warm yellows, reds, and orange. The background is a soft sandy-brown. You feel welcome on the Arby's home page. You feel at home.

FIGURE 4.13   Arby's. (Screen capture from www.arby.com.)

Violets, blues, and greens are cool, peaceful, calming colors that invite images of pastoral, outdoor settings.

Color selection should be part of the overall look of the site. Like the other aspects of the visual character of a site, color should work to help communicate the site's intended purpose or message.

More information on color usage can be found at:

www.websitetips.com/color/#meaning

www.colormatters.com/brain.html

www.pantone.com

Shading and background colors.   Properly used, and with care to ensure that the type is clear and readable, background shading can help visitors recognize page sections more easily. Arby's (Figure 4.13), uses a sand-colored background, which tends to frame and set off the rest of the somewhat darker "warm" colors on the home page.

Organization

The primary measure of a site's organization is *ease of navigation*. Visitors should be able to find their way around the site, moving easily from one

Analyze it

Which two colors would you use as the main ones for each of the following Web sites? Why?

Site that advertises	Colors
1. Western-style country barbecue	
Reasons:	
2. A sushi bar	
Reasons:	
3. An on-the-beach hotel	
Reasons:	
4. A mountain lodge	
Reasons:	

FIGURE 4.14   Dairy Queen. (Screen capture from www.dairyqueen.com.)

page to another and *back*, without having to ask themselves, "Where did I see that?" Visitors who are seeking specific information should be able to find it easily and quickly, without having to drill down through many layers of pages, hunting for the right place to click on each page, scrolling and squinting, to arrive at the intended destination.

Sites with easy navigation use these three general strategies:

1. Organize the information and pages so that important data or functions are no more than two or three mouse clicks away.

2. Include easy-to-see navigation bars or lists with links to the major pages of the site at the top, side, or bottom of *each page*.

3. Provide clear directions to visitors so they know what they need to do next.

The "modular" organization of Dairy Queen's home page (Figure 4.14) makes it easy to navigate and employs the three general strategies. This approach also facilitates the maintaining and freshening of the site because it simplifies replacing existing elements with new ones.

Guidelines for basic Web site anatomy call for *all* of the pages to have a link back to "Home" and a separate link to each of the *main links*, the main channels of information that you offer on your site. These links may be in a "navigation bar" at the top, side, or bottom of the page. *All* pages should have an active e-mail link or a "contact us" link for visitors to request information, place an order, or make a reservation.

Frames

Some sites use a design called "frames" that help keep one part of the page visible while another part changes. In the examples shown in Figure 4.15, the user can click on a link in Part A or B, and the intended page is displayed in Part C. Moreover, the page that appears in Part C can actually be from *another site*.

Visit www.westcoasthotels.com. Notice that the home page is bordered by a frame at the top and one at the left side, both containing navigation links. Click on one of the top or side links and notice which frame changes.

Not everyone is a fan of framed sites. Two factors make the use of framed sites somewhat more difficult than non-framed sites. Jerra Morris, owner/ principal of the Web design firm, Advanced Access (www.advancedaccess. com) points out that some clients prefer non-framed sites to avoid the extra scrolling that frames usually require. Also, without some extra code to link visitors to a printable page, printing pages from a framed site is often either not possible or requires extra steps.

Some search engines (see Chapter 6 for a detailed discussion) may not search some (or most) of a framed site. However, framed sites do have a "non-frames "page, which sets the sizes and names of the frames that search

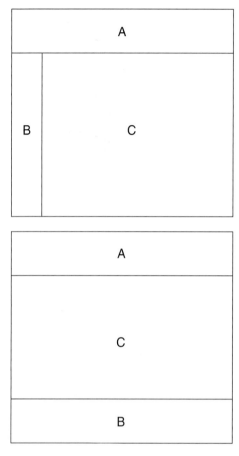

FIGURE 4.15 Two layouts for framed pages.

engines *do* read. The non-frames page may have its own metatags, text, and links. If knowledgeable site builders construct this page, it will have all of the necessary components that are read by the search engines.

Some firms still worry that owners of sites that show up "framed" in the main window may object, because their URL does not show in the address bar of a framed page. Displaying a framed page may imply that the outside framed page is actually on the displaying firm's site instead of a separate site, possibly owned and maintained by a completely separate individual or entity. Some articles have expressed concern about copyright violations. This issue remains to be resolved, but meanwhile, millions of sites use the technique.

Navigation Bars and Lists

How to navigate through a site to desired functions or information should be made obvious to visitors. The easiest way to ensure that visi-

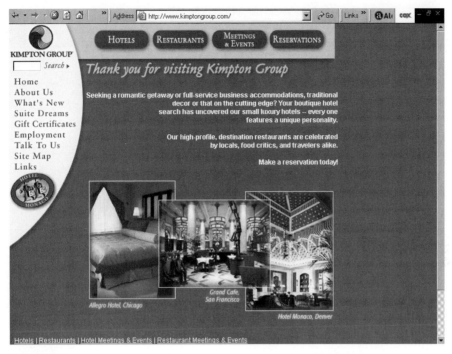

FIGURE 4.16   Kimpton Group. (Screen capture from www.kimptongroup.com.)

Tip	**Viewing Framed Pages**

To view a page that has been "framed" in a framed site, just place your cursor on a blank part of the framed page and right click. This opens a drop-down menu from which you select "Open Frame in New Window" in Netscape or "Properties" in the Internet Explorer browser. Click on "Properties" and you see a "General" page and "Address (URL)." The address shown there (www.whatever.com) is the true address of the framed page. Copy that address and paste it into your browser's location/address bar and you can go to the unframed version of that page.

---

tors can navigate is to include clearly labeled navigation bars or lists of links to the interior pages of the site. Figure 4.16 shows the Kimpton Group's home page. A navigation bar is shown at the top of the screen, as well as down the left side. Users can get to a specific page by using the links at the top or at the side.

Sites that include a great number of pages cannot show links to all of them on their navigation bars without looking cluttered. One useful technique to solve this problem is the placement of links to secondary pages in menus that drop down from the main category links.

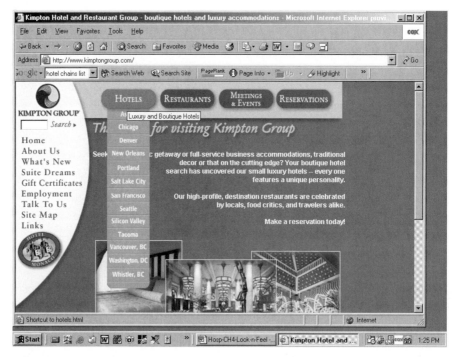

FIGURE 4.17 Kimpton Group with drop-down menu showing. (Screen capture from www.kimptongroup.com.)

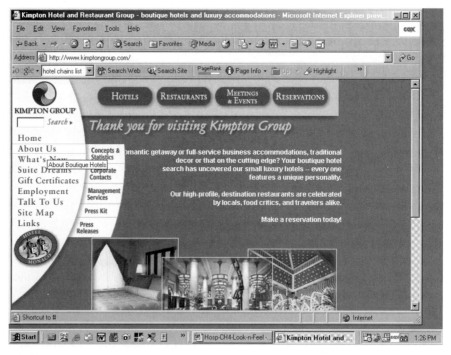

FIGURE 4.18 Kimpton Group with slide-out menu showing. (Screen capture from www.kimptongroup.com.)

The Kimpton Group Web site, which pairs charming hotels with popular restaurants, includes scores of pages. The home page (see Figure 4.16) shows only the most important navigation links for the most needed information.

Dozens of other links lie just below the navigational surface in this site. When a mouse pointer rests over one of the dark buttons/subjects of the top-most navigation bar, a long menu drops down (see Figure 4.17), providing another list of links to choose from.

Rest your mouse pointer on one of the vertical navigation bar links on the left side of the home page and more choices appear. In Figure 4.18, you can see how resting the mouse pointer on the words "About Us" has caused the curved submenu to appear to the right of the main menu choices.

One advantage to using text links, either in a navigation bar or in a list, is that text links can be added, deleted, or reworded in just a few seconds. Buttons, however, are small images, and creating new buttons is more time-consuming. Furthermore, search engines can read text links, but not images. To gain additional search engine value from buttons, site developers add text "mouseovers" to the graphics. Text links and mouseovers add keywords to a page so that it might become more "findable "by search engines.

Because Web site developers can "map" links to any specific image or part of an image, we now see many creative variations. In the screen capture of the 5 & Diner Web site that opened this chapter, for example, the five small record images are actually navigation tools. Click on one, and it takes you to one of five other areas of the site.

Tabs like those on manila folders are used to communicate to the user that certain information will be found by clicking on that folder. Index tabs work well for navigation because we are already accustomed to the concepts of folders and tabs.

Images are often used as links, and can be very inviting and informative. Usually, however, they occupy more space on the screen than lists and bars.

Clicking on any of the three cartoons at the bottom of the Golf Schools Etc. home page (see Figure 4.19) takes a visitor to a new page. The cartoon images create interest and excitement on the site and draw attention to the text words directly under each image. Clicking on the middle image (golf resorts) takes a visitor to a long list of such facilities. The site is nononsense and task-oriented; it gets its intended job done.

Links can be "mapped to" any image, but it's a good idea to ensure that the image is relevant. For example, a casino might map links to the various parts of a craps table so that when a user clicked on a certain part of the table, the resulting page would explain that bet, along with odds and payouts. A golf resort might map links to a map of the golf course so that clicking on a particular area displays information about that hole, such as

FIGURE 4.19   Golf Schools Etc. (Screen capture from www.golfschoolsetc.com.)

the par, length, recommended clubs, information about sand or water traps, or condition of the green.

Site Searches

Yum Foods has provided another common navigation tool for users to find what they seek—a site-specific search engine. See Yum Foods Web page at http://yumfood.net.

A search engine can be limited to search *only* the pages of a particular site, in this case, Yumfood.net. Users type in a word or phrase related to what they want to find, click on the "Search" button, and a list of choices appears. Enter the word "desserts" in the box on Yum's search page and click on "Search." Yumfood.net will return a list of choices, each choice with a link to more information about that dessert item.

Small businesses without the means to create customized search engines can use some developed by Excite (www.excite.com). Also, many companies that host business Web sites provide search engine programming; it's worth asking.

Getting Back from Another Site

Ask for a "Bookmark"

Sites using pages that link to information located on a different site risk losing visitors forever to the outside site. Some pages remind visitors to use the "back button" of their browser, but people who get more than four or five Web pages (or clicks) away from where they started might not return. One way to help them return to a site is to ask the visitor to "bookmark" the page in their browser. The Internet Explorer browser calls this a "favorite." Some programmers take the extra step to make a clickable favorite; that is, when the visitor clicks on the reminder, it creates the bookmark in the browser automatically.

Although this function does not help users navigate a site, it does help them find their way back. These bookmarks are important: using bookmarks and typing in a URL account for more than one third of all ways people access Web pages.

Staying in the Background

Another way to avoid losing visitors is to code each outside link so that a new browser window opens each time a visitor clicks to go to a page outside the original site. The original browser window remains in the background. Operating in the new browser window, the visitors can then wander all over the Web, but sooner or later they notice the background and return to it. And maybe they'll even look through the site further. The downside, however, is that from the *new* window, the user cannot use the back button to return to the original site.

One school of thought holds that you should never offer outside links: all of your links should connect within your site. Look to the purpose and scope of your site to decide whether to include outside links. A site that is intended to provide links to useful information all over the Web, such as vortals, *must* have many outside links.

Tip	Links Can Open a New Window

Here is an example of the HTML code for a regular link to an outside site:

    <a href="www.prenhall.com">An informative site</a>

But, using the following code for the link opens a new browser window and keeps the originating site in the background:

    <a href="www.prenhall.com "target="new">An informative site</a>

In both cases, the link itself looks like this: An informative site.

Analyze it

How many links do you see on this page from the All-Hotels site? See if you can identify 50 or more. How many *types* of links do you see? Name them.

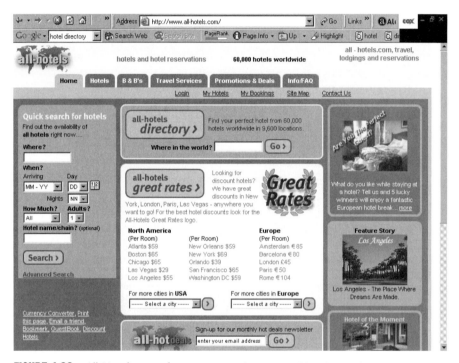

FIGURE 4.20   All-Hotels.com. (Screen capture from www.all-hotels.com.)

Summary

For individual units, as well as huge hospitality chains, the Web is a major marketing tool. A Web site has just a few magical seconds to make its impact for good or bad. The most effective home page is one that communicates its message quickly, is not too busy or cluttered, and uses color and images to build its positioning. Interior pages must reinforce that positioning, be consistent in appearance, and be easy to read.

Once visitors have become engaged with a site, its content and organization must keep them there. The key to effective organization is logical and easy navigation. Using a limited number of layers and clear, directive navigation is critical.

For other businesses, a Web site is simply an adjunct or supplement to other marketing and sales efforts. Such is the case with large national hospitality firms with strong brand awareness, loyalty, and repeat customers who know their products and services well and see their signs and ads everywhere. Yet, even for these companies, the effective use of Web marketing can add to sales. Web users can compare products, services, and companies much more easily via the Web, so even large companies can be hurt by poor Web design and functioning.

Every element of a site's "look and feel" is important in the quest for positioning and sales—every image, every section of white space, every use of color, every link.

Review Questions

1. What is the most important criterion for Web site organization?
2. What are the five general criteria that are key to using the appearance of a site to accomplish the site's goals?
3. What are the three rules about effective Web site organization?
4. Name three features that can help make a site's home page look welcoming.
5. How would you expect a site marketing a seaside bed and breakfast to look?
6. Why is an attractive site less important than one that addresses a firm's goals?
7. Why is it useful to have a site that is different from those of competitors?
8. Why should pages on a Web site have some element that is the same or similar?
9. Is it better to guide visitors carefully from page 1 through page 45 of a site or let them go wherever they wish? Why?
10. Why should a Web page be "directive"?
11. Why is using smaller images better than using large ones?
12. Why does a Web page need white space?
13. What are the dangers of having a cluttered Web page?
14. Why should the length of the text lines not be as long as the monitor is wide?
15. Why is it important to ask visitors to bookmark a site?
16. What is one advantage of using framed Web sites?
17. What do yellow, red, and orange colors usually communicate?
18. Give an example of mapping links to a graphic.

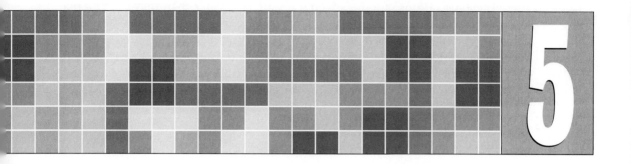

Stickiness

Online Reservations and Other Interactive Functions

Mandarin Oriental, San Francisco Reservations Page. (Screen capture from www.mandarinoriental.com.)

The expectations of today's Web users are far greater than they were even a year ago. A static display of text and graphics, even good graphics, is not sufficient to engage most visitors or draw repeat visits. Web sites must *do* things. In particular, hospitality sites must find ways to involve visitors with fast, useful, easy-to-use interactive tools. Online reservations, orders, and purchases; live chats; surveys and polls; and live events are among the functions that busy programmers have made possible, some of which now seem commonplace.

THE BASICS

The most important function of a company's Web site is communication—not communication that is one-way telling and showing, not the mission statements or the public relations mantras or the glossy brochure-like recitations—but encouraging and enabling visitors to communicate with the company's management and staff, with its clients or customers, and even other visitors to the site. Communication power is the great strength of the Internet today, its highest potential. To the degree that a business can put that power to work on its behalf, it will benefit from its investment in Internet marketing.

To do this requires some form or forms of interactivity and, in some cases, more than a bit of fun. The interactivity must allow visitors to interact with your business and services in ways that are informative, useful, and easy. The communicating may use forms, catalogs, shopping carts, downloads, viewers, or other user-initiated functions that involve the visitor with your company and its services or products. Of these, in the lodging business, an online reservation capability is crucial.

The simplest types of interactivity are e-mail and contact forms (see Part Three for more on e-mail). Beyond these, the key Web functions for Internet marketing are related to:

1. Online reservations
2. Online orders, purchases, and other services
3. Vehicles for direct communication between Web users—functions that enable and encourage the human voice of your site visitors, their friends, you, your company, guests, observers, and a host of others to be heard by one another
4. Online interactions that support selling or enhance site effectiveness by keeping visitors returning for more

Why is this interactivity so important? Why isn't a bright, attractive, artful Web site that proclaims a company or establishment's grandeur and impeccable service sufficient? Why does a site need more than good and plentiful information? The answer to both questions is a compelling one: The marketplace is demanding interactivity—or it will go somewhere else.

In this chapter, you will learn how various functions help your audiences interact with information about your company and its services, with you, and with each other. In the descriptions that follow, remember that the interactivity must be useful, easy to use, service oriented, and clearly related to your business.

BEYOND THE BASICS

Online Selling and Services

Interactive reservation forms, catalogs, order forms, shopping carts, and online gaming are among the types of direct online selling that are now most familiar to Web users. This section discusses the key types of online selling and services being used by hospitality businesses to involve, even captivate, their marketplace.

Interactive Reservation Systems

"Content is king," proclaim Web writers. "Unless you have useful, informative content, all of the gizmos and whirligigs in cyberspace won't help your site!"

"Functionality is king," proclaim Web programmers. "Unless your site can do things in creative ways, all of the content ever written or produced won't help your site!"

What's the answer? You need both. Interactive reservation systems marry content and function to benefit users and sell products and services.

Online travel is booming and that bodes well for the hospitality industry. American Express (www.AmericanExpress.com), one of the world's largest travel agencies, has noted a new stepped-up demand for interactive travel (http://home3.americanexpress.com/corp/latestnews/it-growth.asp). In 2001, the firm recorded a 500 percent increase in reservations made via corporate online booking tools as compared to a year earlier. Interactive travel bookings now represent over 6 percent of all American Express corporate travel reservations made in the United States. And the growth is expected to continue. According to PhoCusWright, a leading travel research firm, online booking of hotel stays will increase to represent 20 percent of all bookings (representing $17.5 billion) by 2005. (PhoCusWright, Inc. [www.phocuswright.com], is an independent strategy and research company that helps its clients understand the online travel marketplace and make competitively advantaged decisions.) For 2003 alone, hotel sales made online were expected to increase 49 percent. Jupiter Media Metrix, another leading research firm, has estimated that nearly 60 percent of online users

FIGURE 5.1   Mandarin Oriental, San Francisco Reservation Request page. (Screen capture from www.mandarinoriental.com.)

in North America research travel online, and half of those make travel purchases online.

Sites that intend to sell products such as hotel rooms or restaurant reservations must do more than provide information, even if it is delivered in a very sophisticated way. To use traditional marketing terminology, they must "ask for the order." Simple ways to do this include displaying a phone number for telephone orders or a printable order form that can be completed online or by hand and then faxed to the Order Department. Even the minimal command for users to send an e-mail to a linked e-mail address to request the product is better than not providing a reservation function at all.

Let's look at the step-by-step making of an online hotel reservation. We are using the reservation system of the Mandarin Oriental, San Francisco for this example. Most hotel reservation systems let consumers make reservations in much the same way. Begin by checking availability (Figure 5.1).

When the reservation system confirms the availability of accommodations for the dates selected (Figure 5.2), it provides the Web user with additional options. The user may convert the money from dollars to some other money, may click on a room photo for more information about the type of room available, or select one of the room choices to proceed with the reservation process. Click-

FIGURE 5.2 Mandarin Oriental, San Francisco Room Availability page. (Screen capture from www.mandarinoriental.com.)

ing on the room image for the second choice, "Bay View Queen," resulted in the pop-up window shown in Figure 5.3. The pop-up window includes one static photo of a room, but some sites include several photos or even a 360-degree "virtual tour" of the room. When the Web user clicks on the "select" button on the Room Availability Page (Figure 5.2), the user is connected to the Mandarin Oriental Hotel Group reservation system.

Some major corporations may develop their own reservation software and databases. Various software development companies, however, have turnkey solutions. Many franchises, such as Holiday Inn or Radisson, select a property management software (PMS) vendor based on price and the ability to create an interface with that franchise's central reservation system. The individual locations then use the vendor or vendors selected by the franchiser. The reservation system used by the Mandarin Oriental Hotel Group is a product called X-TEND, created by HubX. HubX also builds high-end

Room Descriptions - Microsoft Internet Explorer provided by Cox High Speed Internet

Bay View Queen

(Approximately 400 square feet/38 square meters)
These rooms provide fantastic views of San Francisco's famed landmarks toward the bay. Amenities include luxurious queen bedding and features European duvets and silk headboards including a large marble bathroom with shower. Other amenities include color television, CD player and radio with remote control, alarm clock, three telephones with two lines, binoculars, hair dryer, make-up mirror, bathroom scale, vanity stool, bathroom wall clock, choice of cotton or terry cloth robes, Thai silk slippers, twice daily maid service, in-room safe and mini bar, iron and ironing board, umbrella, flashlight, Nintendo video games, complimentary newspaper delivered daily, individual climate control and H2O bathroom amenities.

Superior City View Queen   Bay View Queen
Deluxe City View Room   Executive Corner City View
Bay View King   Bridge to Bridge View
Bay Bridge Mandarin King   Golden Gate Bridge Mandarin King
Dynasty Suite   Taipan Suite
Oriental Suite

FIGURE 5.3   Pop-up from Mandarin Oriental, San Francisco Room Availability page.

Web sites and integrates the reservation systems with those sites. For more information, visit www.hubx.com.

Such reservation systems are not limited to corporations, large chains, or franchises. Smaller venues, such as bed and breakfasts, conference centers, and other enterprises that can make use of reservation systems, may also buy (or lease or rent) a PMS system. For example, John Gardner's Tennis Ranch, a 25-acre Carmel Valley, California, facility with seven guest rooms and five 2-bedroom guesthouses, uses a system created by InnFinity Hospitality Systems. (See the Ranch's reservations/availability page at www.jgtr. com/Accommodations/ResRequest/) InnFinity Hospitality Systems (www. innhs.com) describes itself as a supplier of "PMS hotel software and solutions designed to satisfy the requirements of a wide range of lodging & hospitality venues, including any size hotel, resort, spa, inn, bed & breakfast, meeting/conference center, or corporate enterprise" (see Figure 5.4).

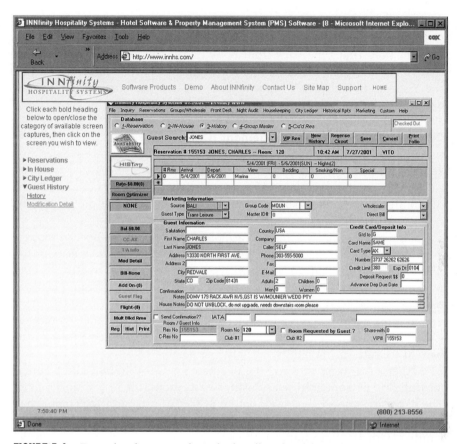

FIGURE 5.4 Example of a screen from the hotel's side of the PMS program. This one is from InnFinity Hospitality Systems. (Screen capture is display resulting from clicking on "Demos" at www.innhs.com.)

Must the software be completely customized for each hotel? How is the reservation system integrated with a hotel's Web site? Beverly McCabe of Infinity Hospitality Services answers this succinctly: "[The set up is] table driven. We enter their pictures and data into their database and the result is customized for their Web site. Clients can choose their own font, backgrounds, virtual tours or different pictures of each room type they wish to offer on the Internet. The product is totally integrated with the client's reservation system, which makes it much easier for the hotel to manage its rates and availability."

Many businesses that use online reservation programs also use travel and global distribution system sites that have certain advertising and search engine advantages. (These are discussed in more detail in Chapter 6.) An online reservation program gives an establishment day-to-day control of available rates, as well as the flexibility of offering all or only part of their accommodation inventory. Beverly McCabe provides this example: "For instance if your most popular room types are Harbor View rooms, you may want to hold that type back from booking on the Internet with the idea that you would make a higher rate with walk-in traffic." These systems load the reservation and guest information directly into the establishment's database, making it conveniently available for marketing use.

Customer relationship management (CRM).   The data entered by a future guest is often maintained in a database for CRM purposes. Sales, marketing, management, and sometimes others (such as the entity's advertising agency) can access and analyze the information. They can plan promotions, discounts, events, and other offerings according to customer preferences, frequency or seasonality of reservations, and other characteristics.

Some reservation systems also ask users to indicate any special requests or preferences, such as non-smoking room, king-size bed, baby crib, or toddler bed. This information, along with all of the other information entered by the user, is saved in the system's database for future use. Some Web sites use the data to personalize the display when the user returns to the site. It might display a message such as "Welcome back, Mr. Malone. Would you like to complete a guest survey?" or "Welcome back, Smith Family. Click here to see our Spring family specials!"

Other advantages of using the database for CRM include the potential for building personalized relationships with profitable reservation makers. The data can support the development of special programs to cement these relationships and increase return business. Also, employees who become familiar with the data improve their knowledge of the clients, and understand their needs.

Effective individualized CRM efforts can be expensive. Some firms use the data more to understand the segments of their market than to build individual relationships. The solution is probably in finding the right balance for a particular establishment or company, individualizing approaches and interactions with the most profitable potential, and planning targeted group programs for other segments.

Reservations by common gateway interface (CGI) form.   One easy way to encourage online reservations is to add a simple CGI form to a Web site. A CGI form is sent by e-mail to the person managing the online reservations, who then verifies availability and responds to the Web user by e-mail or telephone. Although the form may look very similar to the real-time, "live" reservation forms previously discussed, there are several major differences. With the CGI form approach, visitors cannot make a charge directly to their credit card, but they can tell the site owner their credit card information in the form or by telephone or fax. The site owner

Central Reservation Offices (CRO) and Global Distribution Systems (GDS)

How do direct online reservations affect or work with a hotel's CRO and GDS programs?

Most hotel chains have used CRO bookings for years, which relieved the individual hotel locations of much of the time and effort required to create, confirm, and report bookings. Later, the lodging industry followed the airlines' lead and participated in GDS that facilitate third-party bookings by travel agents and others. Although independent and smaller lodging venues did not have the use of a CRO, they could benefit from participation in the GDS systems.

Today's software programs allow the integration of direct, Web-based reservation systems with the CRO database and with the GDS system, which helps to avoid overbooking and minimize underbooking. Companies such as Dallas-based Pegasus Solutions, Inc. (www.pegs.com) provide various technology services to the lodging industry (and others) and their third-party partners. See Chapter 6 for more information on third-party Internet interfaces with GDS data (e.g., Orbitz and Travelocity).

then must enter the information manually into the credit card system. The other major difference is that the Web visitor does not receive an immediate confirmation of the availability or the reservation. Despite these differences, the CGI form is easily created and added to a Web site.

Gift Shop Catalogs

Most large hotels and gaming establishments, and some restaurants and smaller lodging facilities, have gift shops for the convenience of their guests. Some of these may be concessions; others are actually managed by the business establishment itself. With an online presence, even the smallest of enterprises can host a gift shop. Online, many of these take the form of an online catalog. In their simplest form, online catalogs are lists of products or services, usually including a description and often illustrated with product images. Some catalogs may not be interactive at all: they require the user to find the item by reading through the list, then place an order by telephone, fax, or maybe e-mail. Such pages may have been sufficient several years ago, but if your market is at all competitive, you'll have to improve on this.

The Hotel del Coronado in San Diego, California, features 25 galleria shops for tourists and other visitors to browse and make purchases (Figures 5.5 and 5.6). With an online presence, people the world over can browse the shops and make online purchases.

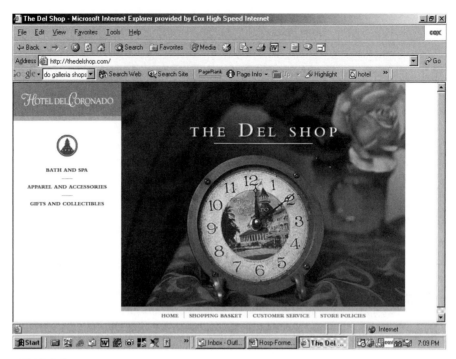

FIGURE 5.5 Hotel del Coronado in San Diego Gift Shop. (Screen capture from http://thedelshop.com.)

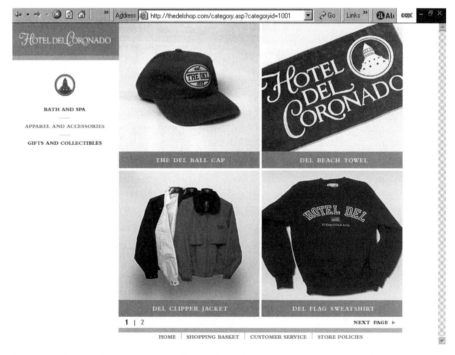

FIGURE 5.6 Hotel Del Coronado items for sale online. (Screen capture from http://thedelshop.com/category.asp?categoryid=1001.)

Software Choices

Literally hundreds of software programs claim to provide all of your Web interface solutions. Here's what just a few of them say about their products. For more information on more products, use your favorite search engine and enter the keywords "online reservations software hotel internet."

INNfinity Hospitality Systems™ (www.innfinityhs.com)

The software includes Reservations, Front Desk Cashier, Housekeeping, Night Audit and Reporting, all as standard modules. Training is a major issue with Front Office Managers as the turn over for front desk positions can be relatively high. INNfinity's use of an exclusive single screen design makes employee training a snap. An Innfinity installed Best Western General Manager is quoted as saying, "when you have a two-week tenured clerk teaching the brand new employee how to use the system, you know the software is easy to use."

INNfinity Hospitality Systems™ provides a one-step Night Audit that runs in less than 5 minutes; automated room blocking by reservation date, rate, room feature request (amenity); Web-Res Internet reservations capability; the ability for revenue splits on package plans; an easy-to-use single-screen design, backed by a powerful, robust, and dependable SQL database.

Guest Tracker 5.1 (www.guesttracker.com)

New Internet / GDS Reservations interface management software helps manage availability On-line and import On-line reservations right into Guest Tracker's pending reservations module. Guest Tracker's software solutions allow larger properties to take advantage of the latest property management system technologies. Guest Tracker Hotel Reservation Software is developed by TCS Hotel Software Inc.

Northwind (www.maestropms.com/products.html)

Using Northwind's On-line Internet Reservation system, ResEze, hotel clients are able to offer their customers:

Interactive, immediate response of availability.

On-line response for your reservation confirmation. If there is no availability, customer can try another date, another accommodation type, or, if none are available, customer can immediately check on another date or simply make other arrangements.

Execu/Tech (www.execu-tech.com/hotel-internet.html)

From Front Desk Check-in all the way to Back Office General Ledger, HOTEL™ by Execu/Tech will provide your property with one complete and seamless integrated software solution. Our internet reservations module turns your HOTEL™ System into a realtime web reservations application!

Try it

1. Visit the Web sites of three companies claiming to provide products that create and manage reservation systems accessed by Internet users on hotel Web sites. (Visit the sites listed earlier or use a search engine to find others.) What are the most common benefits for lodging establishments claimed by the products?

2. You own a small bed and breakfast. Why might you want to add an online reservation system to your Web site rather than a CGI form?

3. What information is gathered by a hotel or other venue when an Internet user makes a reservation online?

4. Just for fun, imagine you want to make reservations to spend a week at the Wellington Springs Inn (somewhere in some mountains in the United States). The year is 1820—no Internet, no telephone, and you have no travel agent. How do you go about making the reservations directly with the Inn? How do you learn whether the Inn will have accommodations for you? How far in advance do you need to make the reservation?

Interactive catalogs use at least three basic components: a "front end" that allows visitors to browse or search for an item; a "back end" database that holds the product information; and a means of ordering online using a shopping cart (discussed later) or order form. Many variations of interactive catalogs are available to suit various products, services, and audiences. The catalogs vary in the appearance, size, content, and sophistication or creativity of the search/respond/order functions. In their own way, the reservation systems discussed earlier are a form of catalog and ordering system combination.

The front end, which is the part that users see and interact with, may present a list of product or service categories for the user to select from. The user clicks on the name of a category and is shown a page with information on the items in that category. A more interactive approach uses a search option that acts as the interface between the user and the database of information. The search option may be fairly simple, such as one in which the user enters an item name or number and the Web site (the site's "system") retrieves the information on the matching item(s), along with a related description, image(s), pricing information, and links to further information.

Shopping Carts

Shopping carts are highly interactive. Users identify items they want to purchase, and the shopping cart keeps track of them. At their convenience, the users "proceed to check out"—they confirm their purchases, the prices,

Sophisticated Search

Some search options are becoming very sophisticated. They use "artificial intelligence" to ask visitors more questions about what they are trying to find. Then, the search engine narrows its focus, retrieves, and displays the matching items. Here's a simple example* of an exchange between a user and a sophisticated search function:

User enters: *hotel*

System displays: *airport or downtown?*

User enters: *airport*

System displays: *How many people?*

User enters: *two adults*

System displays: *King, Queen, twin beds?*

User enters: *King*

System displays: *Smoking? Non-Smoking?*

User enters: *Non-Smoking*

The system then displays the descriptions, technical specifications, and images of the rooms that meet the user's criteria. The user may choose to change the criteria during the process.

This interface is remarkable in the high degree of interaction between the Web site's system and the user, particularly in the high degree of "humanness" of the function.

According to Don Steinberg*, "in a five-month test of this type of 'human' search dialogue for the purposes of selling computers from Acer America's site, Acer's online notebook sales rose by 21 percent . . . using a program developed by Mark Lucente, Former Postdoctoral Research Fellow and Research Assistant, MIT Media Laboratory Spatial Imaging Group."

*This example is adapted from one described by Don Steinberg, "The man with the e-commerce answer," Smart Business for the New Economy, Ziff Davis, February 2001, p. 100.

and any tax or shipping costs, and charge the total to their credit card. Shopping carts typically work in conjunction with a financial institution's real-time credit card processing to check the validity and balance of a given credit card owner's card number. Various forms of security to prevent credit card theft or breach of confidentiality may protect shopping cart transactions.

Part of the reason that shopping carts have become so popular with users is their ease of use (and interactive novelty). With a shopping cart, a user can complete a transaction in a matter of seconds. Shopping carts have become popular with vendors because customers use them and because the programs that operate the shopping carts are relatively inexpensive and easy to install.

The primary steps required to make an online purchase are:

1. The user selects an item and adds it to the order form or shopping cart.
2. The site calculates the amount and asks for the customer's shipping and credit card information.
3. The customer gives the final okay.
4. The order is processed and forwarded to the fulfillment department or warehouse for shipping of the item.

In the hospitality industry, the reservation information is forwarded to a reservation desk and entered into a database.

Increasingly, hospitality sites are selling products directly from their Web sites. In many cases, these are memorabilia items bearing the company's logo, like the ones shown in Figure 5.7.

Online reservations and ordering are not limited to lodging venues. Various food service establishments include CGI forms for reservations on their sites; some also have shopping or ordering capabilities. Consumers can even order gourmet food online from a favorite restaurant and have it delivered hot to their door. In the San Francisco Bay area, for example, MealsToGo.com delivers menu choices to a home or office or to a party in progress at the click of a mouse (see Figure 5.7).

FUNCTIONS THAT ENABLE VISITOR COMMUNICATION

Doc Searls and David Weinberger, two of the "ringleaders" of the Cluetrain Manifesto (see www.cluetrain.com), say,

> The mass production of the industrial world led companies to engage in mass marketing, delivering "messages" to undifferentiated hordes who didn't want to receive them. Now the Web is enabling the market to converse again, as people tell one another the truth about products and companies and their own desires—learning faster than business. Companies have to figure out how to enter this global conversation rather than relying on the old marketing techniques of public relations, marketing communications, advertising, and other forms of propaganda. We, the market, don't want messages at all, we want to speak with your business in a human voice. (The Cluetrain Manifesto, chapter description, p. viii)

Every day, developers are adding new functions to the array of tools that enable Web visitors to communicate with companies and with each other. Increasingly, business sites are adding bulletin boards, chat rooms, online meetings, online seminars, videoconferencing, teleconferencing, and live customer service via individual chat. E-mail and contact forms are now so universal and indispensable that a site without them will soon be lonely.

FIGURE 5.7   MealsToGo. (Screen capture from www.mealstogo.com/.)

These conversational functions or tools are not increasing simply because the developers enjoy creating them (which, of course, they do). Nor does their real significance lie in their novelty. Rather, these tools are filling a key purpose for Web use, the underlying reason for its global expansion—people's natural need and desire to communicate with people. These are the tools that allow Web visitors to communicate with you—a very different function from telling and showing your products and touting your greatness.

These tools also let people get to know you, the you that is the people who make your company what it is. This is the Internet operating at its subversive best. Imagine letting employees spend an hour a week (or some other time increment) in the company's Web site chat room talking with guests, patrons, clients and potential clients, in their own words. Unanticipated consequences might include increased loyalty, appreciation, and creativity—for both customers and employees.

What is wonderful about many of these conversations, especially those among the visitors themselves, is that they often tend to be unvarnished statements of opinion—market research at its cost-effective best.

More About Shopping Carts

If your site sells products, you will want an effective shopping cart system. Because an online shopping cart must work flawlessly from day one, select a firm and software with great care. Always test a number of shopping carts from the front end; that is, as a purchaser, to see how they work from all perspectives. Talk with several customers of any finalists being considered as a potential shopping cart source, asking about their experiences, good and bad, with the company; the installation and set-up; reports; and so on.

Entire shopping cart programs can be purchased for less than $500, not including a real-time credit card processing account. Online real-time credit card processing accounts (or merchant accounts, which require you to have good credit) typically cost 2.3 percent or more on each transaction, an additional $0.20 to $0.30+ per transaction, and about $10 monthly for a monthly statement fee. Merchant accounts are reasonable, but vary in cost that is often based on your credit record.

One of the many firms that sells shopping cart programs is Easycart.com. It offers a system for as low as $399 with instant installation (see www.easycart.com for more information). For custom shopping cart programs, EMK Design at www.emkdesign.com has done pioneering work in this field. A provider of powerful applications in this field is Mercantec, a leader in products and services that enable Internet commerce, at www.mercantec.com. Many such firms provide reports, graphs, and other features. Also, a number of free shopping carts are available (see an example at: www.cowtown.net/stores.htm).

Live Customer Service

You finally find the hotel you seek at the price you want, but you have just one critical question to ask before you are ready to make that reservation. In a bricks-and-mortar store, you could ask a clerk; online, you might have to wait hours (or days) before your e-mailed question is answered. No more. Now, live customer service gives Web users immediate access to a customer service or sales representative. It works very much like AOL's "Instant Messaging," but does not require downloading a program or plug-in. Users just click on your "Talk to us now" button.

This function connects real people in real-time—the cement of the Internet. Many sites have already added a live customer service feature that allows their visitors to interact one-on-one with a real live human who knows all of the answers. Live customer service tools, some of which are free or inexpensive to e-businesses, include a Web button with text that invites visitors to ask for your help. Figure 5.8 shows sample buttons provided by www.humanclick.com.

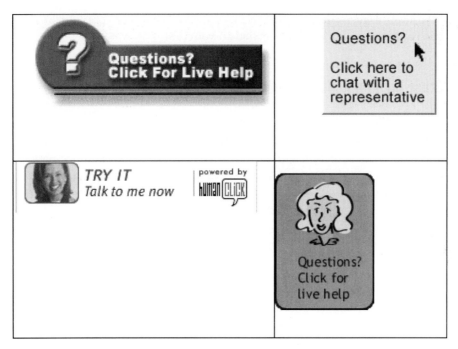

FIGURE 5.8 Sample buttons. (Screen captures from www.humanclick.com.)

Using the services of HumanClick, an early leader in this field, users download and install a free software program that works a chat-room-like split-screen whiteboard. The program signals the user (or someone designated to answer the signal) with an audio or a visual alert when visitors enter the site or when they ask to chat.

The software also provides considerable data about visitors and what they are doing on your site. For example, using your operator window, you receive a real-time view of a visitor's profile, including such information as the name of the visitor's Internet service provider (ISP), the Web pages viewed, length of visit, and so forth. At any point during a visit to your site, you may, in one click, open a chat request on the *visitor's* screen and offer assistance. You can send "canned" answers to the most common questions or create an answer on the spot. You can even take the visitor to other pages on the Web by sending the Web page addresses, which are clickable.

Live customer service may not seem very practical for most entities in the hospitality industry, but services like HumanClick train and employ humans to answer the live questions for you. Charges may vary according to the number of inquiries or time spent with your Web visitor. Answering questions such as "Is there live dance music in the Rua Room on Thursday?" "Do all of your rooms have modem hookups?" or "Are you serving soft-shell crabs yet?" could make the difference between getting a reservation or not.

Also, even a few months of this service can build a history of questions that tells you what additions are needed to your site.

Other Communications Through Writing

Chat Rooms

Chat rooms seem to be proliferating on the Internet with great speed, probably due to the ease of installation and use. The primary difference between a chat room and the live interactions described previously is the number of people involved. Chat rooms can accommodate large numbers of users at one time.

Web visitors can join in a live chat on a Web site with a single click. Using a chat room, customers can discuss industry information or talk with each other about your service. Users may sound off about product problems, try to help each other solve some of those problems, and discuss the need for certain product features—all of which help you improve your products and services. Consider offering a chat room about things to do while visiting your area, good travel activities in the area for families with young children, or the hot rod show that is coming to town.

Such conversations can also help your customers get to know you and your company—with the possible outcome of enhanced product or company loyalty. Why? Because that's what happens when people converse freely with other people, even in this written fashion, rather than just interact with an impersonal Web site page.

Most successful chats follow a schedule so that visitors show up when others are also online. Visitors often like to do the scheduling themselves. Without scheduled times, unless your site has many thousands of visitors a day, chat rooms may sit there unused like desert islands. Schedule and promote a monthly (or more frequent) chat session with the CEO or the customer service manager or a product-marketing director. Promote these chat times in opt-in newsletters, as well as on the site.

Bulletin Boards

Bulletin boards let visitors log in and post questions or statements. Viewing their comments gives you insight on ways to improve your establishment or Web site. To maintain decorum, many firms opt for a bulletin board that either screens out provocative language or can be edited by a manager before the posting is publicly displayed. Never change a negative comment into a positive one—you will be discovered and the situation will only get worse. Rather, if possible, acknowledge the criticism and comment on how it might be corrected.

POLL

If the election were held today, which of the
following would you vote for?

○   G. Davis

○   M. Davis

○   M. Mouse

Click here to <u>Submit</u>

FIGURE 5.9   Poll creation tool.

Polling

Polls give power. Users have the power to give you their opinion. Those opinions give you power to improve—improve your company, your products, your Web site. In addition, many Web visitors *like* to answer polls, especially if the Web page gives instant feedback about the responses. If it is a topic of particular interest, users will return to the site to see later results.

Web page polls (Figure 5.9) can be easily added without requiring the purchase of sophisticated (and expensive) software. Use them to evaluate new hospitality products or service ideas, to determine the importance of various product or service features, or to get feedback on your customer service efficiency or friendliness. You'll be limited only by your own ability to think of questions.

Firms offering free polling applications can be found at www.ezpolls. com, www.visitorpoll.com, www.freecenter.com/yourpolls, www.netvotes. com, and many others. For a list of interactive (and free) polling and other tools, visit www.123go.com/drw/webs/form.htm.

Try it

1. Visit http://ezpolls.mycomputer.com. Create a poll with two questions.

2. Visit www.humanclick.com. "Talk" with one of their representatives via the HumanClick function. Ask the representative how many clicks he or she answers each day. Ask the representative which hospitality sites use HumanClick.

If you have large numbers of visitors daily, you can conduct and post the results of "quick polls" within minutes. These quick polls are the same kind that TV network Web sites use during political campaigns. OpinionPower.com at www.opinionpower.com suggests these uses for quick polls:

- Increase audience interaction
- Increase the time an audience uses your site
- Increase page views
- Increase advertising space
- Learn about your audience as a group, not as individuals
- Use information to better serve your audience
- Provide your audience with information about its preferences

Online Meetings

Teleconferencing

Most telephone users are familiar with teleconferencing, or at least understand the concept. Uncle Harry in Minneapolis, Cousin Sue in Marshville, and Grandma Bess in Kiowa can all talk to each other on the phone at the same time. Computer networking has expanded the scope of the concept—now, the conferencing can take place using a network connection. Once the network teleconference is set up, the users can talk, using a microphone and speakers connected to their computers. More importantly, they can also share computer applications and use a whiteboard that all of the participants in the teleconference can see and write or draw on. Now, your customer service representatives and sales representatives can actually draw pictures to help explain product elements.

One of the earliest Internet teleconferencing programs was Microsoft's NetMeeting. The "new and improved" NetMeeting includes audio- and videoconferencing features, whiteboard functions that allow users to share and edit graphic information, text-based chat, and other functions. For additional information, get the details at www.microsoft.com/windows/netmeeting.

Videoconferencing

Videoconferencing is among the fastest-growing segments of the computer industry. Videoconferencing differs from teleconferencing in that it allows the transmission of video. Participants can use this tool as a one-to-one (two-person) conference, in which case the system is similar to using a video telephone. Small video cameras transmit the participants' pictures to each other's computer monitor, and they use their computer's microphone and speakers for audio.

Videoconferencing can also be used to connect several people at once. Participants communicate in a "virtual conference room," as though they were all at the same table. Reductions in the once-exorbitant costs have increased the use of videoconferencing for company internal and external communications. Still, these systems generally require special network arrangements with an outside provider who outsources the service to the company (and networks its various locations). Just as you see in Hollywood movies, participants sometimes gather in a conference or seminar room, looking at jumbo screens as they participate in the meetings.

Microsoft's NetMeeting supports videoconferencing. Another firm in this field is Webex.com, www.Webex.com, that allows users to hold interactive Web meetings with real-time data and voice and video communications through a standard browser. If your business provides facilities for meetings, conferences, banquets, or other business gatherings, you might consider offering the capability for those clients to participate in videoconferencing or to broadcast their meetings via Webcasting.

Webcasting and Internet Events

Internet "events" are often distributed using Webcasting, which is also often called netcasting or Internet broadcasting. Webcasting is the process of transmitting live or prerecorded audio or video to personal computers connected to the Internet. Webcasting is very much like TV or radio in that it delivers "one to many" communication. The software that enables Webcasting is known as streaming media.

Online seminars

If you want to bring your entire hotel, restaurant, or casino chain's staff up to speed on a new procedure or sales approach, consider Webcasting them a seminar on the subject. The cost of a Webcast, when compared with that of paying for the travel, lodging, food, and expenses to bring employees (or customers, vendors, dealers, or franchisees) to a central location, makes Web conferencing a viable alternative. As travel risks and restrictions unfortunately increase, Webcast may become more common. Employee productivity is also a big factor in online seminars, product demonstrations, or training. Employees can view online presentations from their own computers, saving the time and expense of off-site training. To view an online video presentation, go to: play.rbn.com/?url=rn/rnc/g2demand/0524keynote1_100.rm&proto=rtsp.

Broadcasting a Company Message as an "Event"

Webcasting can be used as an important tool in your internal marketing. Webcasting enables a CEO or other executive to deliver messages to employees of a large firm. Webcasts can be delivered live, but are usually made available from a Web page and are viewable at the user's convenience. Web cast company messages to specific audiences by giving them password-protected access to a specified Web page. Direct the audience to a particular page where they log in and view the full sound and video presentation.

Generally, you can broadcast streaming messages to anyone who "tunes in" on the Internet. Such broadcasts should be well publicized ahead of their release, especially if the release is a one-time-only transmission. If the broadcast will be available online for a prolonged time, as most Web casts are, be sure to list it in directories of "events," such as Broadcast.com at "Yahoo! Events for Business and Finance" on www.broadcast.com/Business_and_Finance.

The Yahoo! Broadcast site (http://broadcast.yahoo.com) offers a large and comprehensive selection of streaming media programming, including live and on-demand corporate and special events from their Business Services customers and live and on-demand special interest shows and Internet-only Webcasts. Yahoo! provides the following Webcasting and audio–visual production services, as well as Web and multimedia development, and consulting.

Webcasting Services
- Live audio and video broadcasting
- On-demand audio and video hosting
- 24 × 7 audio and video broadcasting
- Internet and intranet broadcasting
- "Self-service" audio and video hosting
- Pay-per-view broadcasting
- Secured broadcasting
- Multicasting services

A/V Production Services
- Live Webcast engineering
- Audio/video production
- Audio/video satellite uplinking and downlinking

Tip	Streaming Media

How does streaming media work? Streaming media technologies transmit audio and video from a centralized source, known as a server, to a software client on the user's computer. The software is called a media player. When the user requests a streaming media file, such as a video, the server sends a stream of data to the media player, which plays the data (audio and video) as it is received.

Documents Sent by Autoresponders

An autoresponder is a program that automatically answers any or some e-mail messages or specific commands issued from a Web site. For example, a Web site might have a list of "free reports" of interest to that site's target audience. The user can click in a check box next to the desired reports, enter an e-mail address, and click on "send" or "submit." The autoresponder automatically sends the selected reports to the e-mail address entered by the user. The answers can be long and can carry attachments. These tools are useful for sending large files, even catalogs with thousands of items, to customers or prospects.

Even the most simple autoresponder functions generate two positive results: you are given the user's e-mail address, which you can add to your database for future communication, and your company has sent a message, by request, right into the user's e-mail inbox. This means that after these users have left your Web site, they will see the name of your company, your e-mail address, and information from your site right there in their e-mail. Indeed, this is the advantage of placing such information or reports in autoresponder format over placing the information directly on the site's pages. A variation or compromise might be to put part of the report on the site, with links for "Request the full report by e-mail" available for users to obtain the remainder. Autoresponders do their best work when they are clearly described for the user. For example, "To have our 30-page wine list e-mailed to you instantly, send an e-mail to sales@superduperwines.com."

One familiar form that is routinely used on thousands of sites is the "confirmation" notice that a user receives after filling out forms, either to register as a "member" or subscriber or to order a product, airline ticket, or hotel reservation. Autoresponders are also useful for sending a sample to potential e-magazine or newsletter subscribers, welcome and thank-you letters, ad rates, price lists, and much more.

ONLINE INTERACTIONS THAT SUPPORT SELLING

In some ways, online interactions that do not actually sell products or services are an extension of the "look and feel." Although they may not be as critical as the online interpersonal interactions described previously, they are certainly worth consideration. The objective here is one of attracting visitors and getting them to spend some time on your Web site and then to return to your site. The following are a few to consider.

Downloadable Products

If your hospitality facility happens to be in a scenic area, consider giving Web visitors free scenery-related products for promotional purposes via downloadable files. Sites that use this mode of distribution benefit from

More Interactivity for Your Web Site

If you find yourself addicted to experimenting with your Web site and have long hours on the night shift to play with these functions, here are a few more ideas:

- **Free e-mail.** Offer free Web-based e-mail to your site visitors. Users who sign up for the service will return to your site every time they want to retrieve or send e-mail. Most of these programs use the name of the host site in the e-mail address or add advertising or a slogan to each message sent. This means that users are helping to advertise the host site to their e-mail correspondents.

- **Free calendars.** Calendar programs can be added to a site to allow visitors to create and maintain their schedules. "Members" can check their schedules from any computer connected to the Web, and they must visit your Web site to do it.

- **Opt-in newsletters.** Offer to send visitors timely news of your industry or a regularly scheduled newsletter packed with useful information, tools, or offers. Because visitors sign up for (opt-in) the newsletters, these mailings are not considered spam. This is true even if the mailings contain links that lead the recipient back to pages on your site. The newsletters, or the links provided in them, can include coupons, special limited-time discounts, used equipment sales, deals on blemished products, and so on. However, if the mailings are limited to promotional content, recipients soon will view them as spam. More effective newsletters include content that is rich, unique, succinct, and clearly valuable to the recipient.

- **Free Internet faxing.** This service allows visitors to fax documents usually to the United States and Canada for free from any computer connected to the Web. As with free e-mail and calendars, this service requires users to visit your site.

customers' impulse ordering and their desire to obtain the product in the fastest, easiest way possible. No-hassle, instant gratification reaps many rewards.

Firms that offer free downloadable screen savers make a daily impression on the recipients. You might even find some of your food service providers willing to give you screen saver help. For a list of major food industry firms that offer screen savers, see www.ultimatesavers.com/index. asp?Level1=Promotional.

Many firms create professional screen savers for many different markets and needs. We liked the simplicity of the CassDesign.com home page (www.cassdesign.com), especially the solid positioning line, "Screen Savers that Motivate and Inspire."

Letting your customers download free screen savers may be particularly effective if your facility is in a city famous for a brand-name product that has a following, or if you are near a famous landmark like Mt. Rushmore or Yosemite. You're a seafood restaurant in Big Bay de Noc, Michigan? Offer screen savers of huge pike and muskellunge breaching the water. Are you a lodge in a prime skiing area? Offer downloadable skiing screen savers or links to ski action clips that play online.

Audio Downloads

Audio downloads are not limited to music, although music dominates. Audiobooks can be purchased and downloaded from various sites as well. The sites http://audible.com and www.blackstoneaudio.com are worth examining. Thousands of books have been recorded and are available for download, an extension of the "books-on-tape" concept. Spread information about your region, your Web site, and your establishment by providing downloadable audio "tour guides."

E-Books

Virtually unheard of a few years ago, e-books now inhabit the Web in the offerings of hundreds of online publishers and distributors. At these sites, users can purchase and download a book to read from a computer monitor, a print out, or from an e-book reading device. Visitors can download e-books or request that they be e-mailed.

Offer free or low-cost downloadable e-books that tell the story of your establishment, region, menu, or recipes. Are you located in the Napa-Sonoma or Santa Ynez Valley region of California? Offer downloadable e-books on your area's fine wineries. Do you operate an historic restaurant or inn? Offer downloadable e-books recounting your location's role in local history. Do you pride yourself on being family oriented? Offer downloadable e-books for kids. Is your facility famous for dietary dishes or a terrific health club or spa? Offer a downloadable program for users to track their calories, weight, or activity levels (with your advertising clearly displayed and links back to your online store). Learn more about e-books at www.epublishingconnections.com or www.ebookconnections.com/ReadersPrimer.

Use downloadable files, for example, as an incentive to help build your opt-in magazine or newsletter e-mail list (for further discussion of opt-in mailings and permission marketing, see Part Four). Offer your e-book, screen saver, or other downloadable product as an incentive to get people to complete your online survey, or as a free "bonus" to repeat or frequent customers who make an online reservation, or just as a gift for visiting your site. Preferably, the downloadable item should be one related to your facility, its theme, or your market position.

Summary

Interactive functioning has changed the ways people use the Internet. No longer content with looking up definitions, finding phone numbers, or sending e-mail, users communicate with each other live, make things happen on the Web, control and change things. Effective Internet marketing recognizes these functions and their impact on the marketplace—and uses them advantageously.

The Web tool that is changing the hospitality industry today is the online registration function. Many software companies are offering their variations of this tool for all sizes of hospitality firms. The programs often have the capability of interacting with CRO and GDS programs.

Other important types of interactive functioning include forms that can be sent by e-mail, many types of interactive catalogs, and other tools and activities to increase the interactivity of some sites.

Review Questions

1. What is the difference between a CRO and a GDS?
2. How do Web-direct reservation systems save hotels money?
3. What information is gathered by a hotel or other venue when an Internet user makes a reservation online?
4. What is CRM? Describe how data is used when a hotel has a CRM program.
5. What are the steps a Web user completes when making an online reservation for lodging accommodations?
6. What is the main difference between making real-time, "live," online reservations and using a CGI form for reservations?
7. What are the three main components of an interactive Web catalog?
8. Why would industrial firms making many, many products benefit from having an interactive Web catalog?
9. What does the "front end" of a shopping cart generally refer to?
10. What does the "back end" of a shopping cart generally refer to?
11. How can offering an online e-book as a free download help achieve a site's marketing goals?
12. How can a small shop benefit from selling from an online catalog without the cost of an entire shopping cart system and all of its programming?
13. Why would you want to add "HumanClick" to a Web site?
14. Name some costs that can be saved by using Webcasting instead of in-person meetings.
15. What is an "opt-in" newsletter?

PART TWO

Getting Found

Your Internet presence is worthless if no one can find you. As the Internet has grown to hold billions of pages, the task of ensuring that existing and potential clients and customers find the Web site for your business, product, or service has become more artful. No longer can simply registering with a search engine or listing a site on a directory or even purchasing banner or tile ads on portals secure a particular site's continuous, reliable findability. From Web directory and search engine results, not only do people have to find the link to your site, they also have to decide to *click* on that link to actually get to your information.

With the dot-com visibility, even notoriety, of the past several years, the general public has grown accustomed to hearing and seeing the now-familiar "www" dot-this or dot-that on television, radio, and all forms of print media. Businesses on the Web have adjusted to the idea that they must "advertise their advertising." Web addresses now appear on everything from the wrapper on lettuce to skyline towers, billboards to skywriters, pencils to 747s.

The chapters in Part Two help to ensure that your target audiences find your Web presence by teaching you how to use on-the-Web tools and links, as well as off-the-Web labels, sales collaterals, advertising, or promotion.

The chapters in Part Two are:

Chapter 6   Getting Found: Portals Vortals, Search Engines, and Directories

Chapter 7   Internet Advertising: Links, Banners, Tiles, and More

Chapter 8   Promotion and Advertising: On the Net and Off

LEARNING THE LANGUAGE

The following terms are introduced in Part Two and are used in subsequent chapters. Familiarize yourself with them by reading the definitions provided.

alternative text.   Sometimes called "mouseovers" or "alt tags," this text displays while an image is loading and when the user places the mouse pointer over an image. Unless the Web site owner or creator changes the alternative text, the name of the graphic file, such as house.gif, shows. However, any text may be used, such as "Sam Brown, Realtor® for first-time home buyers in Bowling Green, Kentucky." Some search engines read this alternative text along with visible text to help determine a site's relevance to specific keywords.

banner ad.   Small rectangular, usually horizontal, ad that appears on Internet pages. Banner ads usually link the visitor to the Web site or page of the banner owner (advertiser).

banner exchange.   Reciprocal banner display, characterized by the statement, "I'll put your banner on my site if you'll put my banner on yours." The banners often, but not always, include an active link to the target site, becoming link exchanges.

bridge page.   A Web page that leads visitors to another site; hence, a "bridge." Several sites offer free pages—Tripod.com and Geocities.com are among the better known sources. Often, but not always, these pages carry their own metatags and their URLs can be registered with search engines. Because some search engines penalize such pages in their rankings, the Web savvy put at least some new or different information on each bridge page, rather than just a list of links to pages in the target site.

dealership.   Display of a graphic and link to an e-commerce site in return for a commission on items sold to visitors using that particular link. Sites with large invento-

ries sold in a catalog format are the most frequent offerors of dealerships.

directory.   A list similar to your familiar Yellow Pages®, with links and Web site information organized according to categories. General directories, like Yahoo!, are broad-based and include thousands of topics. Some directories focus on a specific topic and may be considered vertical portals or vortals.

domain name.   The main part of an Internet address, including its extension. In the address www.disney.com/news/pocahontas.htm, for example, "disney.com" is the domain name. Until late 1999, domain names were limited to 26 characters; now they may include as many as 76 characters.

domain name extensions.   Indicate the "top-level domain" (TLD) to which the name belongs. For example: .com indicates a commercial business; .net indicates a company that specializes in networks; .gov is used by government sites (local, state, or national); .org indicates an organization, usually nonprofit; .edu is used by educational institutions, school districts, and schools; .mil stands for military. Some extensions indicate the country where the site is based: .mx for Mexico or .ca for Canada. Early in 2000, .md was added for use by physicians, hospitals, and other medical-related entities. In 2001, more extensions were added, such as .biz, .pers, and .ent.

hidden text.   Text written in the coding of an Internet page that does not display on the site. Common examples are the metatags with title, keywords, site description, and other information that some search engines read and store in their databases.

keywords. Words people enter into search engines to find information on the Web. Most search engines match the words being searched with Web pages that have them. A typical consumer keyword search might be Manhattan, NY real estate. Keywords are also listed in the metatags (hidden text) of Web site pages for reading by search engines.

link exchange. Reciprocal linking between sites, usually without the exchange of any fee or other consideration.

metatag. Code with information about an Internet page or site. These tags explain what the page is about (Meta Title and Meta Description) and provide keywords (Meta Keywords) that represent the page or site content and more. Many search engines use metatag information to determine the ranking of a site in displayed search results.

robot. A program that runs automatically. Some Web pages have hidden text telling robots what to do; for example, "return every 7 days" or "do not catalog this page." (See also spider.)

search engine. An Internet site, function, or program that maintains databases of Internet pages, the keywords, and URLs, and retrieves the information according to keywords entered by users, displaying a list of Internet sites and pages. Examples include Excite, Infoseek, Google, and Webcrawler.

signature link. Text, graphics, and links added automatically to the end of outgoing e-mail messages.

spider. A program that automatically retrieves Web page information for use by search engines; a type of "robot."

sponsor. Site, individual, or company given highly visible credit for supporting a section of a Web site. For example, Goodyear Tires might sponsor a section in AOL called "Tires & Auto Accessories."

tile ad. Small, usually square ads that appear on Internet pages and usually link the visitor to the Web site of the advertiser.

URL registration. Reservation of a primary Internet site address (domain name). Internic, more recently called Network Solutions, is an entity officially authorized to regulate the assignment of domain names.

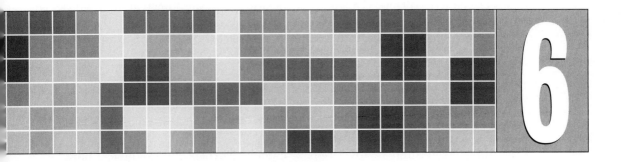

Getting Found

Portals, Vortals, Search Engines, Directories

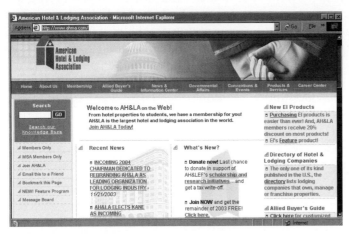

The American Hotel & Lodging Association provides assistance in operations, education, and communications, and lobbies on Capitol Hill. (Screen capture from www.ahma.com.)

The American Hotel & Lodging Association Web site shown above is an example of a vortal. Who is the site's main audience? What does it help its visitors find? Also visit www.all-hotels.com. Who is its main audience? What does it help its visitors find?

Of all the ways that people find information on the Internet, the most common are the links and searching tools on a portal site—a "gateway" to the Internet. Most of the links on a portal are part of the portal's "directory," a list of categories not unlike those in the familiar Yellow Pages® books.

Categories link to subcategories and lists of links to Web sites. Other links take visitors to advertisers or content partners. For example, a portal might arrange with ABC News to provide links to the day's top news stories on ABC's Web site (http://abcnews.go.com). Or, the portal might partner with *CNNmoney* (/money.cnn.com), a financial news network, and provide links to the latest financial stories, stock quotes, and other updates on the *CNNmoney* Web site.

Typically, portals also have a search engine or a selection of search engines for visitors to use by entering words or phrases related to what they are looking for. When someone searches for a product or service you offer, you want the search engines to find *you*. When someone uses a directory, you want to be sure your site is listed.

Portals that focus on a particular topic or audience are called vertical portals, or vortals. Vortals are especially useful for finding or advertising related products and services. A vortal might have links to Web sites that have content related to scuba diving, for example, and include scuba equipment, scuba history, beach hotels, scuba jobs, and scuba experts. One for landscape architecture might have links to sites with content on plant types, diseases, tolerances, landscape design tools, professionals, soils, hardscapes, and yard art. Thousands of vortals serve as portals for the hospitality industry, especially those that target a geographic area. Some vortals have search engines that search only their database. Others have search engines that search the entire Web.

This chapter provides information on search engines and general directories found at portal and vortal sites and other locations on the Internet. Search engines and directories undergo significant changes without warning—technological advances spur new tools and techniques, and seem to do so with speed unparalleled in history. We've updated these pages just before printing, so you will find the most recent information available.

THE BASICS

Search Engines

When a visitor enters words into a search engine, the engine looks into its database of words and phrases and site addresses and responds with a list of links to sites that it "thinks" fit the search criteria. How does it get the words, phrases, and Web site addresses? Basically, one of two ways: Web site owners register their sites with the search engines, and search engines send out programs ("spiders" and "robots") to crawl around the Internet reading the text and the hidden text (especially the metatags) on Web sites and then catalog what they find.

More often than not, these two processes work together in this way: You register your site address, or URL (uniform resource locator), with the search engine (easy to do and in most cases, free), and then, the search engine sends out the spider to find "keywords" on your site. If you have sufficient keywords (but not excessive ones) in your visible and hidden text that match the words that someone enters in the search engine, your site will come up higher in the search engine's results.

Register Your Site with the Major Search Engines

Registering your site with a search engine is easy. Go to the search engine's home page and look for a link labeled "Add URL" or "Add Your Site." Follow the link to the "Add URL" page. Once there, enter the main URL of your site(s), and, if requested, your e-mail address. Most engines also allow the registration of internal pages. Some request a short description. Write carefully! This description will often be the one shown when the engine lists your site. The following are some major portal and search engine home pages:

www.altavista.com	www.lycos.com
www.aol.com/netfind	www.netscape.com
www.directhit.com	www.nbci.com (formerlysnap.com)
www.dmoz.org	www.msn.com
www.excite.com	www.webcrawler.com
www.go.com	www.yahoo.com
www.google.com	www.fastsearch.com
teoma.com	www.search.com
www.overture.com	www.askjeeves.com
www.hotbot.com	www.alltheweb.com/
www.infoseek.com	

Search engines change. Some get absorbed by other engines, such as the combining of the search engine Magellan into Webcrawler. Teoma.com and others have recently begun to compete with Google.com. Goto.com changed its name to Overture.com, and new engines such as Findwhat.com and 7Search.com have been launched as attempts to compete with Overture.

Some search engines clean their databases of addresses on a regular basis. This means that you must reregister your site with the engines every few

How Important Are Search Engines for Driving Traffic to a Site?

Like so many other questions related to the Internet, the answer is, "It Depends." For sites with a very large, broad, and general target audience, search engines might be crucial. The cost to reach a very large unsegmented audience in time, money, and other resources with non-Web approaches could be prohibitive. On the other hand, if the people you are trying to reach can be highly targeted, then search engine results may not be nearly as important as other forms of site promotion.

Let's say you want to generate traffic to a Web site for a very exclusive, high-end country bed and breakfast that caters to dog owners and dog trainers. Your facility provides specialized sheep herding training to champion dogs. You might well find that your print and e-mail newsletters and other promotional activities that are directed specifically to dog breeders, trainers, and owners prove most valuable. Relatively speaking, search engine results may be of less importance to you overall than the newsletter. Nonetheless, search engines may still send you some clients who have somehow not made it onto your mailing lists yet. The following chapters contain more information on reaching your target audiences *off* the Web.

weeks. If you have hired a company to maintain your site, be sure to require that they do this for you regularly.

Use Pertinent, Effective Keywords, Titles, Headings, and Text

The different search engines use different formulas, programs, and strategies for reading a Web site or page in order to catalog it. They might read any of the following or any combination of the following parts of a site or page:

- Site title
- Major headings
- First line of all paragraphs
- All text on the site
- Photo and graphics captions
- Minor headings
- First line of first paragraph
- Alternate text for graphics
- Keywords provided in metatags
- Keyword "density"

By far the most important of these is the metatag for a site's title. An effective title in the source code of a site can be difficult to compose because it must serve two distinct purposes: announcing your site and providing the words that many search engines use to rank one site over another.

Knowing this, you can now make sure that the words and phrases that you think people will use to find you are included in the site's components as often as possible without sounding forced or repetitive.

The most common keywords that users enter into search engines when searching for a product or service are often too general. Users might search for "hotels" and get lists of hotels from all over the world. A more specific and more effective search is, "business hotel downtown Atlanta Georgia." You want the tags and text on your site to be the ones that searchers use and search engines find.

Test Your Position in the Search Engines Often

Even if you hire a company to submit your site address to the search engines, check on them yourself. Go to the engine and enter the keywords that you hope will bring up your site. Are you in the top 10? Perfect! If your site is not on the first page of results and you are serious about Web marketing, then you need help—most search engine users do not look beyond the first two pages of search engine results.

Directories

An Internet directory is an index of links that lead users to information. The index is organized into categories, not unlike your local Yellow Pages®. Users look for the categories that are most likely to contain the information they seek and then "drill down" through levels of information until they find what they are looking for. Just like Yellow Pages®, most directories allow you to advertise on their pages (for a price); some add a plain link to your site free, with charges for enhancements.

Major directories in which you should be listed include Yahoo.com, Looksmart.com, Dmoz.com, About.com, and Galaxy.com. Dozens more, especially regional ones, merit your consideration, especially the specialty ones relevant to your industry. For example, if you operate an inn, you will want to have it listed in directories of inns, as well as more general city directories that list hundreds of businesses for thousands of cities, such as USACitiesOnline.com (www.usacitiesonline.com).

How do you identify the ones for your city, county, state, or region? Begin finding them by using a search engine and searching for the name of the geographic element (e.g., city, county, state, region) along with the words "Directory Add URL." Each directory provides somewhat different instructions for adding a listing, so follow the directions carefully.

Yahoo! (see Figure 6.1) is the most frequently used directory. Estimates vary, but generally indicate that Yahoo! does just over a third of all Internet searches. Getting your site listed *correctly* with Yahoo! is therefore, an important step. Do not even think about adding your site listing to Yahoo! until you have read everything you can that Yahoo! says and that other sites say about doing this. You'll find the key information about adding your site listing to Yahoo! at http://docs.yahoo.com/info/suggest. Read the information and follow the directions carefully. If you make a mistake and Yahoo! indexes you in the wrong area of its directory, correcting the error could take months. The loss will be all the people who could have visited your site, but didn't.

In addition to general directories, list your site in industry-specific directories and vortals. The key directories and vortals for your industry can be found by using your favorite search engine to search for the name of your industry (e.g., hotels, restaurants, casinos), plus the word "directory." Add specific niche or area information if you wish to emphasize those, as in "seafood restaurant directory."

BEYOND THE BASICS

More About Search Engines

Using a search engine is a common way that people find information on the Internet. When someone searches for keywords representative of products or services that you offer, you want the search engines to find you.

How do search engines find a particular site? A combination of ways: Web site owners register their sites with the search engines, and search engines send out programs ("spiders" and "robots") to read the text and the hidden text (specifically, the metatags) on sites and catalog it.

More often than not, these two processes work together this way: You register your site address, or URL, with the search engine, which sends out a spider or other robot to find keywords on your site. If you have the right keywords in your text and hidden text, your site will come up higher in the rankings when the search engine displays the results of a search.

Search engines do not all work in the same way, which is why the job of keeping your site high on the results pages can be such a challenge. Search engines' spiders are programmed in different ways to look for, store, and then report different information from the sites they visit.

How Search Engines Work

The primary goal of search engines, such as Infoseek, Webcrawler, and AltaVista, is to help people find information on the Internet. The engines stay in business by selling advertising, and the advertising rates are related to how many visitors visit and use the engine. Search engine services must be

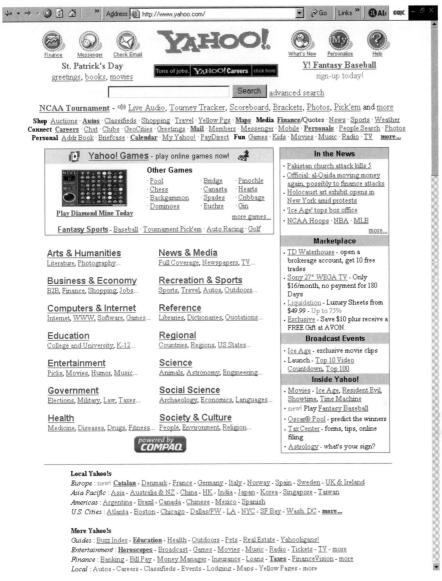

FIGURE 6.1 Yahoo! portal showing a search engine field (immediately below the Yahoo logo) and various categories of the directory. (Screen capture from www.yahoo. com, March 2002.) Reproduced with permission of Yahoo! Inc. © 2003 by Yahoo! Inc. YAHOO! and the YAHOO! logo are trademarks of Yahoo, Inc.)

comprehensive, quick, and useful to their users. Your concern with regard to search engines is that they help prospective clients find you.

Using a search engine to find information is free—to the user. Advertisers, on the other hand, pay handsomely to have their banners, buttons, and

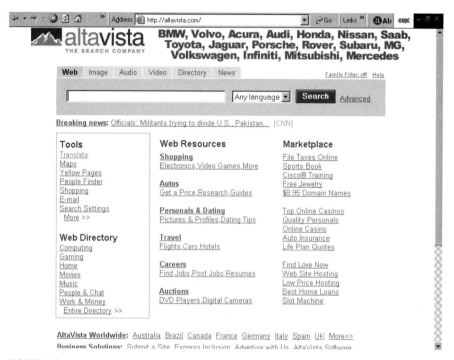

FIGURE 6.2   Altavista.com portal showing search engine box. (Screen capture from www.altavista.com, March 17, 2002.)

other graphics and links splashed around on the pages that users see. How do search engines work? Basically, the user enters a few words or a phrase on the search engine's page, and the search engine responds with a list of links that connect to Web pages. If the words entered are very general, the search engine will return thousands, hundreds of thousands, even millions of links. Fortunately, they only show you 10 or so at a time. Even more fortunately, the search engine shows them to you in order of relevance, most relevant to least relevant, according to the search engine's own criteria.

The results from the search engine also provide a short description of the pages it found. Often, the appropriateness of the description depends on the page itself, not the search engine. A search engine works best when the keywords entered are specific. "PVC pipe Miami Florida," for example, will yield more specific results than "plastic pipe."

Here's an example. Tom Diner in Miami wants to find a local restaurant that serves large steaks. He selects a search engine he's used before—say AltaVista at www.altavista.com. The search page will look much like the one shown as Figure 6.2. Users enter keywords related to their desired information into the box at the top of the screen. The main part of the screen consists of categories that link to Web sites related to those topics.

Mr. Diner must be fairly specific. If he simply entered "steaks," the search engine would find millions of pages related to steaks and the meat industry all over the world. So to focus his search, he adds the words "Miami" and "restaurant." His results page looks like Figure 6.3.

Most search engines and Internet addresses are not case sensitive, although a very few are. Lowercase letters work with almost all of the engines, and frequent users characteristically enter the information without any capitalization.

Information Search Engines Provide

The search engine, AltaVista.com, in the previous example displayed a list of Internet sites that feature steak restaurants in Miami. The results are based on the keywords entered and Altavista's database. The restaurant sites most likely to serve steaks in Miami are shown highest, in most cases, because they included the words "steak restaurant Miami" somewhere on their site.

Now, Mr. Diner selects a site to visit. He scans the titles and descriptions of the sites. The search engine also shows the Web site address (URL) of each site. Some engines assign a ranking or relevancy number alongside each item. For example, "82%" shown next to a site description will mean that the search engine is 82 percent sure that this site is what you are seeking, based, of course, on the keywords entered. Some search engines provide a link to "similar pages" or "more sites like this one." Clicking on such links displays more sites based on the keywords that were used.

Mr. Diner clicks on the link that says "Miami Restaurant and Attractions Guide," which takes him to the Miami dining guide vortal at http://miami.diningguide.net/dt2ste.htm. Now, Mr. Diner can look at dozens of restaurants that were wise enough to be listed in this guide.

Most people who use search engines read the information for several sites listed in the search results and then click on a link to go to a site that seems to be the best fit or sounds interesting. If the site grabs them immediately, they might explore it for a while and bookmark it to return to later. Otherwise, chances are they'll use their browser's "back" button to return to the search results and try another site.

Very few searchers ever look at results beyond the first few results listings in their search for anything. Even fewer look farther than page one of the results. So, tell your Webmaster how important it is that your establishment appear on page one for as many logical keyword phrases as possible.

Knowing this much about search engines tells you that:

■ You want your site to be displayed on page one or at the very least in the top 20 sites listed in the search engine results when your "target" words or phrases are sought.

FIGURE 6.3   Search results from Altavista.com for "steak restaurant miami."
(Partial screen capture from http://altavista.com/sites/search/
web?q=steak+restaurant+miami&pg=q&kl=XX.)

Tip	Meta-Search Engines

"Meta-search engines" search the top-ranked results of other search engines and then deliver all of those summaries or the summaries for the "top 10." Remember, you don't "add your URL" to the meta-search engines. If your site is getting found by the regular search engines, it will come up in the meta-search engines too. Here are five popular meta-search engines and their URLs.

Metacrawler, www.metacrawler.com

Megacrawler, www.megacrawler.com

Dogpile, www.dogpile.com

Debriefing, www.debriefing.com

37.com, http://37.com

- The description of your site that shows in the search results must be stated clearly and must get the user's immediate attention.
- The home page of your site has to convince visitors immediately that they've come to the right place!

Registering Your Site with Search Engines

Registering a site with a search engine is a simple process, and in most instances, it's free. Most search engines have a link on their search page or on their results page that says "Add URL." Sometimes, the link says "Add a Site" or "Suggest a Site." Clicking on that link leads to a form for entering the address of your site and your e-mail address. Some engines send their "robots" or "spiders" to your site to read and store keywords and descriptions in the engine's database.

From SearchEngineWatch.com come these words of caution: "One thing is *not* to rely on Add URL pages. These have been so abused by spammers that the crawlers don't depend on them much for new finds. Instead, they are much more reliant on link crawling. This means that if you build relevant links from good Web sites, you are more likely to be found by the crawlers and included in their listings" (see http://searchenginewatch.com/sereport/01/10-free.htm).

Other engines ask you to enter a short description and keywords that apply to your site. For these engines, write carefully! The description will be used in the listing of your site that is displayed in search results, and the keywords that you write may be the only ones that are used to call up your site. So, make sure that they match words and phrases that people would use when searching for a business like yours.

When adding a URL, check and double check whatever you enter for accuracy. Some engines will inform you that a URL has a mistake in form, such as a comma instead of a period, a missing colon, or a slash going the wrong way. However, engines cannot check the spelling of your URL or e-mail address. If an engine tries to find a Web address that does not exist because it was misspelled, the engine will ignore or delete the submission.

Remember some search engines clean their databases of URLs on a regular basis so that their data is current. This means that you should register your site with the engines repeatedly—every few weeks. If you have hired a company to maintain your site, be sure they do this for you regularly. Otherwise, mark your calendar so you don't overlook this important task.

Can't someone else do all of this URL listing for you? Sure. Finding a service on the Internet to register your URL with the search engines is not difficult. Often, you'll see such services advertised on the search engines themselves, and sometimes, they'll even do it for free. Usually, however, they will charge you a set fee for the service or offer to sell you the related services that they provide, such as Web site maintenance or hosting.

Do they actually perform the work that they promise and repeatedly enter your URL as they say? Most do, but beware. Better to get from them the names and numbers of their customers in your area who have used their service and call those customers to learn their satisfaction levels.

Make the registration of your site address with the search engines part of your Webmaster's job! If you are going to pay an individual or a company to create a site and host it for you, remember to ask them how they will ensure that the search engines find your site and list it in the top 10–20 links on the results pages.

Many Web site designers know how to make a site functional and know how to make it visually attractive, but are out of touch with the latest search engine technologies and how to make a site more findable. (If you suspect this to be the case with your Webmaster, consider showing that person this chapter.)

There are firms that specialize almost exclusively in search engine optimization. And there are software programs on the market that help optimize Web pages so they become more appealing to search engines. See, for example, the functions at www.se-optimizer.com, shown in Figure 6.4. This firm's Optimizer™ analyzes Web pages and points out areas that could be made more appealing to search engines.

Another service that offers to help your Web pages display more frequently and higher on search engine results pages is Position Research, shown in Figure 6.5.

How long after adding your URL until your site shows up on a search engine? You won't see the results immediately. The range is from a few days to many weeks. The same is true for any change that you make to your site

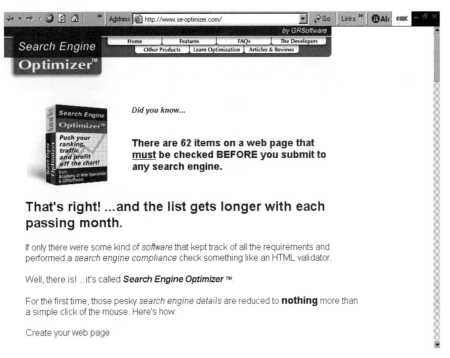

FIGURE 6.4   Search Engine Optimizer. (Screen capture from www.se-optimizer.com.)

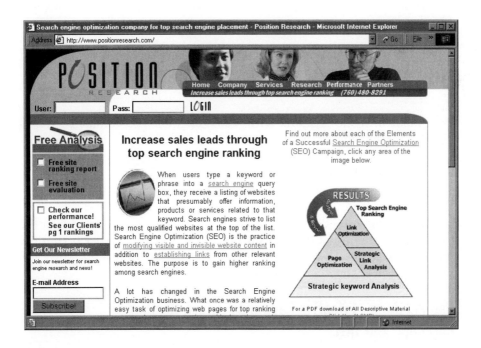

FIGURE 6.5   Position Research. (Screen capture from www.positionresearch.com.)

| TABLE 6.1 | Search engine comparison.* |

Search Engine	Approx. Size	META Tags Support	Spider Support	Popularity Increases Rankings	Submit Time
Alexa	Unknown	None	No	No	4 weeks
Altavista	350 Million	Yes	Yes	Yes	2–5 days
AOL Netfind & Excite	250 Million	Description Only	No	Yes	2–4 weeks
FAST Search	340 Million	No	Yes	Yes	1 week
Google	560 Million	Yes	Yes	Yes	2–6 weeks
GoTo	110 Million	No	No	No	< 3 days
HotBot	110 Million	Yes	Yes	Yes	2–4 weeks
Infoseek	50 Million	Yes	No	Yes	1–2 weeks
Lycos	Unknown	No	No	No	3–4 weeks
Northern Light	265 Million	No	Yes	Yes	2–4 weeks
Snap	Unknown	No	No	No	2–6 weeks
Webcrawler	50 Million	Yes	No	No	2–3 weeks
Yahoo!	Unknown	No	No	No	4–8 weeks

* Disclaimer: The research and findings are independent reviews and should only be used for informational purposes. All search engine sizes and submission times are approximations and may be inaccurate. This calculation and chart is from the search engine information site, SubmitCorner.com (www.submitcorner.com) on its page at www.submitcorner.com/Guide/SE/comparison.shtml. Data were retrieved in June 2002.

that might influence its rank with search engines. The automated robots and spiders that check sites for changes only visit periodically. As the number of sites on the Internet increases, the time between registering and showing on an engine seems to get longer.

Table 6.1 shows a comparison of the average time that it takes key engines to show a site after its URL has been submitted.

Registering a site does not ensure that a link to it will show up in the top 20 or 30 sites listed in the results of a search, however. That part of the picture is related to the content of the site itself, including the hidden keywords that most search engines read.

Use Pertinent, Effective Keywords, Titles, Headings, Captions, and Text

Make your site come up high in search engine results. When someone enters keywords or phrases into the search engine's entry box and then clicks on

Tip	Stay Tuned!

Search engines change their programs without notice. Stay up-to-date on search engines and how to make them work for you by subscribing to the free e-mail newsletters from Web Position at www.webposition.com or from Search Engine Watch at www.search enginewatch.com.

"go" or "search now," the engine checks its database for matches to keywords or keyword phrases. It then reports back, giving the user a list of sites. The more "matches" that a site has in the engine's database, the higher the engine places it in the results list. Some engines penalize sites that attempt to "stuff the ballot box," so to speak. If too many matches occur for a site, or if the matches found are too close together in the text, or if the matching terms are found in fragments rather than in complete sentences (defined as strings of text ending with periods or question marks), the engine might rank the site far lower than it might deserve or remove it from its index altogether.

Assuming that you are not trying to play tricks on the engines, the concern becomes one of ensuring that the engine's spiders and robots find those keywords and phrases on your site.

What are the keywords that people use when they look for information about your establishment or services on the Internet? To find out, use the search word suggestion tool at Overture.com at http://inventory.overture.com/d/searchinventory/suggestion/. There, enter terms that describe your product or service; for example, "seafood Atlanta." The function will show you how many times that term was searched for during the preceding month and associated searches that made use of the core words of that term. The results for "seafood Atlanta" (without quote marks) will look similar to this:

Count	Search Term
99	atlanta seafood restaurant
64	atlanta seafood
39	seafood restaurant in atlanta
31	seafood restaurant atlanta
28	atlanta seafood market

With this information, the Web site designer should include the phrase "Atlanta seafood restaurant" in the critical areas of the site for search engines to read and keep in their databases along with the site's URL.

Furthermore, the site should contain keywords naming the cities served, as well as words and phrases that describe the type of establishment. Keywords should also include the name of the county and any nicknames for the area, such as "The Big Apple" for New York City or "Twin Cities" for Minneapolis/St. Paul.

If a city or region is often misspelled, include the common *mis*spellings of the word as well—such as Misisipi—and mistaken state abbreviations, such as Michigan's MI for Mississippi (MS) or Missouri (MO) or Alaska's AK for Arkansas (AR). To see the frequency of geographical terms (e.g., cities, states, counties) used in keyword search strings, use Overture.com.

Include general product, service, or industry terms among the keywords and the text on your Web pages. Users often combine such terms with the geographical words, resulting in search strings such as "Dubuque downtown restaurants," "Missoula Montana burger recipes," or "Tampa Florida restaurant for sale."

Caution: Never put the keywords on your site without following through and actually adding the data or content that relates to those keywords. If you merely put the keywords, and an engine discovers you doing that, you might get banned for a period of months from that engine.

Try it

Which terms or phrases would you most want to have included on a Web site intended to develop business for a Los Angeles seafood restaurant? Visit the page http://inventory.overture.com/d/searchinventory/suggestion/. Enter "seafood los angeles restaurant." Which phrase had the highest count? What was the count for the top three phrases?

What Search Engines Read When They Visit Your Site: Visible Text and Hidden Text

Each search engine uses its own programming and formulas to read and catalog the information it finds on Web pages. The engines may "read" both visible and "invisible" or hidden text. "Visible" text is what you see when you are looking at a page on your browser. "Hidden" text is the programming code that you see only if you select "Source" from the "View" menu of your browser.

Visible text.   The following list are the most common visible Web page elements that the search engines' "readers," robots and spiders, read on Web pages. Because the engines might read only one of the pieces in this list or they might read several of them, you must be sure that you have used target terms in all of these pieces.

- major headings and subheadings
- the very first line of text on the first page of the site
- the first line of every page and the first line of every paragraph
- all text on the site
- photo and graphics captions

- alternate text" for graphics
- keywords provided in metatags
- keyword "density"

If a site includes ample, relevant content, the key terms related to the positioning of the company, establishment, or service will already be in ample evidence. The list of the ways different spiders read your site has important implications for the wording and organization of Web page headings and paragraphs. Review the following list of questions to help you evaluate how well the text on your site is helping you rank higher in search engine results.

Tip   **Does Your Site . . .**

1. include target words in headings, subheadings, and "click here" text?
2. list the cities you serve on its home page?
3. use at least one target term in every page, paragraph, and sentence?
4. have at least one page with text and links dedicated completely to:
   - menu and specialty food information (e.g., seafood, steaks, pizza, calzones, French chef)?
   - information for travelers (e.g., airport or downtown hotel, motel, beachfront)?
   - information about the area and community you serve?
   - information about your facility that supports your positioning?

Some search engines consider the keywords used in *headlines* more heavily when calculating a site ranking. Also, some engines include the presence of "complete sentences" that contain keywords as a ranking factor—so, whenever appropriate, put a period or question mark at the end of lines of text, because that's how spiders often decide what makes a sentence. To keep track of which keywords people are using to find your Web site, go to Link Tracker at www.radiation.com/products/linktrakker.

Hidden text. Your site has hidden words, or "metatags," which the search engines read. Meta is short for "metadata," which essentially means a "summary of data" or "data about data" that is found in a site. Metatags are a form of HTML code, the underlying code for the World Wide Web. An excellent explanation of metatags and HTML can be found at www.searchenginewatch.com/webmasters/meta.html.

To see the metatags on a site, select "View" from the menu bar of your Web browser and then select "View Source" or "Source" from the drop-down menu. The metatags, plus the coding that tells your Web page where to display images and text, will appear. Metatags are generally preceded in the source code by the word "meta."

The search engines "read" the title of your site, a list of keywords that are supposed to describe the content of the site, and other information contained in these metatags. The metatags that search engines read most often for ranking purposes are those for the site or page "title" and those for your "description." Most engines rank a site higher if the keywords searched are repeated several times among the words in both the title and the description. And many engines compare the words there to the words actually on the site to be sure that Webmasters are not just "packing" the metatags with extra keywords.

The following is an example of a firm's metatags (www.search enginewatch.com).

```
<html>

<head>

<title>Search Engine Watch: Tips About Internet Search Engines &
Search Engine Submission</title>

<meta name="description" content="Search Engine Watch is the
authoritative guide to searching at Internet search engines and search
engine registration and ranking issues. Learn to submit URLs, use HTML
meta tags and boost placement.">

<meta name="keywords" content="listings search engine watch Web
site, danny sullivan editor internet.com using meta tags improving
placement, how to submit urls to major internet search engines
Webmaster's guide, rankings search engine registration tips for
searching better reviews, tutorials technology report free newsletter,
news articles placement engine submission online help
www.searchenginewatch.com">

<LINK REL="stylesheet" HREF="/css/text.css" TYPE="text/css">

</head>
```

Another type of hidden text is "alternate text" (also called mouseovers and alt tags) for photos and graphics. Search engines cannot read pictures or graphics, so a photo of a staff member showing one of your rooms to a group tour ground operator is not going to help you with search engine rankings. However, many search engines do read the hidden "alternate text" that is attached to images.

To see the alternate text for images, rest your mouse pointer on an image; you will see either a file name, such as "photo.gif," or some text, such as "Our New Orleans hotel services concierge provides friendly assistance." This alternate text is displayed only briefly. If you don't specify alternate text when the page is created, the file name of the image is used. See Chapter 4, Figure 4.4, for an example of alternate text.

Why bother adding target words to these hidden text areas? Because some search engines read and catalog the words in the alternate text, increasing the likelihood that the site will be found by users of the engine.

Many search engines and directories do not rely entirely on automated spiders and robots. These engines also use human assistance to evaluate the relevance of Web sites and add them to the database.

How Does Your Site Rank? Test It with Various Keywords

One way to determine whether search engines are finding your site and whether your URL appears on the first or second page of results is to check each search engine yourself. Go to each engine, enter the keywords you think visitors might use, and then look for your site listing. This process may be somewhat time-consuming, but it is also very instructive. If your site is not represented to your satisfaction, it's time to talk with your Webmaster.

Some software programs check your ranking in the search engines for you. Such programs can be found at www.jimtools.com and www.bcentral.com/products/free.asp.

You can also check your site's ranking on various search engines automatically by using the free limited edition of the rank-checking product found at www.siteowner.com/pafree.cfm?LID=228.

After you enter your Web site's URL and the keyword or keyword phrase that you believe most consumers would use for your product or service, the program gives you a page showing how your site ranked on various search engines. The results show which engines listed your site and where it was positioned on the results list.

If all this business about metatags and invisible codes sounds too difficult, don't worry. Most executives don't do this work themselves. Instead, they hire someone—a Web site design firm, a technician, an in-house or outside Webmaster, a technician at a local ISP firm—to construct a Web site, add or delete pages, and make updates and changes to them.

Be sure to communicate to your Webmaster that you want your site to be kept current—*including* its metatags, which must stay consistent with the keywords your target audience visitors use.

Table 6.2 shows the crawling, indexing, and other characteristics of Alta Vista, FAST (AllTheWeb), and Google. It also covers crawler-based results from Inktomi that feed portions of AOL Search, HotBot, and MSN Search. FAST Search covers crawler data used by Lycos.

Another way to check a site's rankings is to use "top-10.com," which can be found at www.top-10.com/free.html. (This site might not function well with older browsers.) Follow the instructions and then fill out the

Tip	Watch Searches in Progress

You might gain some insight into the terms that people use to search the Internet by viewing the keywords that people are searching for—"live." Go to any of the sites listed and watch the search entries.

(Caution: Words are not typically censored for you. However, some of the sites listed will give you the option of filtering out "adult" terms.) You will notice that most people do not use very specific keywords for searches.

www.altavista.com/sites/search/real_searches

www.askjeeves.com/docs/peek/

www.metaspy.com/

www.kanoodle.com/spy/

www.galaxy.com/info/voyeur.html

http://searchenginewatch.com/facts/searches.html

form, paying special attention to the keywords the form requests. These keywords can be ones currently on your site, or you can enter other combinations to see how well your site does with those. Or, you can check on your competitors.

After you fill out the form and submit it, Top-10 will send your report immediately or in a few hours, depending on how busy the site is. The report will help you evaluate how well the keywords on your site are working for you. Remember, your goal is to do all you can to have your site listed on page one if at all possible, or on page two (typically within the top 10–20 positions) of every search engine's summary pages.

Search Engines Rank Sites by Popularity

Every time a site links to you, it helps your site get found on the Web. According to the search engine information site WebPromote.com at www.webpromote.com, "If you have more sites that link to your page than your competitor does, your page will rank more highly on the engines. Numerous links will not only improve your rankings, but you will also improve your traffic (following links is the second most popular way people find new sites). Furthermore, on ... HotBot and Lycos, link popularity also determines whether the engine will crawl deep into your site and index more pages or not. Do not ignore this step, no matter how hard it sounds (www.webpromote.com/wpwsrch/detail.asp?aid=2&iid=aug1999vol3&rw=1&cl=1&sortorder=).

TABLE 6.2   Major search engine crawling and indexing characteristics.

Crawling	Yes	No	Notes
Deep Crawl	FAST, Google	AltaVista, Inktomi, Teoma	
Frames Support	All	n/a	
Image Maps	AltaVista	FAST, Google, Inktomi	
robots.txt	All	n/a	
Meta Robots Tag	All	n/a	
Link Popularity Helps Deep Crawl	All	n/a	
Paid Inclusion	All (including Teoma) except . . .	Google	
URL Status Check	— See Checking Your URL & Search Features Chart —		
Indexing	**Yes**	**No**	**Notes**
Full Body Text	All	n/a	Some stop words may not be indexed
Stop Words	AltaVista, Inktomi, Google	FAST	
Meta Description	All except . . .	Google (rarely uses)	
Meta Keywords	AltaVista, Inktomi	FAST, Google	
ALT text	AltaVista, Google	FAST, Inktomi	
Comments	Inktomi	Others	
Stemming	— See Search Features Chart —		
Ranking	**Yes**	**No**	**Notes**
Meta Tags Boost Ranking	Inktomi	Others	
Link Popularity Boosts Ranking	All	n/a	Very important at Google
Spam	**Yes**	**No**	**Notes**
Meta Refresh Google, Inktomi	AltaVista	FAST	
Invisible Text	Others	FAST	
Tiny Text	AltaVista, Inktomi, Google	FAST	

Source: http://searchenginewatch.com/webmasters/features.html

How Many Links Point To Your Site?

To see how many sites have links to your site, go to AltaVista (www.altavista. com) and enter your query this way: link:yourdomainname.com. So, a firm with the URL www.AceHotel.com enters link:acehotel.com. The search results show how many sites AltaVista found that contained links pointing to that URL. Searching for link:sonesta.com/boston finds 21 pages pointing to www. sonesta.com/boston. (For comparison, searching for "link:marthastewart.com" finds about 5,600 pages pointing to her site. Searching for "link:ebay.com" found nearly a half million links to eBay.)

Another method of determining links is found at LinksToYou at www.linkstoyou.com. There, you enter your URL in their "Links To You" counter. Searching for the URL www.booksonrealestate.com produced the following:

www.booksonrealestate.com	
AltaVista	found **5** links to you.
AltaVista	found **5** links to you *excluding* your own links.
Hotbot	found **11** links to you.
Fast	found **9** links to you.
MSN	found **16** links to you.

Based on this exercise, you can see how logical it is for a search engine to rank a popular site (one with many links pointing to it) ahead of one in the same category with fewer pointing links.

Search engine formulas may consider not only how many links point to your site, but also how important those sites are in terms of size and how many links point to *them*. Another factor is how closely related to the core business of your site are the sites that contain those links to you.

What can you do to benefit from the "popularity factor"? Add your URL to every site you can find in your industry and on large and small directories and lists that allow free and purchased text links or ads. If you do this, and if a competitor had a site precisely equal to yours in every way except link popularity, then yours, having far more links, will cause most engines to rank your site ahead of the other.

One leader of these popularity sites is Google (www.google.com). Google explains its page-ranking methodology this way:

> PageRank capitalizes on the uniquely democratic characteristic of the Web by using its vast link structure as an organizational tool. In essence, Google interprets a link from page A to page B as a vote, by page A, for page B. Google assesses a page's importance by the votes it receives. But Google looks at more than sheer volume of votes, or links; it also analyzes the page

Try it

1. Visit AltaVista at www.altavista.com. In the search box, enter link:restaurants.com. How many pages did AltaVista find pointing to restaurants.com?
2. Visit LinksToYou.com at http://linkstoyou.com/CheckLinks.htm and enter restaurants.com. What additional information did you receive at LinksToYou.com?

that casts the vote. Votes cast by pages that are themselves "important" weigh more heavily and help to make other pages "important."

These important, high-quality results receive a higher PageRank and will be ordered higher in results. In this way, PageRank is Google's general indicator of importance and does not depend on a specific query. Rather, it is a characteristic of a page itself based on data from the Web that Google analyzes using complex algorithms that assess link structure.

Of course, important pages mean nothing to you if they don't match a user's query. So, according to Google, it uses text-matching techniques to find pages that are both important and relevant. For instance, when Google analyzes a page, it looks at what those pages linking *to that page* have to say about it.

The Open Directory Project

Like Yahoo!, the Open Directory Project (ODP), www.dmoz.org, uses human editors to decide which sites are relevant to a particular topic or category. Because the editors actually look at the sites submitted for inclusion in the search engine's database, the results given to the users are more likely to be pertinent to the search, at least in theory. In other words, using human editors has the potential of creating a better search engine or directory.

ODP's editors are volunteers familiar with various specialties and geographic areas. As the Internet grows, so does the number of volunteer editors. ODP says about itself, "As the Internet grows, so do the number of net-citizens. These citizens can each organize a small portion of the Web and present it back to the rest of the population, culling out the bad and useless and keeping only the best content." (Volunteer editors present their qualifications to ODP before being approved to edit a given ODP category.) See Figure 6.6 for an example from ODP.

Sites submitted for a particular category are evaluated and added (or rejected) by the editor for that category. To ensure the quality of site additions and to avoid favoritism or other abuse, other editors oversee editors. If an editor is found to be selecting all or only the sites of friends, for example, that editor is replaced.

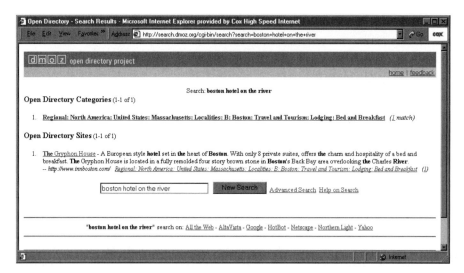

FIGURE 6.6   ODP search results for the keywords "boston hotel on the river." (Screen capture from http://search.dmoz.org/cgi-bin/search?search=boston+hotel+on+the+river.)

Besides its potential for creating a high-quality, comprehensive directory, the ODP is important because many other Internet search engines and directories share its comprehensive database. This means that if a site is not included in the ODP database, it may well not be included in several others. The ODP powers core directory services for some the most popular portals and search engines on the Web, including AOL Search, Netscape Search, Google, Lycos, DirectHit, and HotBot, and hundreds of others (http://dmoz.org/help/geninfo.html). Because the ODP is now the source of information for so many other engines and directories, you cannot afford to miss inclusion in this database.

To learn about registering a site or becoming an ODP volunteer editor, visit http://dmoz.org/about.html. Read and follow ODP's site submission directions carefully. Just as when submitting to Yahoo!, you must first find the category in which you would most like to be listed and submit your URL from there. Unlike Yahoo!, however, you can submit many pages from the same Web site. Pages or sites may be listed in several ODP categories, as long as the pages are relevant and provide, in the editor's opinion, adequate content. For example, a page with nothing but lists of links might be less likely to be added to the ODP than a page with both original content and links.

"Pay-Per-Click" or "Keyword Bid" Search Engines

Unless you have superior Web skills or a exceptional Webmaster, your firm will probably not be ranked as high as you would like on most search engines. But you can buy your way to the top.

There is a way you *can* rise to the top of a few search engines—every time. But it will cost you money. "Pay-per-click" or "keyword-bid" search engines, such as the one at www.overture.com, auction their top positions for specific keywords. The higher up you want your site's presence to appear, the more it will cost you. Each time a user clicks on a "sponsored" link on a keyword-bid search engine, the owner of the site pays the amount bid for that link. So, if you bid 10 cents for a keyword phrase (which might or might not be enough money to earn you the *top* spot, depending on other bids) and Overture.com visitors click on your link 100 times in a week, that costs you $10. When no one has bid on a term, the keyword-bid engine simply ranks and displays sites like any other search engine.

To find out what the top keyword bids are for your product or service, just go to Overture.com (www.Overture.com) and search for the name of your product or service. Include a city or town name if your facility has a local emphasis. The city name plus product name or a type of service (e.g., airport hotel, pizza, sandwich shop, motel, bed and breakfast) is generally the most often searched for keyword phrase used when people are searching for businesses in a particular city. For example, "oakland seafood restaurants" or "seafood restaurants oakland" and even "oakland ca seafood restaurants" will be used rather than just "seafood restaurants." A business seeking a dominant position in its entire industry, or the entire country, on the other hand, would leave off the term that defines a geographic area and use the generic terms by themselves. "Hilton," the corporation, at www.hilton.com, should leave off the city reference on its umbrella site that serves the entire corporation. Conversely, The Dana Point Hilton All Suite Inn should include the city name of "Dana Point," as well as perhaps adding "California" and "Orange County" to its name to form a wide array of logical search terms.

What's the biggest advantage of ranking high in Overture.com? Sites that rank high also reach about 75 percent of the people who use other search engines. Why? Because Overture.com, while being a top-10 search engine, is partnered with dozens of other major portal and search engine sites, and scores of medium to small ones, that prominently display links to companies in the top Overture positions to their visitors.

Keeping a site in the first or second place position on Overture has several other advantages. Overture claims that the #1 position gets from three to five times the clicks of secondary ones. Furthermore, Overture's top two (and typically top *three*) results are displayed, along with other engine results beneath them, on America Online (http://search.aol.com), which has 30 million members; Microsoft's Internet Explorer (80.5 percent of Web users use this browser; see www.cnet.com/software/0-7287394.html?tag=dir for browser information); the Microsoft Internet Explorer default home page (www.msn.com); Earthlink; CNET (www.cnet.com); Netscape Search (www. netscape.com); and many more large portals, as well as hundreds of small engines and sites. At least 75 percent of Web users visit some function of these huge sites daily, so a firm's chances of gaining wide positioning on the Web by having a high position on Overture is multiplied by a huge factor.

Another bid-based site worth investigating is Sprinks.com (www. sprinks.com). Sprinks' top-ranking sites results are *also displayed* on (your-industry)-related search results at About.com (www.about.com), one of the most frequently visited U. S. sites with 33 million monthly visitors (according to media auditor, MediaMetrix, at www.mediametrix.com/data/thetopjsp? language=us). About.com covers more than 450 topic-specific sites, many of which relate directly to the hospitality industry. Moreover, About. com's premier CitySearch™ service serves all of the key cities listed below. If you are located in one, you definitely want to have a link in the CitySearch™ "restaurant" section of About.com pointing to your facility.

Albany, NY	Metro Detroit
Atlanta, GA	Miami/Miami
Austin, TX	Beach, FL
Baltimore, MD	Milwaukee, WI
Boston, MA	Minneapolis/
Chicago	St. Paul, MN
Cleveland, OH	Nashville, TN
Columbus, OH	New York: Brooklyn
DC/ Capital Region	New York: Queens
Dallas, TX	Orlando, FL
Greater Philadelphia/	Phoenix, AZ
So. Jersey	Pittsburgh, PA
Hartford, CT	Portland, ME
Houston	Portland, OR
Huntsville, AL	Reno/Tahoe, NV
Indianapolis, IN	Salt Lake City, UT
Kansas City, MO	San Diego, CA
Las Vegas, NV	San Francisco
Little Rock, AR	Santa Cruz, CA
Long Island, NY	Seattle/Tacoma, WA
Louisville, KY	St Louis, MO
Manhattan	Tampa Bay, FL

(Source: http://about.com/citiestowns/.)

Prominent on the page for every city is a box similar to the one shown in Figure 6.7, which produces pages of restaurant and entertainment links. DiningGuide.net (Figure 6.8) offers worldwide restaurant search capabilities.

For hoteliers, About.com offers considerable information about hotels, reservations, resorts, destinations, vacations, and much more.

MetroSearch.com

In your town

- ## Restaurants
- ## Movies
- ## Bars/Clubs
- ## Events

FIGURE 6.7 Sample city search box.

Try it

1. You work for The Red Lion Hotel chain. The keywords in the metatag of the home page of the company Web site include: Red Lion, inns, lodge, motel, motor hotel, motor inn, breakfast, complimentary continental breakfast, hotel, rooms, suites, accommodations, lodgings, guest-rooms, and travel.

   Use the keyword suggestion tool at http://inventory.overture.com/d/searchinventory/suggestion to see if The Red Lion is using the same keywords in its metatag as the ones Web visitors use to search for motor hotels, motor inns. What would you recommend, if anything, to the company's Webmaster?

2. Use the tool at http://linkstoyou.com/CheckLinks.htm to check the popularity of The Red Lion's Web site at www.redlion.com. Now, use the same tool to check the popularity of Howard Johnson's Web site at www.hojo.com. Which motor inn's Web site has more links going to it? Now, use the same tool to check the popularity of your own company's Web site and a competitor's Web site. How many links did you find? Which site is doing a better job of getting links pointing to it?

FIGURE 6.8 DiningGuide Network for Restaurants Worldwide, a "vortal."(Screen capture from http://diningguide.net.)

Other bid-for-position sites include Findwhat.com, 7Search.com, Search-Hound.com, Kanoodle.com, OneSearch.com, SimpleSearch.com, and more than 250 others listed at www.payperclicksearchengines.com.

More About Directories

Portal and vortal sites are often a combination of a search engine and a directory (in addition to advertising). An Internet directory is an index of links that lead users to information. The index is organized into categories, not unlike your local Yellow Pages.® Users look for the categories that are most likely to contain the information they seek and then "drill down" through subcategories until they find what they are looking for. Two special types of directories are those specific to an industry and directories in community (city, state, regional) information sites.

Most directories depend on human input for the listings and categories. Many sell primary link positions to sponsors or partners. If, for example, you were to click on the category "New York State > New York > Lodging" shown in Figure 6.9 you would be immediately escorted to the page shown in Figure 6.10. There you are presented with another set of drill-down choices to make in selecting *exactly the kind* of lodging that you

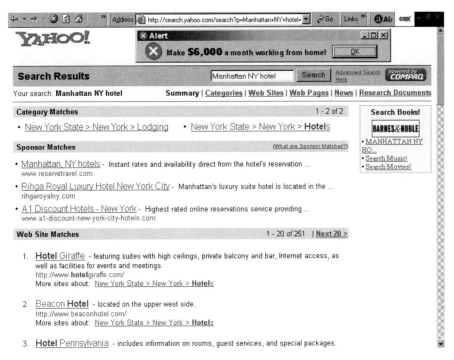

FIGURE 6.9 Yahoo! search results. (Screen capture from http://search.yahoo. com/search?p=Manhattan+NY+hotel+.)

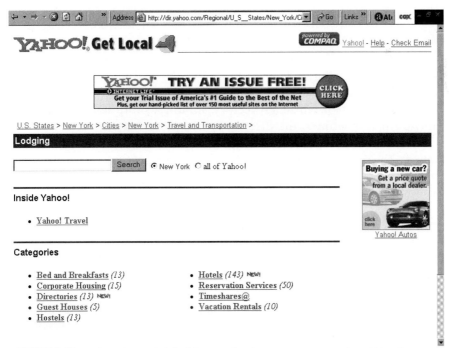

FIGURE 6.10 Yahoo! New York lodging results. (Screen capture from http://dir.yahoo. com/Regional/U_S_States/New_York/Cities/New_York/Travel_and_Transportation/Lodging/.)

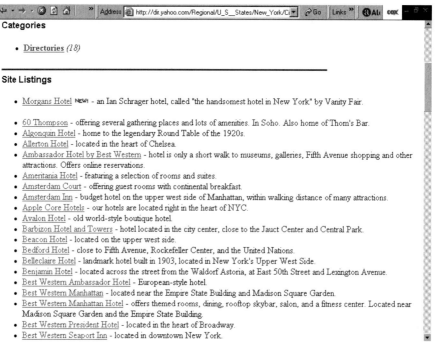

FIGURE 6.11   Yahoo! New York hotel listings. (Screen capture from http://dir.yahoo.com/ Regional/U_S__States/New_York/Cities/New_York/Travel_and_Transportation/Lodging/ Hotels/.)

are seeking. If you click on the category "hotels," you are presented with yet another, and final, list to choose from, as shown in Figure 6.11.

To have a site listed in a directory, submit a short description for the entire site. Sometimes, the directory's editors review sites and write the descriptions themselves. Because the search function of a directory looks only in the descriptions submitted, not in the actual sites, changing a site has no effect on its ranking in the directory. Changing the description, however, might. Changes to Web sites that help improve its ranking with a search engine will do little to improve the position of its listing in a directory. Naturally, an attractive, well-organized, functional site with good content might be more likely to get included with a good review than a poor site.

Visit the 4Internet directory at www.4internet.com. Once there, drill down to find specific cate-gories and cities. 4Internet's restaurant subdirectory is located at www.restaurants.com; its New York City restaurant subdirectory is found at http://restaurants.com/US/Metro.asp?Metro=New+York; and the Brooklyn subdirectory of the NYC subdirectory is located at www.restaurants. com/US/USAlphabet.asp?Metro=New+York&City=Brooklyn.

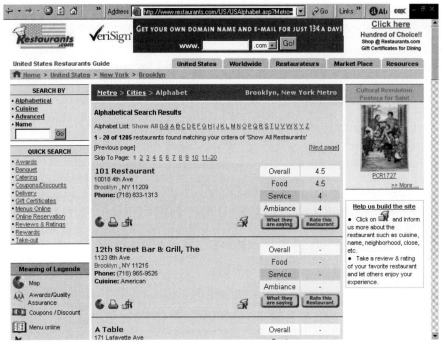

FIGURE 6.12 Restaurants.com. (Screen capture from www.restaurants.com/
US/USAlphabet.asp?Metro=New+York&City=Brooklyn.)

From that subdirectory (Figure 6.12), you can see a map showing the
restaurant's location, send them an e-mail message, read ratings of the restaurants from its patrons, create a rating report on the restaurant, and more.
Although this site does not currently offer links to the Web sites owned by
the restaurants listed, it may do so soon.

Thousands of other directories are on the Internet. Many contain a special section for your industry, often subdivided into state, county, or city sections. Some are called "yellow pages" and show only local telephone company
listings. Others, however, will let you add your listing at any time. See, for example, Verizon's United States Yellow Pages® at http://superpages.com/cities/
and note the link at the bottom, "Add or Change Your Listing."

Yellow Pages® and business directories give users minimal data for making
decisions on selecting one company over another. Nonetheless, millions of people monthly use such sites to find businesses and professionals, so you should
be in them—at least in the ones that relate to your state, county, and city. The
following is a list of large "yellow pages" or "business directory" sites. Visit the
sections of these that serve your area and enter your data. It will help position
you above all of the firms that did not take the time to do it.

Verizon Super Pages,
http://superpages.gte.net/

Smart Pages, www.smartpages.com

Freeality, www.freeality.com

Info USA, www.abii.com/

Info Space, www.infospace.com

Look Smart,
www.looksmart.com/

Internet Oracle,
www.internetoracle.
com/findc.htm

World Pages,
www.worldpages.com/

Bell Southern, US
http://yp.bellsouth.com/

Zip2, www.zip2.com/

Listing the Web site for your lodging, dining, or casino property with much larger Web sites is not a formidable task. Best of all, most people restrict their online experience to a very small number of sites. So, having your hospitality site listed in only a few places can have a large impact on people finding your site and patronizing your establishment. About that tendency people have to visit only a few sites on the Web, Cyberatlas at quotes Alexa Research as saying:

> The top 50 search terms account for only 2.73 percent of all search term page views, which reflects how diverse people's interests are," said Jason Maxham, lead data miner at Alexa Research. "By contrast, the 50 most popular Web sites receive 25 percent of all traffic—that's more than eight times as concentrated as the search terms. This concentration reveals that in the bigger picture, people still converge on the same batch of sites. (http://cyberatlas.internet.com/big_picture/traffic_patterns/article/0,,5931_588851.00.html)

Yahoo! A Special Animal

The leading portal began in 1995 as a hobby of two Stanford University graduate students to help them find sites on the then "brand new" World Wide Web. Now, the firm they started is worth several billion dollars and growing. Their company is Yahoo!, the oldest and most frequently used of the directories. The founders chose the name Yahoo! because it was easy to remember and connoted excitement; they added the exclamation point to make the name stand out even more.

Technically, Yahoo! is a "directory" of Web sites, rather than a search engine, but for our purposes, that's not important. Let's repeat the important part: Yahoo! is the most frequently used of the directories. (Mostly because it was there first—the first rule of "positioning.") The majority of searches begin at Yahoo! This means that your site listing in Yahoo! is very important for your Internet findability.

Figure 6.13 the results of a Yahoo! search for "Boston Restaurants." Because about half of all Web searches begin on Yahoo!, you stand to lose a great deal of business if you are not listed there.

FIGURE 6.13   Yahoo! search results. (Screen capture from http://search.yahoo.com/ search?p=boston+restaurants.)

As mentioned in the Basics section of this chapter, do not attempt to add your site to Yahoo! until you have read everything you can that Yahoo! says and that other sites say about this. If you make a mistake and Yahoo! indexes you in the wrong area of its directory, correcting the error could take a very long time. The loss will be all of the people who could have visited your site, but didn't.

Yahoo! staffs a giant team for processing the tens of thousands of weekly Web site submissions. To them, "aggregating information" means doing whatever it can, within reason, to keep abreast of "what's happening" (in Yahoo!'s words) on the Web.

With Yahoo!, you must decide exactly where you want to be listed before adding your URL. Say your firm is in Davenport, Iowa, and you want to be listed geographically in Yahoo! You would go to Yahoo! and search for "Davenport Iowa (name of your product or service)" (no quotes). Yahoo! will give you two types of matches: "category" matches and "site" matches. When you click on the "Site Match" link, you get the list of firms who successfully listed their sites where they ought to be in Yahoo! If you wanted to be on this page, you would click on "Suggest a Site" in the bottom right corner of the page and then follow the directions.

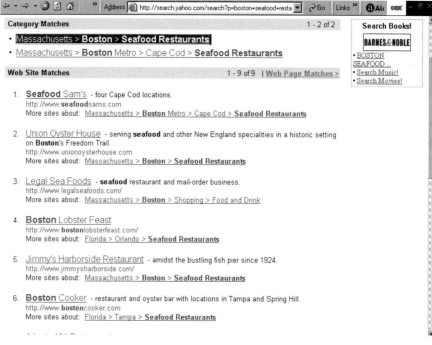

FIGURE 6.14   Results of Yahoo! Web pages search for Boston seafood restaurants. (Screen capture from http://search.yahoo.com/search?p=boston+seafood+restaurants.)

Try it

Visit www.yahoo.com and search for the products or services your company offers. To narrow the results, do the search again with the name of your city. Did you find your company's site? Where does it fall in Yahoo!'s directory structure?

"Boston seafood restaurants" is located in the Yahoo! directory under the heading:

Massachusetts > Boston > Seafood Restaurants.

And a search of Yahoo! Web pages displays the page shown in Figure 6.14 for "Massachusetts > Boston > Seafood Restaurants."

How Many People Find Your Site Using a Search Engine or Directory?

Various programs or services will track your site's traffic and tell you how many visitors accessed your site, which search engines sent them, how long they stayed, and other data. Ask or pay the company that hosts your site to give you "log statistics." In some cases, they might have to install a traffic reporter on your site (and charge you for it) so you can get the information. You can also buy and install your own program for tracking your site's traffic, but this is not always a simple project.

Visit www.webtrends.com/wt_main.htm and read about Web Trends' traffic programs, or visit www.websidestory.com or www.hitboxprofessional. com and download a free traffic analyzer. One way or another, try to get useful statistics about visits to your site. Why?

Because if you know what content *captures* on your site is most appealing to (most looked at by) your visitors, you can emphasize that information, page, or approach. If you know which sites' links the visitors used to get to you, then you know what types of sites you want more links on. And if you know general traffic statistics, you can evaluate how well your "getting found" strategies are working.

| **Tip** | **Yahoo!** |

Yahoo! has a directory called "Yahoo! Get Local" for virtually every key city in the United States. For many hospitality sites, "Get Local" is the best place to get found on Yahoo! For more help on making your Web site submission to Yahoo!, and other directories, visit the following:

> http://searchenginewatch.com
>
> http://searchenginewatch.com/webmasters/index.html#essentials
>
> http://searchenginewatch.com/webmasters/directories.html
>
> http://searchenginewatch.com/webmasters/yahoo/
>
> http://searchenginewatch.internet.com/webmasters/work.html
>
> http://searchenginewatch.com/webmasters/paid.html

Note, Yahoo! and several other search engines are now charging commercial firms to register with them. In most cases, this is well worth the cost, but check carefully before signing up so you know what you are getting.

Summary

The primary tools on portals and vortals are search engines and directories. Hundreds of thousands of Web users rely on these tools to help them find information on the Internet. Although users find Web sites in other ways also—television and radio advertising, newspapers, magazines, direct mail—search engines and directories are responsible for enough directing of Web traffic to warrant attention from site owners.

Web site addresses become part of a search engine's or directory's database when site owners register the site URL. Some search engines send out a spider or robot to crawl the Internet, finding and cataloging sites, but most of this is the result of someone registering a site with that engine.

Search engines read and catalog various bits of text on the Web sites they visit. They read some or all of the hidden text of metatags and mouseovers, the beginning lines of pages, the beginning lines of paragraphs, links, and sometimes whole pages.

Some search engines rank sites according to their popularity; that is, how many other sites link to the site being ranked. Other search engines sell positioning on their results by allowing site owners to bid on the top positions for particular keywords.

Directories usually look and behave more like the print directories that we've always known. They present lists of companies or Web sites according certain categories.

Review Questions

1. What is the type of site most frequently used to find Internet information?
2. What are the two most frequently used sources for people to find Web data?
3. How is a vortal most like and unlike a portal?
4. A directory is similar to what kind of printed publication found in most homes?
5. Can a portal include one or more search engines? Why is this good?
6. Which kind of tool for finding information uses humans to categorize sites?
7. How does a search engine's spider or robot work?
8. Does the Web have millions or trillions of Web pages now?

9. If you market locally, why is it important to include your city name in your metatags?

10. What are just two directories that you should be listed in?

11. Why must one be especially careful when entering a URL into Yahoo!?

12. Is Altavista.com a search engine or a directory or a portal or all three?

13. How does having many links point to your site help you on search engines?

14. What does a meta-search engine do?

15. Why is it important to correct typos when adding your URL to sites?

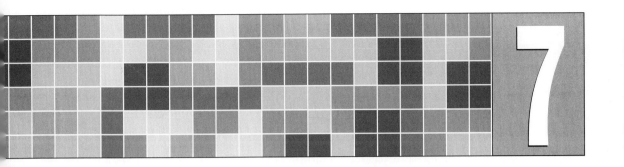

Internet Advertising

Links, Banners, Tiles, and More

Many hospitality industry executives who begin to build an Internet presence for their firms and individual locations are surprised to learn that if their Internet presence is going to work for them effectively, they're going to have to advertise it.

"Advertise my advertising?" Yes. Advertise your advertising. Even if a site enjoys superior ranking in search engine results, those results alone are insufficient to ensure that prospective customers find the site and then elect to explore it.

If, of course, yours happens to be the only firm in the country with a Web site for your particular product or service field, or if you are a Hilton, Marriott, McDonalds, or Burger King, you may delay this worry—for a while. The better strategy is to build Web dominance while you can. On the other hand, if firms in your industry or regional area are already reaping the benefits of a strong Internet presence, you may find that your site, especially a site for each of your individual units, has tough competition. In this case, you'll have to find other ways to win the visibility your site—and business—deserves.

As you may have already noticed, the Internet is such an individualized mosaic that defining, describing, or understanding its components is not a simple process. For every generalization that we make, we find numerous exceptions. Although this delights the creative left-brain folks, it makes the job of Internet instructors (and writers) more complex.

THE BASICS

Listings and Enhanced Listings, Banner and Tile Ads

What They Are

Many sites offer a free listing or link "presence," as well as links that you can buy. To add a link to your site from sites where they're offered, look for the words "Add URL" or "Link Your Site," or something similar. Usually this link takes you to a form to complete and submit to the site. When you fill out the form, be sure every word is spelled correctly and your URL and email address are correct. This is no time for a mistake that will keep people from reaching your site (or a glaring error that might embarrass your company). Further enhancements of your marketing presence on a directory page or other Web site can take the form of ads—usually banner or tile ads. Banner ads tend to be wide but not very high—like a skinny person lying down. Tile ads (also called "block" or "button" ads) are usually smaller than banner ads and are square or rectangular. Banner ads today are standardized for efficiency and transportability from one Web page to another. Sometimes, a banner or tile ad is very attention-getting—animated and colorful. But a small square box with plain text in it is also considered a tile ad.

The primary objective of a banner or tile ad is to motivate the visitor to click on it and visit the advertiser's site. A second important objective is to build brand awareness of a name or product through repetitive "impressions" made on a Web user. At the end of 2000, more than 99 percent of the people who saw banners or tile ads ignored them; that is, the click-through rate for banners was less than 1 percent.

Some banner ads, however, perform extremely well. Why? Their design and placement is such that they give exactly the right message to the right audience on the right page in the right page position at the right moment.

What They Cost

The price range for links and banner or tile ads varies widely, beginning with free and increasing to tens of thousands of dollars. A site successfully selling banner ads that produce qualified leads probably charges for the advertising based on the total number of "impressions" that the ad delivers. "Impression" sounds like something that actually "makes an impression" on a Web site visitor, but, in fact, "impression" is a term used in print advertising.

In the context of a Web site, the word "impression" might more accurately be called "a *chance* to make an impression." A Web site visitor does not have to actually see or read a tile or banner ad for it to be counted by the Web page owner as an impression. The ad simply has to be there on the page where the visitor *could* see it. Does that sound like you might be buying smoke and mist? Some people think so. Nobody (except media firms) is completely satisfied with this method of charging for online ads. Watch for more debate about better ways to display and charge for ads.

Where to Put Them

We could just say, "everywhere you can," but, although this answer has some validity, it isn't very helpful. One approach that some find useful is to prioritize first, second, third, and so forth, "tiers" of advertising. Identify, for example, big sites that have the most "unique visitors" or offer the most "page impressions" and that are tied most closely to your product or service as the first tier. Then, look for happy surprises—effective Web sites that don't charge much for advertising. Some site types to consider for the addition of a link or ad are: community information sites, "specialty" sites, ISPs, media sites, directories, industry association sites, your firm's or home office's site, and leading online magazine sites.

Community information sites, vortals, and specialty sites. The number one consideration when placing advertising on the Web is where your target audiences spend their Internet time. Where on the Web do your audiences look for information about hospitality-related firms? If your business offers local services, one answer to this questions is "community information sites," followed by county (or parish) and state sites. Companies or professionals who capitalize on this, and whose competitors do not, will ultimately come out far ahead. You may have hundreds or thousands of national or worldwide locations, but ultimately, consumers want to know what's available in their area or an area they plan to visit. It may be the greatest oversight in the lodging and dining field that so little advertising is placed on geographically specific Web sites that act as portals to hospitality in a state, county, and especially a city.

The previous chapter discussed how visitors use vortals and other specialty sites devoted to a particular topic or theme. If your positioning is related to a topic or theme, then search these sites for opportunities for linking or advertising. For example, restaurants that feature vegetarian or "healthy" meals might advertise on health or fitness education sites or sections of local community Web sites. A bed and breakfast that is part of a farm or horse ranch might advertise in the "Equestrian Spas" directory or "Horses Allowed Bed and Breakfasts" or a "Farm Locations" guide. Some examples include:

Equestrian spas: spas.about.com/cs/equestrianspas/index.htm

Horses Allowed Bed and Breakfasts:
bandb.about.com/cs/horses/index.htm

Maine Farm Locations:
travelwithkids.about.com/gi/dynamic/offsite.htm?site=http%3A
%2F%2Fwww.mainefarmvacation.com%2Fmap.html

Online directories and "yellow page"-type directories. "Yellow page"-type directories that every business unit or location should consider include the Verizon Super Pages, Netscape Web Directory, Netscape Yellow Pages, the Thomas Register, YellowPages.com, AtHand.com, Big Yellow, and others. Why? Because people who have used their telephone company's Yellow Pages® for years feel comfortable using online "yellow pages." Their comfort level with the concept of "yellow pages" is high, and new Web users, in particular, look there. In fact, in February 2002, 1.75 million searches for the words "yellow pages" were performed on the bid search engine, Overture.com, alone. Firms large and small, local and national, do everything possible to get listed on these pages with exact wording and other information that builds awareness. Enhancements such as bold face type, active links, or tile ads are sometimes too expensive for small companies, but the basic listing might be free.

Interest-related directories.   Identify directories that are related to any prominent feature of your business or local area. Is your restaurant located on a pier, in a harbor, or near a sport fishing center? Consider placing a link or ad in the online fishing or fishing equipment directories. Do you own an inn in ski country? Evaluate sites that post ski conditions or that sell ski equipment or clothes. Do your food servers sing opera while working in your Italian restaurant? Place a link or ad on sites related to opera.

Trade and industry associations.   Many trade and industry associations— local, state, national, and international—now have Web sites with information for members and the public. Some association sites offer members a free or low-cost "profile page" or "electronic business card." These opportunities on trade association Web sites are valuable because they give a firm visibility within their industry, and often referrals or cross-selling can result.

Trade association sites, such as those of the National Restaurant Association, the California Restaurant Association, and others, sometimes also offer enhancements to a firm's name or a link in their directories. Don't settle for being just one of the firms listed in a "me too" fashion among many others on such sites. Enhanced listings and ads in trade association directories make a firm stand out in its field, and the benefit gained usually exceeds the additional cost. This strategy positions a business compared to similar businesses in the minds of Web site visitors.

Parent firm.   Most large hospitality firms have corporate or company-wide sites that include pages for divisions, subsidiaries, and individual locations around the world. Is yours a local entity of a much larger firm? Be sure your parent firm's site has a link to your subsidiary, division, or individual location's site (and vice versa).

Oddly enough, even major multinational firms may lack comprehensive links to the Web sites of their worldwide local units. Valuable business may be lost at the local level by this oversight.

Portals and search engines.   Search engines (see Chapter 6) offer many opportunities to enhance a company's Web visibility. Some of these, such as Overture.com and Sprinks.com, allow users to bid on keywords. The high bidders for a keyword or group of keywords have their sites listing displayed higher on the list.

Another search engine approach to keyword enhancements is to sell and display a keyword-triggered text-only ad on the results page. This ad appears only when a certain keyword is searched by the user. How often people using a search engine actually see these ads in the far right column of the search results page is a matter to be studied; however, this "context-relevant" approach has great appeal: the ad appears only to those people who have expressed an interest in a particular phrase. This "self-selection" approach is far more effective, and possibly more cost effective, than displaying ads at random to any user. Visit RealNames.com, Sprinks.com, and DirectHit.com for examples.

Reciprocal Links and Banner Exchanges

Reciprocal links and banner exchanges are exactly what the terms imply. Reciprocal linking is, in short, the "I'll link to you, if you'll link to me" strategy. Banner exchanging is a variation of that—"I'll put your banner on my site, if you'll put my banner on your site." Both strategies provide ways to increase the likelihood that people will find a particular site. As an added incentive, the number of links on the Internet that take people to a specific site can result in a higher placement in some search engine results for that site. This is called "popularity ranking" (see Chapter 6).

With whom do you set up reciprocal links, and where? How do you go about exchanging banners? Are these strategies worth the time and effort?

Reciprocal Links with Other Businesses

Most companies do business with many firms that do not compete with them. Some are suppliers to the businesses; others are vendors to that company's customers or end-users of its products. Some may be wholesalers, dealers, retailers, distributors, or franchisees. Search the Web to find the firms in such categories that have a strong Internet presence. (If you can find them easily, so might others.) Then, send them e-mail inviting them to exchange links or banner ads with you. The cost of doing this is your time, and the win–win potential exists for both parties.

Banner Exchange Services

"Banner exchange" firms can help increase a site's visibility by displaying a banner on a number of Web sites in exchange for displaying a rotating banner of theirs—actually, of one of their clients. Usually, a participating site gets a half a banner exposure in return for a certain number of times that someone clicks on the exchange banner. Some banner exchange firms are more generous, giving two views of your banner for every three views that your site provides theirs. The banners of all participants in a banner exchange are the same size so they can be rotated within the "banner frame" placed on the sites of the banner exchangers.

The bother, cost, and reduced speed in page loading associated with a banner exchange are seldom worth having more people who are unlikely to be buying a niche-related product see the banner. The presence of an exchange banner can lead to a slower displaying page and increased design costs. Worse, different banners showing up on a particular page could confuse visitors as to why the banner is there or what site they are really visiting.

Affiliations and Sponsorships

Two other forms of banner or link exchanging are affiliations and sponsorships. With affiliations, a link from one site takes visitors to some other site. If the visitor buys something at that other site (e.g., a book, CD, or poster), the referring site gets a commission. Note that having an affiliation banner on your site does not bring visitors to your site. In fact, it sends your hard-won visitors off to some other place on the Internet. Affiliations are probably not worth your time and energy for the small commissions they may pay. An exception is a *bona fide* store or a store section that provides a convenient shopping service to visitors as its primary function and that links to many affiliated, commission-paying sites.

Sponsorships can be time-consuming but effective. Basically, a sponsorship is the recognition on a site or site segment that it is "sponsored by" a certain person or business. Sometimes, the sponsor actually creates the page(s) or provides the information that is hosted on another site. (That's the time-consuming part.) Ideally, the page or information makes the sponsored site more valuable and more useful to visitors.

Here's how a sponsorship might develop. Let's say that Darrell Holcomb proposes to the owners or Webmasters of a high-traffic community site that his quality Bed and Breakfast will create an information section (delivering content or design or both) on regional parks for the community site. In return, Darrell requests that the community site display a banner at the top of the new parks section crediting his business for sponsoring the section as a community service—with a link to Darrell's site, of course.

Signature Links

Most e-mail programs provide for creating a "signature" that is added to the end of outgoing messages. The signature can be as simple as the sender's name, which isn't terribly useful. However, signatures can provide additional contact information, an invitation to participate in a new sales promotion, a service tip, or just about anything else that a message can have—including links to the company's Web site or particular pages on that site. Signatures are usually automated; that is, they attach themselves to outgoing messages without additional steps. Eudora and some other email programs allow users to create various signatures and then select which one they want to add to any message. Depending on how a company uses email, this can be one of the most targeted and effective linking mechanisms available.

BEYOND THE BASICS

Listings and Enhanced Listings

Many community information sites, real estate directories, specialty sites, and other related sites will list a Web site address (maybe linking, maybe not) for free or for a fee. To add a free link from sites where they're offered, look for the words "Add URL" or "Link Your Site," or something similar (as you do for search engines). Usually, this takes you to a form to complete and submit to the site.

The page shown in Figure 7.1, accessible through the California Restaurant Association (CRA) Web site at www.calrest.org, has a link that says, "Add Restaurant." Once you add your restaurant or restaurants, the link and information is accessible to other site visitors.

An added incentive to add a restaurant link to Restaurantrow.com is that this site enables consumers to make online reservations at the participating CRA restaurants. Visitors can see menus and photos of restaurant interiors, get directions, download restaurant information to personal digital assistants (PDAs), or e-mail the information to someone else. Adding a restaurant listing to Restaurantrow.com is worth the time and effort.

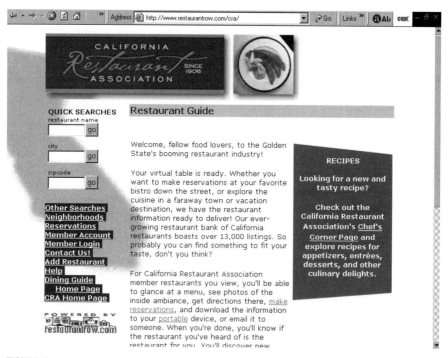

FIGURE 7.1   Restaurant Row. (Screen capture from www.restaurantrow.com/cra/.)

Marketing Opportunity?

Large national hotel and restaurant chains seem to forego advertising on local area Web sites, even those serving the nation's top cities. This marketing opportunity for local establishments, who might dramatically increase their guest count by becoming more visible at the local level, is sure to be temporary.

Becoming obvious in local directories and on other sites can be a financially viable means for a local business to compete with the advertising of well-known entities. Millions of people look at state, county, community, and other local Web sites to find hospitality sites, and the ones they find have a higher likelihood of getting the trade.

Visit The Restaurant Directory at www.therestaurantdirectory.com/Illinois-rest.htm for another example. When we checked, three restaurants in Illinois had listed themselves in the "Restaurants in Illinois" section of the nationwide Therestaurantdirectory.com's site. Someone from each of the three restaurants visited this site, clicked on "Put Your Business Here," and entered the text that resulted in an ad being shown on this page. The cost for one of these ads is $19.95 per quarter, or $79.80 for the year.

When completing such listing forms, be sure every word is spelled correctly and the URL and email address are correct. Errors in addresses result in discarded entries, misdirected links, or undeliverable e-mail. Errors in descriptions result in lost opportunities, and worse.

If the form asks or allows for a site description using a specified number of words or characters, type a draft of the description using a word-processing program first. Use the program's word counter and other features to make sure the description is the best and most accurate possible with the number of characters (usually counting a space as a character) allowed. Proofread it yourself; spell checkers don't catch everything. Then, copy and paste the description into the form.

Some sites allow you to enter a name for the link, in addition to the site address. Some also allow a 15- to 30-word or 90- to 150-character description beneath the name. Before writing this, think of the best (truthful) thing to say in this limited space to get people to come to your site. The number of words is limited, so try different combinations to make sure that every word counts to the maximum. This is where a marketing plan and the unique market position or branding statement become important. What position should the business, product, or service occupy in people's perceptions? What are the site's main emphasis and primary goal? Who is the target audience? What are they seeking when the message appears? Do you want to attract seniors, businesspeople, golfers, tourists, affinity groups, Japanese tour buses? Be certain of all of this first (see Chapter 2), then give the link a name and a description that best empathizes with target audience desires and that communicates the intended marketing positioning.

Some directories offer a plain listing or listing-plus-link for free and provide listing "enhancements" for a charge. An enhancement might be bold typeface, different colors, boxes, stars, a location above other entries, or more space for additional descriptive text. Hospitality businesses with local markets should ask community Web sites in their area if they offer bigger, more visible links for a charge.

Visit www.vegdining.com and search for Denver veggie restaurants. In the results, notice that several vegetarian restaurants in Denver have listed themselves on this nationwide Web site where people can locate such restaurants in most cities. If yours is a specialty restaurant, search on the Web for city, state, county, national, and international sites that list similar restaurants, and then evaluate the listing possibilities.

A firm can have an "enhanced" presence in Vegdining.com by becoming a sponsor. For example, the vegetarian dating service shown in Figure 7.2 became a sponsor and as a result, was blessed with their own "veggie ad" appearing prominently on the site's sponsor page.

VeggieDate.com

Tired of dating carnivores? Try VeggieDate.com, the premier vegetarian/vegan/macrobiotic dating and networking service. Meet other like-minded individuals with the click of your mouse. Now with over 2800 listings. Free 30-day trial, six month membership only $9.95, full year membership only $14.95!

Visit our Web site: www.VeggieDate.com

FIGURE 7.2   VeggieDate.com. (Screen capture from www.vegdining.com/News/Sponsors.cfm.)

Buying Search Engine Enhancements

Bid-for-Position Search Engines

What? *Pay* a site's way to the top of summary pages on certain search engines? Yes. As mentioned in Chapter 6, some bid-based search engines give the highest ranking to the web site whose owner pays the most money for each click-through. Site owners (or their Webmasters) bid on specific keywords, such as "Staten Island electronic assembly." When a user enters those keywords into the search engine, a link to the site of the highest bidder is displayed at the top of the list, followed by other sites in the order of the amount of money paid by the site owners for those keywords. If no one has bid for a particular word or phrase, these search engines work just like the others, displaying the most relevant sites first. Another variation, and a major advantage, of bid-based search engine results is that the bidders can create their own wording for the listing's title and description, which may or may not be the same as the title and description in the site's metatags (see Chapter 6). Although bidding for position appeals to some site owners, note that it creates havoc with the popular notion that search engines were always meant to stay "objective." Conversely, many experts believe that bid sites produce better results because people willing to pay to have their sites dominate may actually have something more worthwhile to offer.

Tip	CPC vs. CPM

Always use caution with "cost-per" terms. "CPC" is significantly different from "CPM." CPC refers to "cost per click." With sites like Overture.com, you pay only for click-throughs; that is, you pay only when someone not only sees, but also actually clicks on, the link leading to your site. This is paying on a "cost per click" (CPC) basis.

CPM refers to "cost per thousand" (impressions). With CPM, you pay for each time a user sees the page your ad is on, whether or not that user clicks on the link to go to your site.

Overture.com.   The early and acclaimed giant of bid-based search engines, GoTo.com, has changed its name and is now located at www.overture.com. Its clients pay Overture.com anywhere from one cent to many dollars each time a user clicks through a paid-for link to visit their site. If a site owner wants to be the first link that shows up for keywords that are already "owned" by another site, the owner may outbid that other site. The previous top bidder's link then moves below the new high bidder's link. Overture.com says that links at the top get three to five times as many click-throughs as other links on the same page.

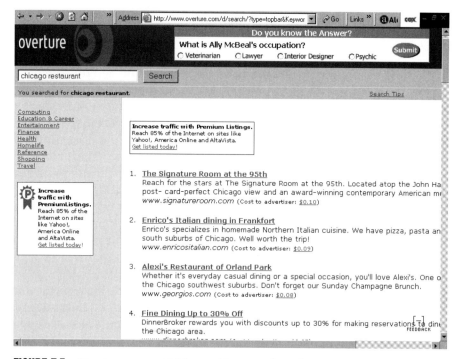

FIGURE 7.3   Overture.com, a bid-for-position search engine. (Screen capture from www.overture.com.)

At a cost of $0.10 per click-through, The Signature Room at the 95th, located atop the John Hancock Center in Chicago (at www.signatureroom.com) has positioned itself to appear first (at least in March, 2002) on Overture.com in the results for "Chicago restaurant" (see Figure 7.3). Notice that only one cent separates the top three bidders, who can repeatedly leapfrog each other to stay in the first positions that a searcher sees.

How do you decide which keywords to bid on? Overture.com makes it easy to see how often Web users search for specific words by using their "Suggested Search Terms Tool" at inventory.overture.com/d/searchinventory/suggestion/. The assumption here is that if people use certain keywords on Overture.com, they use the same keywords on other engines such as Yahoo!, Netscape, and Lycos.

Figure 7.4 shows part of the Overture display that resulted when the words "Chicago restaurant" were entered into the Suggested Search Terms Tool. The words "Chicago restaurant" were sought nearly 20,500 times in March 2002 on Overture.com. The same terms were likely searched for on bigger search engines like Yahoo!

A Chicago restaurant might bid on one, several, or all of the listed search terms. The higher the bid, the higher the site will come up on the

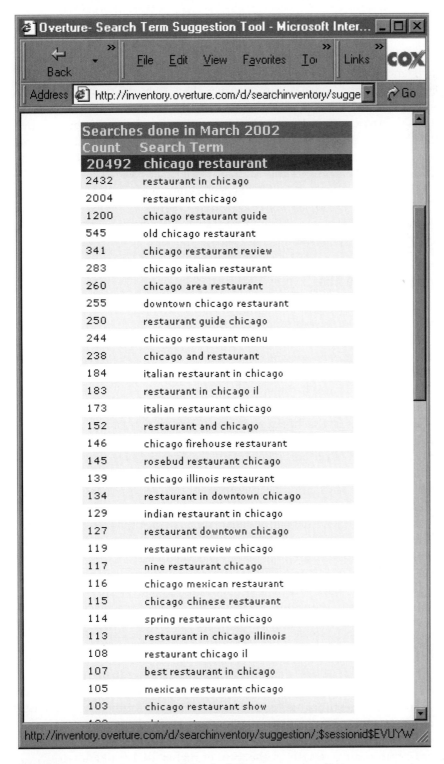

FIGURE 7.4 Keyword search statistics for "Chicago restaurant." (Screen capture from inventory. overture.com/d/searchinventory/suggestion/;$sessionid$EVUYWVIADCTHACQVLPMASYQ.)

search result pages of Overture.com. Furthermore, many of the biggest search engines have agreements with Overture.com to display Overture.com results higher on a summary page than they do their own search results.

On Overture.com, a deposit of $25 gets you started. Similar, but smaller, bid-based search engines are Sprinks.com (www.sprinks.com), 7Search (7search.com), and Findwhat.com (www.findwhat.com), which in April, 2001, started displaying its top results on the major search engines of Excite.com (www.excite.com) and Webcrawler.com (www.webcrawler.com). A list of more than 250 keyword-bid search engines is provided at www.payperclicksearchengines.com. Information is also available at websearch.about.com/cs/payperclick.

Banner and Tile Ads

With varying degrees of effectiveness, some site owners advertise using banner or tile ads. Banner ads tend to be horizontal rectangles. Tile (or block) ads are usually smaller squares or rectangles. Some small tile ads are called button ads. Whereas banners used to be *de rigueur* on the Web and are still used extensively, the use of smaller tile and button ads has grown significantly. Web sites that sell tile ads like them because they are easy to align and fit into almost any format.

On this page of the hotel directory Web site, Choice Hotels International has purchased a tile ad that is hard to miss (see Figure 7.5).

With banners or tile ads, the primary goal is to have the consumers click on it to visit that site. Another objective is to build brand awareness of a name or product through repetitive presentations of the name or logo to viewers. Media analysts, in 2000, generally believed that more than 99 percent of the people who see banner ads ignore them, explaining the average click-through rate (CTR) for banners and tile ads of less than 1 percent. According to *The Industry Standard* magazine (December 18, 2000, p. 123), banner click-through rates during 2000 for at-home surfers approximated 0.05 percent and for at-work surfers, it approached 0.25 percent. By March 2002, it had become common knowledge that the average CTR (www.netvisitors.com/htmls/banners.html) for banners was fixed at 0.05 percent.

Some banners and tiles, however, perform very well. Their design and placement give exactly the right message to the right audience on the right page in the right page position. Remember: Although banners are small, they are actually "little billboards," and designing effective billboards is as much an art as a science. The creative people who read the latest reports on effective billboard design and who put considerable effort into designing banner ads will reap positive results in the form of higher click-through rates.

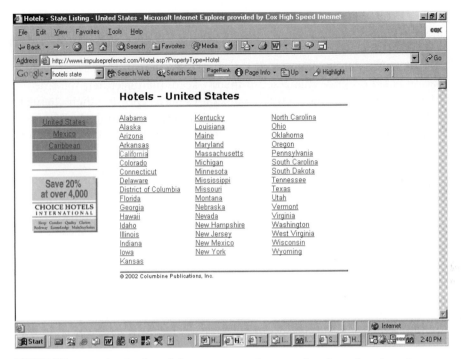

FIGURE 7.5   Impulse Preferred. (Screen capture from www.impulsepreferred.com.)

Context-based Advertising

Another tactic that Web firms are developing to increase click-through rates for banners is called "contextual" or "context-based" advertising. Using this strategy, a media firm, such as DoubleClick.com (www.DoubleClick.com), might track a certain Web site visitor to discern his or her online habits. If the user visits, say, five pages in a row that deal with a certain type of content (e.g., articles, tips, hints) on outdoor camping, then on the sixth and subsequent pages, many or all of the ads that appear for this visitor will be for camping-related products such as tents, camping stoves, hiking boots, or backpacks. Context-based advertising is based on the theory that a person who exhibits a preference for particular content will be more receptive to ads showing related products.

Watching the Competition

During 2000, a number of firms formed to help businesses keep track of what their competitors do on the Web. RivalWatch (www.rivalwatch.com) sends crawlers to competitors' Web sites where they gather information by category, product assortment, price, and types of promotions being offered. RivalWatch customers can then use this data to modify their own offerings.

ARS Competitor Tracking Services (www.arsl.com/CTS/Printers/Digital Cop/digitalCopiers.htm) provides a similar service for tracking product information based on price changes. It primarily keeps manufacturers informed of the day-to-day tactical moves their competitor's make, allowing their clients to make educated marketing decisions in their product planning. As Web competition increases, watch for a growth in services that track online competitors.

Animation

Animation helps catch the Web visitor's eye, and newer banners feature many interactive tricks, including video. Expect to see much testing of different sizes and shapes of banner and tile ads during the next few years as advertisers race to break through the less-than-1-percent-click-through-rate barrier.

Better-performing ads generally overtly invite the consumer to take some action: "Click here," "Don't click here," "Stay Somewhere Awesome in Downtown Houston!" Or, they make an arresting offer: "Hotel Rooms for 65 percent off!" or "Win a New Buick!" Look at the entry page of HotelDiscount!com at www.hoteldiscounts.com and notice how many times you are told to click here or go there. The ads make offers to visitors to entice them to click onto another site.

A banner or tile ad must be excellent in both design and message to produce results. Those made by a firm specializing in small-space Internet ads are often worth the price. Should you use a traditional advertising agency? Only if they have a long record of accomplishment in designing Internet ads, and even then, have your firm's most careful decision makers interview the agency's clients about the results that the ads produced. Some ad agencies that had the tools and experience to prepare them for Web-related advertising have lagged behind in the world of cutting-edge web site and Web ad design.

Sizes

Web ad sizes do have some standardization. At last, there are agreed-upon standards for the size of banners and tile ads. The Internet Advertising Bureau (IAB) has proposed standard banner sizes, now endorsed by the Newspaper Association of America (www.naa.org). (Smaller sites, eager for ads, will still run banners of almost any size; however, most large sites set pricing according to standardized sizes.)

Most sites that host advertising stipulate a maximum file size for an ad, generally somewhere between two and seven kilobytes (KB). Smaller files mean faster page loading onto the visitor's screen, which can influence whether a visitor will wait to see the entire page or click impatiently to go elsewhere.

Sites that are more technologically sophisticated offer options: displaying an ad on a specific page in a specific position 100 percent of the time, or rotating the ad's display with other ads in that same, or another, position. Buying ads that rotate in a particular position decreases the cost, but it also reduces the ad's visibility because it does not appear for all visitors. Sites offering rotating banners and tile ads are often the ones that millions of people visit each month, and although a banner rotates with others, the huge volume of visitors ensures many views, even in rotation.

Several Internet sites evaluate banners (and other images) and help reduce their file size. For the most part, these are subscription services, so that you pay a monthly fee and have unlimited use of the tools. Optiview.com (www.optiview.com, formerly Gif Wizard), for example, will "read" a site and assemble a list of graphics and links. Then, it analyzes each of the graphics, ranks them by potential savings in file size, checks for duplicate graphics, and, based on the user's selections, actually reduces the file size of inefficient (bulky, bloated) graphics.

In addition to optimized images, OptiView SiteScan provides the following:

- Identification of broken links
- Identification of duplicate images
- Compression of individual images on your web site
- Compression of individual images on your hard drive
- Image editing tools

Sites such as Optiview changed names frequently in the past. Some begin as free services, then convert to subscriptions. To find current sites, search for "gif optimizers" on your favorite search engine.

Advertising Costs

Advertising costs on the Web vary tremendously. Large "content sites" like About.com charge anywhere from under $10 to $25 or $35 or more per thousand impressions. Note, however, that some firms are willing to negotiate. Watch for "specials" and "new advertiser programs," and always ask about promotions they might be offering firms in your budget category.

As the definition of your target audience becomes narrower, the cost of online advertising for that audience increases. The most expensive banner ads are those that appear on pages frequented by a very tightly defined audience. For example, a hotel with a target audience of people planning a trip to Orlando, Florida, might request that its banner appear only at specific times. The banner might appear only on the next page a visitor sees after performing a keyword search that included the phrase "Orlando" or, even more specifically, "Orlando vacations."

Ads can be targeted for even more narrowly defined users—for example, ads can be programmed to appear only for married visitors between 40 and 55 years of age with an income over $100,000 per year who live in New Jersey Zip codes and who visit art museum Web sites. More parameters selected for a target audience are, naturally, tied to higher charges by the media firm or web site. Such sophistication usually requires the assistance of professionals, and any number of media firms will help. Firms such as DoubleClick (www.DoubleClick.net) help clients define their target audience and plan the placement and frequency for running ads on their networks of Web pages to reach that audience.

The least expensive banner ads are those that target no specific audience at all. Such ads appear on a "run of schedule" (ROS) basis, appearing on various Web pages, perhaps in rotation with ads from other firms. In all cases, however, the advertiser is given a guaranteed total number of impressions for its dollars. When that number is reached, the term of advertising typically ends and the ad no longer appears unless it is renewed. Also, the more clicks it takes a visitor to reach the page carrying an ad, the less that ad will cost. Thus, ads on the top of the home page of a site generally cost the most; ads on pages five clicks away cost considerably less.

Where to Place Ads on the Web

Travel Vortals

Hotel chains, franchises, and membership groups develop cooperative arrangements and partnerships with the various leading airline travel and reservation sites. The big three travel vortals are Expedia.com, Travelocity, and Orbitz.com, followed by Yahoo! Travel and several others.

Hotels enjoy considerable prominence on travel Web sites such as Travelocity (see Figure 7.6). Cooperative agreements and partnerships typify the relationships between such travel sites, the airlines, and national hotel and restaurant chains, as well as rental car firms.

Advertising Online to Local Markets

One key element to advertising your site, and sometimes your business, is the purchased and free ads and links on as many regional, county, and city Web sites as you can afford. Many lodging and dining businesses do not yet take advantage of the fact that consumers today look on community Web sites to find local community information. Not only do local contacts tell visitors where to stay, they themselves may have an occasional need for lodging (e.g., in between the sale of a home and moving into a newly purchased one, or during fumigation, disasters, or major home repairs). All types of

FIGURE 7.6   Travelocity. (Screen capture from www.travelocity.com/Lodging/
0,,TRAVELOCITY//Y,00.html?HPTRACK=mpc_hot.)

restaurants rely on a certain amount of business from local residents and
visitors. Local directories are the logical locations for visibility.

Independent hotels, motels, inns, and other lodging facilities find advertising on local directories to make intuitive good sense. Large corporate entities sometimes, however, focus on broad, big-budget, wide-range advertising,
and need reminding that their many locations may benefit from local advertising. Parent company Web sites should link to the sites or pages for their
various locations. In this way, link exchanges can take place with local firms.

In a word, go local. Be everywhere online in your own community that
you can.

One advertising task for restaurants is to become a favorite dining place
for community opinion makers, those who are the chairpersons, presidents,
directors, forepersons, chamber of commerce members, church leaders, and
so forth. On the Web, initiate ways to give visibility to local leaders. Some
sites do this inexpensively by creating a community section with links to
city emergency phone numbers, city-related Web sites, parks, recreation, social services, local government, and even the local organizations in the cities
and the names of their leaders.

Add a link (including a title and 25-word description) to the local Rotary (or other) Club chapter's site on your site and then ask the Rotary president to go to your site and check the title and description for accuracy.

Serve charitable groups through catering, food donations, and making your facility, or its various dining and meeting rooms, available for free or at a greatly reduced rate for licensed, nonprofit organizations.

What's the logic of doing this? It goes back to pioneer opinion researcher Elmo Roper's (www.ropercenter.uconn.edu/intro.html) beehive theory of opinion making—you don't have to influence the opinions of everyone; you just have to influence the opinions of those (at the top of the beehive) that everyone *listens to*.

According to a survey (see full text at www.gvu.gatech.edu/user_surveys) done at the Georgia Institute of Technology, the following are the ways that people in the United States find out about Web sites:

- Search engines – 85 percent
- Links from other sites – 89 percent
- Printed media – 62 percent
- Friends – 66 percent
- Newsgroups – 30 percent
- Email – 32 percent
- Television – 33 percent
- Directories – 58 percent

These data indicate that links (including banner and tile ad links) from other sites are slightly more valuable than search engines in bringing people to a site.

Should you advertise on the sites that have the most visitors on the Web? Although well-known general interest sites such as Discovery.com, CNN.com, or ABCnews.com have millions of visitors daily, their "news-weather-sports-oriented" visitors are probably not looking for information related to lodging or eating. Also, the cost of advertising on those sites is often beyond the budgets that most small- to mid-size businesses, such as an individual B&B or restaurant, allow for Internet advertising. Therefore, the better approach is to advertise on sites where a target audience spends its time looking for local information or for product-or service-related information. Where is this? They spend a considerable amount of time searching city, county, and state sites in their nearby geographic area for goods and services they need to keep their business and personal lives running smoothly. If you have advertised on these regional sites, they will find you. And because 48 percent of online small businesses gain customers within a 50-mile radius of their operation, it pays to consider advertising on local sites.

Consumers routinely visit city, county (or parish), or state sites to learn the schedules, phone numbers, addresses, or Internet addresses of local businesses, clubs, churches, schools, chambers of commerce, city festivals, city offices, stores, utility companies, services, hotels or restaurants, or even casinos. Almost every North American city of any size today has one or more "city" Web sites, and most have business sections that list local businesses in their directory's categories.

Visit some community sites—whether city, regional, or some other area—to get an idea of content and advertising. To find city sites in your area, check Official City Sites at officialcitysites.org/country.php3, which provides a directory of city sites, organized by state. Knight Ridder, the large newspaper publisher, also operates a national network of regional portals in 58 U.S. markets through its Digital division. Those sites are listed at www.realcities.com (see Figure 7.7). A company might wish to advertise on one or many of Knight Ridder's Real Cities Web sites.

About its target marketing, Knight Ridder says, "At Real Cities, we offer you a broad range of targeting options—from content- and category-specific offerings (business or lifestyle) to geographic opportunities (local residents of a specific region). You can even pinpoint your targeting to a particular time of day, day of the week, or to a consumer's online browser or computer operating system."

You will find other examples of city sites at the following locations:

www.neworleans.com

www.omaha.com

www.jacksonhole.com

www.orlando.com

www.baltimore.com

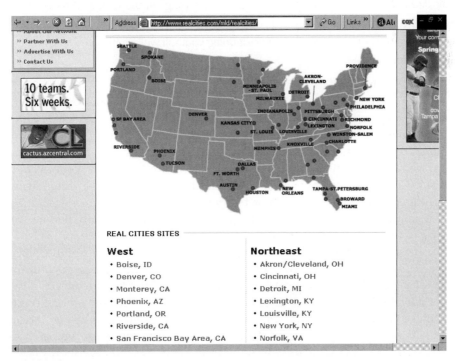

FIGURE 7.7 Real Cities from Knight Ridder. (Screen capture from www.realcities.com/mld/realcities/. Shows top portion of screen only.)

www.darien.lib.ct.us

www.bennington.com

Some "official" city sites operated by city governments do not allow commercial advertising or links. However, chambers of commerce Web sites often do offer links, especially to their members.

To find out how to advertise on a particular community Web site, look for a link on the site called "advertising," "how to be listed in this site," or something similar. That page will give details, an email address, and sometimes a phone number.

Tip — Be the First

If the local community-information Web site lacks a business section and the owner does not plan to add one, all is not lost. Ask the owner about the best place in the site for your link. The owner may propose something tailor-made for your business. If possible, meet the owner in person to discuss the advantages and importance of adding a directory to the site that is more audience specific. If it works out, you may well be the *only* firm listed in your category for a very long time.

Community site owners eventually position themselves to earn money from having many firms pay to be in their directory, so maybe you can negotiate "top billing" in the new section of the site. Maybe you can be there forever, if you are first, no matter how many other firms sign on later. (This is another example of how a big part of *positioning* yourself well on the Web has much to do with being there *first*.)

Regional cable companies that offer fast Internet connections have created county, regional, and large city Web sites for the areas they serve. They also provide their customers with a custom Web portal site, which might "push" consumers to places where your link(s) or ads would reside. Visit OCNow.com for an example of a county Web site owned by a cable company (Cox Cable, www.cox.com). The portal page within OCNow.com leads visitors to pages or sections for each city in the county. A business that markets countywide in Orange County, California, might want its banner or link to appear on this page.

If a firm markets only to certain Orange County cities, it should place ads just in the cities served. Clicking on a category in the center column, takes the user to a related page on which you can *also* buy an ad.

On the "restaurants" page of the countywide site, OCNow.com, serving Orange County, California, diners can search for restaurants by city, price, or cuisine, or merely click on "The Best of O.C. Restaurants" by type such as steaks, burgers, pizza, or sushi. In some cases, such sites tend to list only their

Try it

1. Go to OfficialCitySites.org (officialcitysites.org/country.php3) and click into the site to find the links for Golden, Colorado. Visit the city site and the chamber of commerce site. How do the two sites differ with regard to advertising?
2. Find the Web sites for *your* city in CitySearch.com (www.citysearch.com) and look for a business category. If specific categories are not shown on the first page, check the site's directory, index, or site map to see if a business section is somewhere inside. Go there. This is where you want your firm's link or ad to be.

advertisers as among the "Best" restaurants in the county. Conversely, some county and large city sites take pride in objectively ranking restaurants and hotels, either using their own editors or by allowing site visitors to evaluate places where they have dined stayed.

Local newspaper sites are also good candidates to consider if they have sections related to your business.

State Web sites

Visit Arizona.com. From the cities page of this statewide site, visitors can click to a city and find hotels, restaurants, casinos, and other local business information. Near the top of the page is a text that reads as below.

Arizona Hotels & Resorts-Lowest Rates Guaranteed! Save up to 50% on hotels, motels & resorts throughout the state. Visitors can view individual hotel Web pages with pictures and information. Check rates, availability and make secure online reservations!

Such ads can increase the likelihood of Web traffic and increased business for the participating hotels, motels, and resorts. Having rates and availability information along with online reservation functions makes the service particularly attractive to users who want comparisons and like to make decisions at their own convenience.

The business or industry sections of some state Web sites offer links and banner or tile ads. Because many state sites operate as "portal" or "entry" points to the whole state, they are often more interested in charging national advertisers for large ads rather than charging smaller businesses pennies by comparison for small ads. Some state sites maintain business directories. Check your state's pages and look for "Add URL." Then, add your firm's site. Some sites add the links free; others charge a fee. On those sites that charge, look for links saying things like "Advertise Here" or "About Advertising."

Magazines

Most well-established print magazines already have Web sites, and advertising on them is easy. Contact the Web advertising representatives from the magazines in which you already advertise by e-mailing them from the magazine's Web site.

Many online magazines and the online versions of print magazines that serve a particular industry are ideal places to advertise a Web site because the magazines shape their content and advertising for a target audience. If your firm subscribes to *Standard Rate and Data* (www.srds.com), check to see whether the magazine profile matches your target audience.

Good reviews are as good as gold! Want to get dozens of online magazines to review your in-hotel, at-resort, or independent restaurant? You can, and the secret to success here is being a squeaky wheel with the online magazines covering the dining and lodging world. One key, of course, is having something truly and undeniably distinctive to serve those who visit your establishment because any one of them could post a consumer evaluation of your restaurant or hotel.

The Zagat Survey (Figure 7.8) is a nationwide guide to thousands of restaurants, where diners place evaluations of dining establishments where they've been pleased or *displeased.* Just one bad consumer evaluation could dissuade people from visiting a given location. See also the popular site Epicurious.com.

Some Web sites send their own editors and reviewers out to experience restaurants and rate them for their online publication, Web site, or print magazine. Invite various review editors by name to visit your establishment to see for themselves. Repeat the invitation on a regular basis so that you get their attention. Some reviewers receive hundreds of requests (or more) each week.

Internet Service Provider Sites

Some Internet Service Providers (ISPs) offer customers a link on their site. This link can be valuable because ISPs typically offer a default home page used as a personal home page by thousands of customers of the ISP. Businesses that market in rural areas may be luckier than their urban peers in finding ISPs that offer free or nearly free links. A particular firm may be the only one or one of very few in an industry to be listed on the entire ISP site for a city or region—a definite positioning advantage!

ISPs in some rural areas often serve several small cities, each with its own city Web site, for example, mid-Michigan's Maple Valley Computer Center at www.mvcc.com. Check the ISP home page to see all of the cities it serves, then visit one.

FIGURE 7.8 The Zagat Survey. (Screen capture from www.zagat.com. www.zagat.com/ Search/Details.asp?VID-1&PID-1&LID-44&SPH-stone+crab&ST-2&NDPH-&CRT-name+contains+%27%27stone+crab%27%27&RID-20829)

Yahoo! and Other Mini-Stores

Many advertising benefits can be gained by operating a mini-store offered by Yahoo! or other portals. Yahoo!'s stores benefit greatly by being, of course, in Yahoo! with its millions of daily visitors. "Yahoo! Store" (store.yahoo.com) users pay a flat rate depending on the size of the site. There is no per-transaction fee, no start-up cost, and no minimum time commitment. However, it is yet another way that hospitality can use to improve their visibility and accessibility on the Internet.

Reciprocal Links and Banner Exchanges

Reciprocal links and banner exchanges provide ways to increase the likelihood that people will find a particular site. Furthermore, most major search engines place a site higher in their summaries based on how many pages link to it—another reason to get as many links to a site as possible. Visit www.linkstoyou.com to get an idea of how many sites already link to yours.

Dear (Name of Firm) Webmaster:

Because we are not competitors but sell to the same target audience, perhaps we can set up a valuable win–win situation.

Would you be willing to put a free link to our firm on your Web site at http://hisfirm.com if I put a similar free one for you on our site at www.myfirm.com? We could both enjoy increased exposure at no expense.

If you'll send me your text, I'll put it on our company site within four days at no cost to you, ever! Or, you can edit the sample that I wrote for you, showing a suggested format, and send it back to me.

Cordially,

> Your Name
> Your Title

Enc. Sample ad text, written in our format
(Title That You Want On Your Link)
(25-word description)
(Your Web site URL) (Your e-mail address and phone number)

Vacationing in Ft. Lauderdale?
Before you leave, reserve dinner at Our City's Finest Seafood Restaurant
www.WottaPlace.com
E-mail: Harry@WottaPlace.com
Toll Free: 888-555-5555

FIGURE 7.9   Sample e-mail message.

Reciprocal Links

Search the Web to find industry-related firms who have a strong Internet presence in areas you serve. Then, send them an email inviting them to link with you. A sample message is shown in Figure 7.9.

Some commercial sites actively seek reciprocal links and will give you a free link only if you give them one; for example, Seniors Search at www.seniorssearch.com. Some sites require that their link be placed on the home page of the reciprocating Web site. If this interferes with a home page design or loading speed, the Webmasters of the sites might negotiate. Sometimes, pointing out to them that you have created a special links page that is accessible from a prominent link that is on your home page will satisfy them. Then, be sure to follow through with what you promise, because they will check.

Individual hotel or restaurant sites (or pages) that offer local nonprofit, women's, youth's, and other community and civic groups links that take people to these organizations stand to benefit by asking for the return favor. Also, by placing ads on local online Web sites or local printed or emailed newsletters in your community, you may build personal referrals, reviews, and links. Organizations to consider for reciprocal links and ad placements include:

- PTAs
- Schools
- Sports teams
- Class Web sites of high school seniors
- Nonprofit, charity-minded organizations
- Women's and men's clubs
- Service clubs (e.g., Rotary, Lions, Kiwanis, Junior League)
- Churches
- Affinity groups of all kinds

Banner and Link Exchange Services

Banner exchange firms can help increase a site's exposure by displaying a banner in rotation with others on various Web sites. The banners of all participants in the exchange are of the same size. Unfortunately, a banner can appear on any one of thousands of the exchange firm's participating Web sites—most of which are not related to a particular business, target audience, or geographic area. Moreover, exchangers have little to say about what products or services appear in the banner frame that stays fixed (ideally, they request, prominently positioned) on their site, although a site can specify "non-porno" banners.

To participate, you must have a banner or tile ad of specific dimensions and file size, usually 7 kb or under, which, to be effective, may require the services of a fairly skilled designer. Bottom line: It's probably not worth the bother, cost, and reduced page loading speed on a site just to have more people who are unlikely to be interested in your facility see your banner.

The exception? For some firms, banner exchanges are a smart tactic. For example, if a well-known restaurant, a chain of hotels or restaurants, or a renowned chef is selling (nationwide) a recipe book called, *Recipes from Spago, Chinois, and Points East and West*, then the book could apply to anyone, anywhere, and a "shotgun" marketing tactic such as a banner exchange might be valuable. However, remember that the number of times that a banner is displayed depends entirely on the number of times that the exchange banner is displayed on the reciprocating site. If a site lacks heavy traffic, it won't gain much from a banner exchange program.

For full information on how Microsoft's bCentral establishes and manages banner exchanges through its free Banner Network, visit www.bcentral.com/services/bn/default.asp.

Affiliates

Some companies, especially booksellers and software companies, pay a commission for sales they gain that originated at another site, referred to as an affiliate or dealer. It works this way: You put their icon on your site, and for each person who clicks on the icon, goes to their site, and then places an order, you get a commission—usually 5 percent or more of the sale amount.

Casino Affiliations

Casinos may pay online affiliate Web sites from 25 to 40 percent commission per player, sometimes for the life of the player. Incentive programs keep the players coming back and technical and marketing support are given to the entrepreneur. Table 7.1 shows the commission rates offered affiliates by FortuneAffiliates.com.

Online casinos use pop-up ads on Gator.com, the popular free program that automatically fills out contact and credit card forms for you on Web pages. They send spam email, they run pop-up, banner, and tile ads on other Web sites. For some Web users, the advertising seems to be everywhere, and non-gamblers often find such intrusions immensely annoying.

The tactic that casinos use in advertising themselves with unsolicited e-mails and garish, in-your-face ads is a statistical one: If they reach enough

TABLE 7.1 Commission structure from FortuneAffiliates.com.		
Tier:	**Commission:**	**Your Potential Earnings:**
1. $0 – $15,000	25%	$3,750
2. $15,001 – $30,000	30%	$8,250
3. $30,001 – $500,000	35%	$172,750
4. + $500,001	40%	Unlimited

(Source: www.fortuneaffiliates.com/commissiontable.htm)

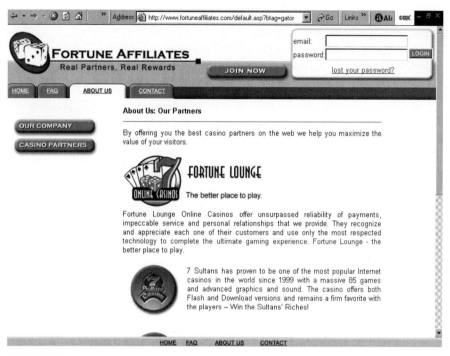

FIGURE 7.10   FortuneAffiliates.com. (Screen capture from www.fortuneaffiliates.com/default.asp?btag=gator.)

people (millions), they will get a certain number of online casino affiliate candidates. They can afford to do this only through mass e-mailing and Run-of-Schedule (ROS) advertising on high-content sites where their ads target no particular audience and are, therefore, relatively inexpensive.

Fortune Affiliate's ad (Figure 7.10), generated when the word "casino" or phrase "casino affiliates" is entered at Gator.com, offers a handful of casino choices to prospective affiliates. The casino sites themselves are rich with state-of-the-art graphics, Flash programming, animation, realistic casino sound effects, and as many as 50 separate games from which a player can choose.

Gaming is a significant business on the Web. Online gaming revenue rose from $800 million to over $2 billion in 1999. By 2003, it is estimated that the online gaming industry will top over $6 billion in revenues. See, for example, www.ownacasino.co.uk for more information.

Regulation of casinos.   Many regulations govern the advertising of U.S. land-based casinos. For example, commercial casinos can advertise their restaurant and entertainment venues, but not their gambling activities.

Church bingo, Native American tribes, and state-run lotteries, however, are permitted to advertise gambling.

According to www.casino-gambling-reports.com, Title 18 of the United States Code §1304 includes the following provisions:

> Whoever broadcasts by means of any radio or television station for which a license is required by any law of the United States, or whoever, operating any such station, knowingly permits the broadcast of, any advertisement of or information concerning any lottery, gift enterprise, or similar scheme, offering prizes dependent in whole or in part upon lot or chance, or any list of the prizes drawn or awarded by means of any such lottery, gift enterprise, or scheme, whether said list contains any part or all of such prize, shall be fined under this title or imprisoned not more than one year, or both.

A number of exceptions undercut the original sweeping scope of this section of Title 18. The exceptions include state lotteries; fishing contests; gambling conducted by an Indian tribe pursuant to the Indian Gaming Regulatory Act; a lottery, gift enterprise, or similar scheme by a not-for-profit organization or a governmental organization or conducted as a promotional activity by a commercial organization. Additional exceptions include horse racing and off-track betting.

Advertising casinos.   The general recommendations for online advertising of hospitality sites apply to advertising gaming establishments. To help identify casino target audiences, many Web sites offer profile information on gamblers, particularly on problem gamblers (see the Ohio State University study on this at ohioline.osu.edu/flm01/FS24.html).

One way to encourage target audience members to visit an online casino is to email them using opt-in mailing lists. People on an opt-in email list have already shown an interest in gaming by "opting-in" to some other site on gaming and stating that they are willing to receive more information about gaming. This means that they are proven target audience members, a group that is more likely than the general public to visit a gaming site. Generally, these mailing lists are rented for a fee, often from so many cents per address per mailing. Many times, the firm that has the list does the e-mailing for you. Read more about mailing lists in Chapter 9.

What are the costs to you of adding affiliate marketing to your site? Every image or word added to a site increases its loading time for visitors, and Web visitors are not patient. Adding new icons to a Web page inevitably requires some level of redesign or reorganization of the page. Worse yet, if visitors click on an icon to go buy something, you have just enticed them away from your site. So, is it worth adding affiliate icons? Probably not, unless your site is logging hundreds of visitors each day who aren't interested in your main product or service field anyway.

On the other side of the transaction, however, if you are a nationwide marketer of consumer products, it may be worth your while to set up your own network of affiliates. Your icon on hundreds of other sites can help build brand awareness. The sales monitoring technology and bookkeeping, however, are somewhat intimidating for most businesses.

Some of the best known non-gaming affiliate relationships are Amazon. com (www.amazon.com), 1–800-flowers (www.1800flowers.com), and Omaha Steaks (www.omahasteaks.com). The affiliates information shown in Figure 7.11 for 1-800-Flowers.com shows how a typical affiliate program works.

Sponsorships

Sponsoring a section of a site usually refers to providing the content and maintaining a section of a high-traffic site in return for the display of logos or links in that section, sometimes to the exclusion of competitors. Sometimes, sponsorship refers to the payment of a large fee to have company information displayed and the company cited as the sponsor somewhere on the page(s). For example, a local hotel or restaurant might sponsor a tourist information section of a city or community Web site. Why would a hotel or restaurant with its own Web site do this? Primarily for the traffic that the city or community Web site enjoys.

Although sponsorships on sites with the traffic and market power of very high-traffic sites may be too expensive for small firms, sponsoring a

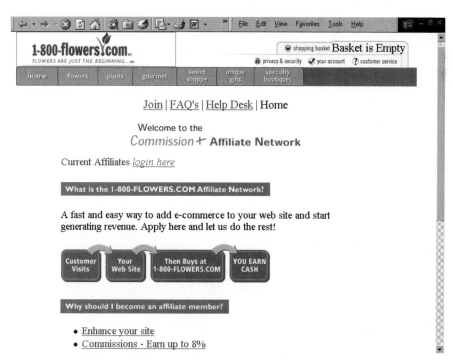

FIGURE 7.11   Affiliate program from 1-800-Flowers. (Screen capture from www.1800Flowers.com, Affiliate Program tab.)

section of a community site may be worth investigating. Chambers of commerce and city, state, or county Web sites or portals are likely candidates. Other community sites that might entertain such an offer include a local historical society, city recreation program, city government, local ISPs, local clubs and organizations, a visitors' center, local moving and storage firms, and other sites tied to a local or regional market.

How does a company ask about being a sponsor? Call or e-mail the organization to identify the decision makers. Then, contact them and offer to provide all of the content for a special section about your industry or product category on their site in exchange for being listed as the sponsor. You may have to sell them on the idea of even creating a special section; they need to understand how it can produce revenue or traffic for them.

Signature Links

Any time your hospitality firm (corporate office or local city unit) sends out an e-mail, it should have a "signature" at the end. Here is how one online dictionary of Internet terms, Marketingterms.com (www.marketingterms.com/dictionary/sig_file/), defines a signature: "A short block of text at the end of a message identifying the sender and providing additional information about them. . . . For business use, SIG files often include a mix of contact information and business promotion. This may include the sender's name, job title, company name, phone #, fax #, e-mail address, Web site address, tag line and brief benefits of your products or services."

Your signature should contain your contact information, including phone, fax, and other phone numbers, plus a repetition of your email address. The use of graphics can be an effective addition if they are small files and you are sure that the recipient's e-mail program will display them properly.

According to 185red.com, by 2003, 140 million people, or 62 percent of the U.S. population, were to be using e-mail (www.185red.com/docs/email_tips.pdf).

Because people who stay at hotels and who dine out often are in the higher socioeconomic brackets where Internet access is very high, a high percentage of hospitality customers are able to receive e-mail.

Clickable e-mail addresses and Web site URLs at the end of e-mails that you send out are valuable for pointing attention back to your site. Once users click on a link in your signature, they are taken to a specific Web page on your site where you might describe special offers, coupons, weekday promotions, special events, or a musical performance by a famous group at your facility, whether lodging or dining.

Bridge Pages

Some firms believe in optimizing a number of Web pages so that when people search for a certain keyword phrase a page will come up, often instantly, redirecting the searcher to another page, which may or may not have anything to do with the original keyword phrase.

If the final page reached *is relevant* to the keywords the searcher used, search engines are not usually upset by bridge pages. But what if the bridge page was set to come up when millions of people searched for "Britney Spears" and redirected the people seamlessly to the home page of Ace Hotel and Restaurant? In that case, the search engines would probably ban Ace from their engine or at least reduce its findability.

Bottom line, if you use bridge pages, be sure to have an experienced expert create them. For further information on how bridge pages affect findability, see the information at SearchEngineWatch.com (searchenginewatch.com/webmasters/).

Tracking Ad Performance

The effectiveness of an ad should be measured. Statistics on link performance, such as impressions and click-throughs, tells you the degree to which an ad or combination of ads is driving visitors to your site. Increases in visitor communications, downloads, purchases, or other actions following ad placements indicate the degree to which an ad (or combination of ads) is working in conjunction with your site content and functions to help you reach site goals.

One helpful approach is to conduct a 30-day test before committing to a long-term ad purchase. This lets you track performance and adjust an ad or link before you commit large amounts of money. You can track many types of visitor and site behaviors, but only a few concern you as a banner advertiser. These include:

- Impressions or page views—the display of a page containing your banner ad on a visitor's monitor. You must rely on the page owner's statistics for data on impressions.
- Click-through rate—the percentage of users who clicked on an ad. Calculate the CTR of an ad by dividing the number of clicks on the ad by the number of impressions.
- Referral—the page last visited by a user before entering your site. By capturing referral data, you discover which sites—and which marketing tactics, such as banner or tile ads, text links in directories, or links in the text of a paragraph—are sending you visitors. Various programs will capture this information for you, such as those offered by HitBox at www.hitbox.com.

Summary

Creating and launching a Web site is only the start of Internet marketing. The next critical activity is getting people to visit the site and use the information and tools there, including interactive communications, purchasing, making reservations, signing up for a gaming newsletter, and so on.

Online advertising encompasses a range of tools, including listings and enhanced listings, banner and tile ads, affiliations and sponsorships. Depending on their placement, some of these can be created without cost; others can be extremely expensive and feasible only for large firms.

Where are links and ads best placed? On sites frequented by the target audience. These may include portals and vortals, area (city, county, state, region) community information sites, online magazines, online stores, and exchange and auction sites.

Online advertising should be evaluated. The most common means of evaluating are impressions and click-through rates. Other measures include comparisons of visitor communications, reservations made, downloads, purchases, or other actions taken before and after the placement of a link or ad or combination of ads.

Review Questions

1. Why do site owners have to "advertise their advertising"?
2. What percentage of online small businesses gain sales from their local area?
3. Describe the difference between a listing and an *enhanced* listing.
4. What are two objectives of most banner ads?
5. What percent of people who see banners actually click on them?
6. Give two examples of "specialty sites."
7. What is one disadvantage of exchanging banners with other sites?
8. What kind of search engine is Overture.com?
9. What is the difference between CPC and CPM?
10. How does the context-based presentation of banners or tile ads work?
11. How do standard banner sizes make planning online advertising easier?
12. Is the price of advertising that reaches a carefully defined target audience higher or lower than advertising to a larger but more general audience?
13. Why does an ad on a page that is five clicks away from a home page cost less?
14. Why are ISPs a good place to advertise for some firms?
15. Do people use search engines or links more often to find pages on the Web?
16. Why are affiliations to sell the products of another firm not usually worth creating on a business site?

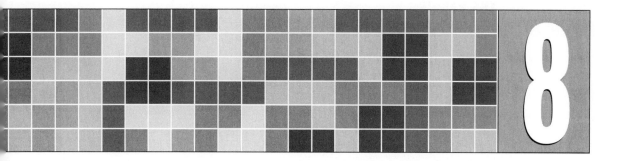

Promotion and Advertising

On the Net and Off

If your phone number is there, put your e-mail and Web site address there too.

More? You mean there's more *besides* advertising? If you're serious about Internet marketing, then, yes, there's definitely more. Businesses in the hospitality industry are blessed with large audiences. When it comes to reaching them, however, it's a mixed blessing—one that requires considerable prioritizing and planning.

Some of the tasks to reach your target audiences are common sense, inexpensive, and easily done—and you would probably think of them and do them anyway. Tasks like adding your Web site address and e-mail address to your business cards, letterhead, and envelopes; flyers; post cards; invoices; and print ads seems obvious, but can be easily overlooked.

Other tasks discussed in this chapter are also matters of common sense and are inexpensive, but not so easily done. Newsletter articles, press releases, and other public relations efforts require time and effort, both in their preparation and in their placement. This chapter provides step-by-step guidance for obtaining effective target market visibility.

THE BASICS

Public Relations

Professionals define "public relations" as "good performance, publicly appreciated." *What* about your performance is good? *How* can you obtain public appreciation for it? One method is to use "publicity," which is a major tool of the Public Relations profession. Here's one approach to getting publicity.

The first step involves identifying the good performance that a business wants to highlight. "Good performance" should spring from strong points—from *positioning*, from *branding*. What has the company or the business owner, entrepreneur, or employee done that educates people about using or choosing its products or services? Or that helps them solve a problem or answer typical or unusual industry questions?

Let's say you are the best Italian restaurant in an area with three Italian restaurants that are so-so—and you suddenly publish the recipes for your best menu choices. News? If you are making this information available for free on the Internet, maybe so. Or maybe you're the golf resort that has added panoramic or 360-degree virtual tours of every fairway to your site for all to see. Or maybe you're the Coastal Hotels chain that has set up a volunteer group to keep the southern California or Myrtle Beach shorelines clean. Keep thinking; you'll find it—the "hook."

The next step begins the process of obtaining public appreciation. Write a one-page summary of how your inn is using the Internet to provide valuable and much-needed information on family safety while traveling. Or write a one-page summary of how your Chinese restaurant manager helped a chef from Beijing find, preview, purchase, and occupy the perfect location for his restaurant supply firm, featuring low-cost equipment imported from China. Or write about some other topic that builds on a unique market position and related activity.

The key is to get the critical information down on paper (or into a word-processing program or e-mail) in a short form. This is not the final article—it is just information that will interest a newsletter, magazine, or Web site editor in the story. This may, of course, be the entire job of a staff person in a larger company, or it could be hired out to an advertising agency or promotions firm. But for smaller to mid-size hospitality firms, the job usually falls to a sales manager, an owner, or a vice president.

In large hospitality corporations with hundreds of locations worldwide, the job of getting local publicity is usually that of the local manager. In some cases, the corporate promotional and public relations staff develop programs that the manager can use or modify for local print or other media.

At the third step, someone in the company sends, takes, or e-mails the summary to the editor of the local paper; the local, state, or national trade or industry magazine; business journals in the area; magazines and newsletters of all groups related to the industry; and even to the magazine or newsletter published by the firm itself. Besides getting public recognition in print media, you should target Internet sites that will publish the recognition and link to the company site. News services, e-newsletters, and eZines (Web magazines) are often hungry for content.

More Visibility

Where else? Don't overlook these opportunities to mention the company's Web site: Internet bulletin boards, news groups, chat rooms, and "usenet"; business cards, flyers, seminars; conferences and talks at community functions; vehicle door signs, grocery-cart panels, shopping mall kiosks, and bus stop benches and shelters; waiting rooms, lobbies, cash-register counters, and front windows of your own nationwide dealers, representatives, distributors, franchisees, and other businesses listed on your site. You will think of many more. Use your imagination and your knowledge of your business and its strengths, its position, the community, and its target audience.

BEYOND THE BASICS

Many marketing professionals believe that editorial matter is seven times better read and remembered than ads. In the ad industry, writing and placing articles and news releases or press releases to gain "free" publicity typically costs about one tenth of the cost of buying display ads. When promoting a site and services, most small to mid-size businesses need to allocate considerable time and resources to articles and press releases. In many cases, the editorial content is a major reason people subscribe to magazines, newspapers, and online newsletters.

More About Public Relations

If, as advertiser lore would have it, "public relations" is "good performance, publicly appreciated," a business or person actually has to do or say something newsworthy (even sometimes meritorious) in order to get public appreciation (publicity).

Being "newsworthy" is not as momentous as one might think—you need not rob a bank or donate a new wing to the hospital. "Newsworthy" means facts that are timely, interesting, or educational to the audience that receives them.

The most common news releases issued by manufacturers and industrial companies for customers and potential customers announce new products or services, or talk about people joining the business or being promoted. Releases for the industry and investors often announce new company leadership, resources, attainment of sales goals, or acquisitions or mergers. Less common but powerful are releases that report how a firm or a representative of the firm used its product or service to solve a problem for a customer. Such case histories can help position a firm as an industry leader, an "authority" on solving customer problems, a company that understands its customers' needs.

Getting Local Publicity

Once you have a content-rich Web site at the local level, every piece of promotion and advertising that you do can direct consumers to that site, which has all of your offers, benefits, coupons, or discounts. You can serve the community in a way that the hospitality industry has not done before, and in return, your business stands to reap the rewards of local referrals.

News releases are fairly easy to prepare and submit to local media. Some suggestions for news release topics for local lodging establishments include announcements of:

- The addition to the staff of a new experienced manager (along with short biographical notes)
- Winning of an industry award
- Plans for or the opening of remodeled rooms, lobby, pool area—did you use environmentally friendly materials, local contractors, energy-saving insulation or power sources?
- New or significantly expanded concierge service
- Extensive local tour service from hotel
- Free limousine service to local spas, golf courses, or other sites

Ideas for news release topics for local dining businesses include announcements of:

- Hiring a new chef
- New menu, mentioning main entrees, specials for seniors, children, business lunches, banquets, etc.
- Famous dish recipes revealed
- New manager or owner
- New service such as make reservations online, order for pickup or delivery online, set up banquet online
- Useful additions to your Web site, such as the nutritional information for menu items
- Extended hours
- Awards
- Singing waiters, dinner theater, midnight suppers, or other special entertainment or services

Suggested news release topics for gaming establishments include announcements of:

- New report on odds—loose slots
- New games or machines
- New dining features, hours, chefs, etc.
- New management
- Online version of popular games

Try it

Write a news release, not to exceed one page, on one of the topics listed previously.

Articles Give Credibility

To get news articles about a business or service published, you have to capture the interest of a reporter, editor, or Webmaster. Ask yourself, "What does this establishment do that is interesting or useful for its target audiences to know?" "What has it (or its staff, workers, management, vendors, or products) done lately that those audiences could benefit from knowing?" or "How can we educate people about (something) in a way that helps them?"

Ask those questions in the context of positioning or branding (see Chapter 2). What has this business done that is interesting and related to its market positioning, such as the "family buffet with plenty for everyone," the "world's best gourmet hamburger," or the "second home for seniors"?

Sometimes, writing the headline helps you write the story; for example:

- "Local Hotel Offers Online Travel Safety Brochure"
- "XYZ Restaurant Launches Consumer Food Safety Tips on Web site"
- "Small Town Inn Helps With Lake Cleanup"
- "Apple Orchard Restaurant Announces Free Cobblers for Kids on Tuesday"
- "Local Resort Golf Pro Addresses Area Youth at Career Day Event"

Try it

Write a one-page summary of an event, activity, or accomplishment. The summary should include the reasons why the publication's audience (not necessarily the firm's immediate audience) would be interested in reading the feature article. Describe the "angle," the point of view that should be inherently appealing to the audience that the publication reaches. Without an angle—a reason why the story should be published—you will not get very far with editors.

Hospitality businesses that market locally send a summary—by e-mail, snail mail, or personal delivery—to a local paper (to the attention of the newspaper section editor most likely to be interested in the subject, or, lacking such a section, to the editor of "features" or the "general interest" section).

Corporate offices of large lodging or dining entities that market nationally send such a summary to editors of print and online publications for the industry; area business journals, newsletters, or magazines of related professional organizations; organizations that it supports; area commerce magazines; and industry columnists. The last group, columnists, is often ignored, but just a mention by one of them in a well-read column, or one that is syndicated nationally, can draw valuable attention to your firm.

A firm that is a division or wholly owned subsidiary of a bigger firm should contact all of the publications in which the parent office or corporation places advertising.

Note that the summary does not have to be great literature. Recipients use the summary to evaluate the merits of doing a story on the solution, event, or other information included. If they like the summary, they might call for an interview or some additional information and then write the final story themselves.

Local Media

Local newspapers are often quite generous with their publicity in specialty sections, especially for their advertisers. If you are assigned the task of getting an article in the local media, you should talk to the advertising reps from local newspapers and business journals in which the company advertises. Advertising representatives have considerably more impact on what editors run in smaller papers than they do with the larger papers. For the individual local units, this can be a job for an assistant manager.

Sending out your publicity items in the proper format makes editors more receptive to your submissions. The format shown in Figure 8.1 is a standard one used for years in public relations. Note how an editor can scan the top fifth of the press release in seconds to know the story's subject immediately. That is why writing headlines for the editor's eye is important, even though the editor will, in most cases, rewrite the headline to his or her own liking.

Getting publicity into occasional or periodic special sections, which are often primarily vehicles for the newspaper to sell more advertising, can be relatively easy. The representatives for these sections have considerable influence regarding what goes in such sections, and sometimes, the newspaper employs special editorial staffs just to compose these "advertorial" sections.

Although the articles in these sections sometimes seem "puffy" and may tend to over-sell the subject, they draw attention to a business's announcements. Often, just writing an article about the tons of fish a fish and chips cafe has served to date or about a chef's charity work as "the ad hoc menu designer at the local homeless shelter" is sufficient to move a story into print.

Company Letterhead

For more information, contact:

Jake Lamotta, PR Director   **News Release**

(800) 555-5555   **For Immediate Release**

Jake@Riverdine.com

Thomas J. Geller Joins Riverdine Restaurant

As General Manager,

to Spearhead Renovation, New Menu, and Catering Service

City, State—June 23, 2004—Thomas J. Geller, with more than 18 years experience in restaurant management, has been named general manager of ABC Gourmet Restaurant, the largest, oldest, and best-known dining facility in Bigcity County.

Geller is spearheading a new and significantly expanded menu and catering service recently announced by FoodServer, Inc., the parent company that owns Riverdine and 35 other similar magnificent-view theme restaurants. Foodserver, Inc. (www.sitenamehere.com) is the country's leading theme restaurant specializing in view-intensive dining.

Previously, Geller was manager of FoodServer's ABC Restaurant in Cleveland, Ohio, for eight years. Before that, he was manager of the world famous Chateau Lodge Restaurant, atop Victoria Peak in Hong Kong. Geller says, "We're installing all state-of-the-art equipment for both our dining room and new catering service. Nothing of this caliber has been seen in the entire country and we can hardly wait to introduce it to the Orange County community about two months from now."

Geller also owned his own gourmet restaurant for four years and before that was an executive chef with the BordenFine Restaurant chain.

Chad Hallock, President of FoodServer, Inc., says, "We are most gratified to have found a seasoned industry veteran such as Tom Geller. Because his

---

FIGURE 8.1   Standard press release format.   (continued)

career spans virtually every aspect of the dining business, he becomes a valuable addition to our team as we prepare to launch many new services during the next two years."

Riverdine Gourmet Restaurant is a subsidiary of Foodserver, Inc., a division of Purita Foods. The local and extensive website of Riverdine Gourmet Restaurant is at www.RiverdineGourmetsitenamehere.com. The national website of Foodserver, Inc. is www.sitenamehere.com.

Riverdine Gourmet Restaurant is located at 4050 W. Bates Ave., City, State 99999-9999—Telephone: (800) 555-5555

FIGURE 8.1   Standard press release format (continued).

If you are part of a business that has a sales or marketing director, ask what criteria the company uses to publish articles on individual employees, or discuss company successes in its widely distributed corporate or local newsletter. In many firms, especially at the corporate level of a hospitality firm, and particularly regarding casinos, an attorney must approve all publicity items before distribution.

Bacon's Publicity Checker (newspaper or magazine version, see www.bacons.com) and Gebbie's, Inc. (www.gebbieinc.com) provide lists of publication editors and contact information. Read more about publicity at www.free-publicity.com/faq.htm. Look over the many resources at The Public Relations Society of America, www.prsa.org, and its links to other resources there. Check, too, the Writer's Resource, InkSpot.com at www.inkspot.com.

When researching facts for a publicity item you're writing, check for published media articles on the same subject at www.findarticles.com.

Contacting Editors

One way to know what editors want to see or announce about an industry, business, product, or service is to ask them. Editors, however, are usually busy trying to meet deadlines with the next day's (or week's) material. When you call, have your "pitch" down to 15 seconds or less—"Fred, Tomorrow morning, 100 of our 102 employees are going to show up at work wearing chicken suits to promote our new line of frozen Blazin' Chicken dinners." Or, "Fred, Our San Diego residents can now get two-for-one weekday rooms for their out-of-town guests, or for their family, at our BlueBird Hotel on the bay. This beats any other hotel offer in the city. I can send you the story now."

Pay attention to the relevant sections of the publication for several weeks or more to develop a sense of topics and "hooks" that have successfully gotten printed. Emphasize a story's "angle" when you talk with or e-mail an editor. The first thing an editor looks for is the "hook."

Call editors only about articles, not about news releases. Figure 8.2 includes examples of acceptable scenarios of query calls or e-mails to an editor.

Smaller Publications

For businesses with an audience that includes middle-income families, getting an article in miscellaneous local tabloid "throwaways" and "driveway" publications can be easy and worth the time invested. Because the editorial staff of such publications is usually very small, they may view an offer of free written material as a cost-effective blessing. Your firm's Web site address should always be included. Better yet, post a larger (more details included) version of the same article on your Web site and ask the editor to include a link to it in the story. Leave the article archived on your site for all future visitors to read.

Becoming a Columnist or Contributor

Editors of entertainment-oriented e-mail and Internet and print newsletters often seek valid content in time to deliver it to their subscribers from one deadline to the next. Some entrepreneurs help them by writing a guest column. Your firm could provide such a guest columnist. Sometimes, a simple case history story, for example, about how you solved a problem for a guest or how the Heimlich maneuver was used to save a patron's life (especially if the manager then organized and supported life-saving training at a local fire station) can gain pages in on- and offline newsletters.

A business or professional that is an expert in a field or specialization qualifies as an "authority" in the eyes of the trade magazine, business journal, newsletter, and online eZine publications. (Generally, in large companies, executives have Public Relations staff write their "by-lined" articles and columns.) Following are some tips on having a guest column or article published (these procedures vary widely—they are guidelines and tips, not rules):

1. When the editors agree to print an article from you or your company, send them an outline, not the final article. This way they can approve the outline before you write the "final" text.
2. Always ask how many words the article should have.

Dear Bob,

Hard-to-Get Flu Shots Available Tuesday at Local Gourmet BoffoBurger
[Headline for print communications only.]

I'm Fred BrickandClick from the local Gourmet BoffoBurger restaurant. On Tuesday, the 21st, ten days from now, we will have nurses on hand to administer flu and pneumonia shots. Most hospitals and doctors in this area will not have flu shots for yet another month. But we will and at only $15 per shot. We were hoping that, as a community service, you might help us spread the word about this valuable program that we are offering. What would you like to see—a news release? Or would you like to interview one of our people who could come to your office? We think this is important and want it to go well. Full details are on our Web site at (give URL here).

* * *

Dear Bob,

Citywide Flying Disk Tournament Benefits Boys & Girls Center
[Headline for print communications only.]

I'm Fred Manager from the local Been Inn. As you know, last year we worked with the city recreation department to fund and build the new Frisbee-type "disk golf" course for public use. Next Saturday, we will be hosting the first annual citywide "disk-golf" tournament to benefit the Boys and Girls Center. In what format would you like us to give you the details of our announcement? We want to do this the right way for you because your coverage will have a lot to do with how much money we can raise for the Boys and Girls Center. Full details are on our Web site at (give URL here).

* * *

Dear Bob,

Battered Spouse Organization Surprised by $15,000 Donation from Food Servers and Other Inn Employees
[Headline for print communications only.]

Your county business journal readers might be interested to know that our 55 inn staffers collected, and are contributing, over $15,000 this year to our local battered spouse organization, Paula's House. Paula's House executive director, Susan Ganner, said that she was astonished because this is the largest single local donation they have received to date. We think that this donation can serve as a good model for your many business readers. Presentation ceremonies will be held next Tuesday, Oct. 14, at Paula's House. Susan is most receptive to being interviewed. How should we give you what you need for your readers?

Full details are on our Web site at (give URL here).

FIGURE 8.2   Acceptable queries or e-mails to an editor.

3. Polish the article before sending it to the editor. Have colleagues read it and give their critique before you submit that final version. (Be prepared. Critical feedback is not always easy to accept gracefully. Keep that in mind when you select your helpers.)

4. Be sure to include your Web site's URL in the text of the article. This helps drive visitors to your site whether your article appears in a print or online publication.

Some business writers have become the "regular columnist" for trade news in their industry, although this tends to be truer for smaller trade magazines than for larger ones. Still, it does not hurt to approach larger trade and online sites with a proposal. Bill Gates of Microsoft has no trouble getting columns placed—but neither should leaders and managers of businesses in other niche markets, including lodging, dining, and gaming managers.

Tip	Legal Review?

Some firms require that their legal department review any written material that is sent out for publication, particularly comments made by CEOs and other top management.

These columns add visibility for the business's Web site because each column should carry a Web address, plus photo(s) and contact information. An executive, manager, or chef appearing as an authority enhances the firm's market position and industry reputation. Moreover, every time an article or column is accepted, it gives the writer and the company more credibility with editors when getting the next one placed.

Epicurious Magazine and its Web site post a list of authors. Visit the site www.epicurious.com and you will see that some of the authors are also chefs or owners of restaurants. Consider getting your PR people to interview your chef and see about getting articles and recipes in some of the leading print and online food Web sites.

Tip	Columns by the Batch

To help get approved as a specialty columnist for a publication, write four or five columns and deliver them all at once to the editor. Sending several columns in advance shows that you know your topic, and the editor will have several weeks of columns before having to worry about whether you will meet their deadlines. Remember that positioning works best when you get there first. If you don't get a column published, eventually a competitor will.

Will a publication's editors let small business owners or managers in mid-size hospitality businesses write a regular column? It depends. Some local papers might charge a modest "fee" for publishing each column—usually to avoid problems in their relationships with other prospective columnists, especially those who are advertisers. On the other hand, many eZines look for a leading firm, or even a good individual writer in their industry, to provide expert content that gets a temporary prominent location (and then becomes archived on the site, thus being available for years.)

If the publication or online magazine or newsletter agrees to such a "columnist" arrangement, the writer should focus the columns on tips, "how to," and educational subjects valuable to the audience. Columns are usually short (ask for an exact length—maybe 1,000 to 2,000 words).

Try it

Olden Days Book Publishing in Smallville, YourState, publishes and distributes books on the history of YourState. The company publishes books on state history and town history, as well as architectural, economic, social, political, family, and religious histories. Olden Days will soon release a new book entitled *Early Dining Establishments and Saloons in Smallville*. Your restaurant is going to give free copies to the first thousand patrons.

1. Write a press release for this new book.

2. Make a list of the newspapers and magazines that you will send the announcement to.

Publicity on the Internet

Online business newsletters and Web sites routinely publish articles on ways to provide better service. Consider the benefits of publishing your own newsletter. Walter Mathews' 187-page book gives considerable advice on how your hospitality firm can use newsletters to market itself better (www.chipsbooks.com/rsnewslt.htm). The book shows how to:

- Develop a brisk, engaging writing style
- Select editorial content that captures readers' attention
- Create an attractive newsletter design
- Plan the look, length, tone, and frequency of your publication
- Negotiate with printers
- Build a mailing list of the people most likely to respond to your message
- Use and select among a variety of distribution options, including mail, fax, and the Internet
- Measure your newsletter's impact on business

Check to see which large organizations and associations are leaders in your industry. For lists of associations, visit the American Society of Association Executives at www.asaenet.org.

Every industry now has its own online newsletters, many of which are extensions or versions of trade magazines that operated long before the Web began. To find newsletters in your field, search for "business newsletter lists" or "(your industry's name) newsletter lists." Much useful information about Web commerce, e-marketing in general, mailing lists, and more is available at Dr. Ralph F. Wilson's site: www.wilsonweb. com (see Figure 8.3).

FIGURE 8.3   Web marketing information site. (Screen capture from www.wilsonweb.com.)

Local Web Sites

City, county, and state Web sites often need content in the form of helpful hints for their sites' visitors. To approach these sites, e-mail the designated editorial or advertising person listed for the target city, or the Webmaster, and attach a summary of your article idea. Explain why their visitors might interested. Or, offer to perform some service for the site in return for a small mention and a link to your firm's site. Figure 8.4 shows a sample request.

Dear Fred,

The section of your Web site on "Our city's scenic spots" is terrific. Those 10 photos are magnificent. Did your photographer daughter take them? Some people might like to know more about each photo than is covered by the brief captions. I am offering to write a paragraph or two about each picture for free, in return for a small paragraph of credit.

After I have written the descriptions for the images, would you let me have a paragraph near the middle of the page of photos that says:

> Photo descriptions by Lamont Cranston, Night Manager, Shadow Restaurant. "The Shadow" has been here for 77 years. For a special Shadow discount coupon and more info, click <u>HERE</u>.

I can have the captions to you within a week. Please reply by e-mail or call me at 800–555–5555.

Sincerely,

Lamont Cranston

ShadowKnows@ShadowRestaurant.com

FIGURE 8.4   Sample request for a link.

Usegroups

Usenet and its many newsgroups ("usegroups") and online forums use the Internet to enable people in a particular industry or profession or who share some other interest to discuss topics of mutual interest, ask and answer questions, and, in general, learn from one another. Participating in these groups may give you a forum for drawing attention to your business.

Exercise considerable restraint if you choose to use this forum—observe the "netiquette" (www.albion.com/netiquette/) that applies among most newsgroup participants. Blatant advertising of your services will be sure to draw fire.

Note that usegroups can be very time-consuming, and the benefits may be negligible. Consequently, usegroup participation rightfully earns very low priority in the repertoire of Internet marketing tools. The "Internet FAQ Consortium" (www.faqs.org/faqs/usenet/what-is/part1/ and www.faqs.org/faqs/usenet/what-is/part2/) describes Usenet as "a worldwide distributed discussion system." The Consortium document continues:

> It [Usenet] consists of a set of "newsgroups" with names that are classified hierarchically by subject. "Articles" or "messages" are "posted" to these newsgroups by people on computers with the appropriate software—these articles are then broadcast to other interconnected computer systems via a wide variety of networks. Some newsgroups are "moderated"; in these, the articles are first sent to a moderator for approval before appearing in the newsgroup. Usenet is available on a wide variety of computer systems and networks, but the bulk of modern Usenet traffic is transported over either the Internet or UUCP [don't ask].

A typical Usenet scenario is when someone makes a statement and others comment on it. Newsgroups are generally topical, and they deal with every imaginable subject.

Most usegroups, also known as newsgroups, are searchable by topic, usually by entering "usegroups" into a search engine along with a topic name or by entering "alt. (nameoftopic)" (no parentheses and put a space between the dot and the topic name) in the browser's location box. Using a browser's location box, the format "news:alt.(yoursubject)" also works. Enter, for example, news:alt.autos or news:alt.marketing and hit the Enter key. The browser will return a list of related newsgroups that you might want to explore.

To find extensive information on newsgroups, visit Google at http://groups.google.com/. You can learn the basics at http://groups.google.com/groups?group=*&hl=en. Furthermore, Google offers a complete 20-year Usenet Archive with over 700 million messages, and you can browse their complete list of groups at http://groups.google.com/groups?group=*&hl=en.

Tip	**E-mail Address for Usenet Mail**

Before you join a usenet, you will be asked to create a screen name that newsgroup people will see, and to provide an e-mail address for receiving the responses to your postings. Usenets can deliver hundreds of e-mails a day, so having a special e-mail address to collect them—one that is separate from your normal e-mail address—is a very good idea to avoid being overwhelmed. One of the free Web-based e-mail addresses is good for this purpose. These are offered by Yahoo!, Hotmail, and others. Just use your favorite search engine to search for "free e-mail."

Bulletin Boards and Guestbooks

Thousands of local ISPs, business groups, state and national business associations, plus community, county, and state Web sites have bulletin boards where people can leave messages for others to see. As a rule, users go to the "Bulletin Board" Web page, enter their identification information, and then enter a message for all users to see or only for persons sharing a certain password. For the hospitality industry, bulletin boards offer a very low return on the investment of time. The exception to this rule is a local community bulletin board specifically devoted to local dining, which is not common.

Web site guestbooks tend to be less effective than selected testimonials from guests or patrons, especially if they are celebrities, local leaders, or other people known to the target Web audience. The problem with "live" guestbooks is their use by dissatisfied guests or patrons who may exaggerate a negative experience.

Web Site Administrators

Making the acquaintance of the owners or managers of key local and national Web sites can have significant benefits for small or medium businesses. At the very least, establish an e-mail relationship with them. If you really like their site, tell them so. Tell the site's owner that you would like to be the first to know of any new promotions or link enhancements that are offered. Tell the owner that if he or she ever has any questions about your industry, to ask you—no strings attached. Write an article about the current or upcoming state of your marketplace or write a series of helpful tips for those who buy from your industry and give the article to the site owners to post, free, on their site.

Why? Because your competitors most likely will not think of doing this, especially for the more local and smaller regional Web sites. If yours is the only firm helping them better serve their audience, site owners may well turn to you for advice, notify you when they have new advertising opportunities, or even refer people to you as valuable resource or vendor to them. They begin to help you improve your marketing position.

Get to Know the Owners of Large Industry-Based Sites

Get to know the owners or managers of key national Web sites in your field. Send them an e-mail thanking them for building such a terrific resource for your industry and for busy people like you. Rarely do the builders of huge and valuable business-oriented Web sites receive such e-mails from corporate executives or managers. They will remember. A good place to start is with your own state's lodging, dining, or gaming association's executive director and Webmaster.

The National Restaurant Association site (Figure 8.5) provides a list of all state restaurant associations. BeverageNet.net provides links to additional industry associations, restaurant chains, and online sponsors at www. beveragenet.net/links/sra.asp.

Try to become reasonably well acquainted with the owners and editors of the major Web sites and newsletters that reach your key audiences. If you are the owner or manager of a small business or a regional manager of a hospitality chain, or even the CEO of Cendant, make a point of contacting Web site executives well ahead of the next industry trade show or convention and ask if they'll have time to see you or one of your team members. If the site owners are coming to your town for a convention, seminar, or trade show, offer them a tour of your facility. Stand out from your peers who rarely acknowledge anybody. Just remember that standing out from the crowd is a big part of positioning yourself and your firm in an industry. You are creating a personality for your business, and that personality is part of positioning.

Why? To build a win–win relationship that benefits everyone. In addition, key hospitality industry Web site staffers may have the power to give your locations a special placement or promotion on their site.

FIGURE 8.5   National Restaurant Association. (Screen capture from www.restaurant.org/ states/.)

More Ways to Advertise

All of your business's printed materials should have its Internet marketing information clearly visible. On menus, direct mail offers, receipts, invoices, brochures, flyers, and other materials that provide sufficient space, add a box with text that directs readers to your site.

Make an entire print brochure or flyer an announcement of helpful resources to be found on your site. Offer the audience strong and specific reasons to visit. For example, if you cater to frequent travelers, you could list topics that include:

- How to pack luggage to avoid wrinkles and protect delicate objects
- How to help avoid lost luggage
- What to take with you on every trip you make
- Why duct tape is the handiest thing you can take on trips
- How to select the right bag for each kind of trip you take
- Find weather delay times at every airport
- Tips for ordering tickets, making hotel and restaurant reservations online
- Top travel sites for vacationers, business travelers, and family vacations
- Find the cheapest air fares
- Frequent flyer mileage and how to use it the best

Include some humor. Why humor? Because (surely you must have noticed) many corporate Web sites are incredibly boring. The primary reason for promoting a business, service, or product on the Web is to get more visitors to come to your site. Visitors are not going to return to a ho-hum site.

Use your creativity to identify ways to increase the visibility of your site. The following are a few ideas:

- Display the unique market positioning statement (UMPS) or brand prominently on your business cards, letterhead, ads, flyers, brochures, product wrappers, and boxes along with the e-mail and Web site addresses.
- Advertise your site in publications that your target audience reads. Announce features that are unique in the industry and that offer tools, hints, tactics, shortcuts, or resources of value to your audiences.
- Hold seminars for target audiences—perhaps a free "How to use the Internet and e-mail to get more sales" at your city's or hotel's next trade show. Provide handouts, business cards, and other materials that list your Web site, what it has for visitors, and your e-mail address.
- Exchange or share visibility with firms or merchants favored by your target audiences; for example, put merchants' coupons or

announcements on your Web site, and the merchants put a display on their sites or in their stores promoting your facility.

Some strategies that have the potential to increase visibility are not widely used or are only used regionally. Among these are advertising on screen-clips that run before and between movies (you have a captive audience) at local theaters; bus stop advertising on the shelter posters and benches; car door signs; and a Koelzer favorite, grocery-cart ads. Local grocery shopping-cart advertising is often overlooked as a way to build visibility for Web sites.

For most grocery-cart ads, you pay a fee to a firm that has the rights to such advertising in various grocery stores in your area, and that firm puts your ad on the carts. Often, the ad is placed next to a store map or aisle directory on the cart—where shoppers look for item locations.

Stores in suburban areas average anywhere from 100 to 250 shopping carts; mega-groceries may maintain 500 or more. Costs vary widely, according to the number of carts, regional pricing, and the size of the ad. Get statistics from the company that sells the ad space in your market area(s). Compare the cost to that of your general newspaper ads for a specific area for six months to help you decide. Make similar comparisons for other types of "public" advertising.

Rolling Billboards: Signs on Vehicle Doors

Hospitality businesses with their own delivery vans, shuttle services, or other vehicles have a mobile advertising advantage. Such vehicles should carry both the URL of the company Web site and an e-mail address. Moreover, along with the URL, include a positioning statement or a reason for people to visit the Web site; for example:

Get Tips for Healthy Eating at www.ABC-restaurant.com

or

Order from the Widest Menu in Town at www.ABC-restaurant.com

Providing a reason to visit the site along with its URL is more effective.

A Final Word on "Getting Found"

Webmasters or managers obtain site traffic statistics various ways. The company hosting the site will usually provide "log statistics" for a fee. They use a tracking program or "traffic analyzer." Businesses maintaining their own sites can purchase and install their own program for tracking their site's traffic.

Such programs not only indicate how many visitors accessed the site, but also what site or search engine sent them there, what browser they were using, their location, which pages they visited first or second, how long they lingered on each one, and more.

Why is this valuable information? Because if you know what types of sites users were visiting before they came to your site, then you'll know what types of sites to advertise on and target to get your site more visibility. You'll know what types of sites to spend your time and money on, rather than guessing. Furthermore, you can evaluate how well your "getting found" strategies are working.

A Rule

Here's a simple guideline: If your phone number is there, put your e-mail and Web site address there too.

Are you reaching your traffic goals? Which strategies, links, or ads are working to bring visitors to your site? Which are not? For example, if your Webmaster changes certain keywords in the metatags on the company site, traffic data might indicate whether this has affected the number of visitors. Conversely, if you can't determine the effect on traffic, how do you know that you're adding the right words and tags?

Yes, you can deduce increases or decreases in traffic to some degree based solely on the fluctuating number of e-mail inquiries that you receive. But you could be getting hundreds of visitors to your site who don't send you an inquiry. And here's the rub—they might send you an e-mail inquiry if only your site were designed or worded a bit differently.

Right now, you may have no idea which page your visitors go to after seeing your home page or how much time they spend on each of these succeeding pages. If you knew, you would be better able to modify the prominence of your pages to your advantage.

Tip   Traffic Analyzers

Topics covered by one version of the Web Trends (www.webtrends.com) traffic analyzer include the following statistics:

Most requested pages, least requested pages, top entry pages, top exit pages, single access pages, top paths through site, most submitted forms, most active organizations, top authenticated users, most active countries, summary of activity by day, activity level by day of week, activity level by hour, technical statistics, forms submitted by users, client errors, server errors, most downloaded file types, organization breakdown, North American states, most active cities, bandwidth, most accessed directories, top referring sites, top referring URLs, top search engines, top search keywords, most used browsers, Netscape browsers, Microsoft Explorer browsers, visiting spiders, most used platforms, and glossary.

Another source of useful information about site traffic analysis is HitBox at www.hitbox.com. If you are at a smaller firm with a limited budget, you'll be glad to know that one version of the HitBox traffic analyzer is free.

Try it

For each of the fictitious Web site addresses listed that correspond to a restaurant with a similar name, write a "hook" to motivate that site's target audience to visit the site.

Example: For www.foodforthenest.com, a family restaurant, you might write "FoodfortheNest.com Contributes to Fund for Endangered Birds."

1. www.Family-Reunion-Dining.com

2. www.HealthyFoodMenuDiner.com

3. www.hugeburgershack.com

4. www.DungenessCrabHeaven.com

5. www.DetroitGourmetPizza.com

6. www.LaFranceGourmet.com

Summary

In many ways, promotion on the Web is very similar to promotion anywhere. You have to emphasize positioning or branding, along with what you can offer the customer or client that is of value.

Put your firm's phone numbers on everything that you print or publish; do the same for your Web site and e-mail addresses.

Professionals define "public relations" as "good performance, publicly appreciated." Much of getting your firm promoted is common sense. It makes sense to send editors news releases and articles about your firm, especially because this space usually costs so much less than ads purchased in the same media.

Be creative about identifying alternative places to promote your site. Grocery carts, theater screens, on the tailgates of city vehicles, on buses, towed airplane banners, hot air balloons, barges on the river or the lake, banners with smileys cut in them and hung across main street, trucks with billboards on them parked on the street near the entrance to your city's biggest trade show or annual festival—how many more can you add to this list?

Review Questions

1. What is "good performance publicly appreciated"?

2. What does "newsworthy" mean in the context of public relations?

3. Why would a restaurant at or near a golf course want to show 360-degree views of the golf course on its Web site?

4. Which is better remembered—an ad or an editorial item?

5. What is powerful about an article or column (perhaps by a hotel manager or restaurant chef) that describes a problem solved by your service or one of your staff?

6. Why does an audience give you more credibility when they read a favorable article about your firm or its products?

7. Why is it easier to get publicity into local media than into national media?

8. What is meant by a story's "angle" or "hook"?

9. Can newsgroups be time-consuming or do they save you time?

10. Is advertising encouraged in usegroup postings?

11. Name two services that Web site owners can provide to your firm.

12. What should go onto all your business cards, fliers, brochures, e-mails, and newsletters—basically, on everything that your company publishes about itself?

13. Why should you offer specific reasons for your audiences to visit your site?

14. How can adding some humorous or lighthearted content improve many Web sites?

15. What is the value of displaying your URL and a tagline on your firm's vehicles?

16. What does it mean to offer something valuable *to the audience at hand?*

17. Why would you announce a special new addition of Web site content to your audiences?

18. Name two things that you can learn about your Web site visitors from the site's traffic statistics.

PART THREE

Effective E-mail

Effective marketing in today's world means that you must communicate by e-mail—you *must*. Even if you have no Internet presence—no Web site, no listings on Web directories, no pages in a mall—you must be able to communicate via e-mail.

1. Your clients, guests, and patrons, present or future or both, want to communicate with you by e-mail.
2. E-mail is fast. You can ask and answer questions, send marketing information, keep your clients updated continuously. This means that, through a series of messages, you can build rapport with prospects that you could not build using regular mail.
3. E-mail gives you many features that make your communications more effective, including forwarding messages; sending messages to custom lists of your clients and prospective clients; sending webpages, links to webpages, photos, attachments of reports and proposals, and much more.

E-mail tends to be much more conversational than other written communications. Why? Because e-mail users are accustomed to fast responses. When e-mail assumes a conversational style, your readers can ask you questions about your message right away. And they expect your answers right away.

Using a conversational style can lead to some sloppiness, however, which can result in missed opportunities and a poor impression. Opportunities are lost when a writer just doesn't take time to ask "one more question," add "one more point," clean out extraneous and distracting comments to make the message more understandable, more useful to the reader, or provide needed information in the response. If you don't provide good information, the business next door—the one using e-mail—will.

The chapters in Part Three are:

Chapter 9 E-mail Marketing
Chapter 10 E-mail Mechanics
Chapter 11 E-mail Preparation

LEARNING THE LANGUAGE

The following terms are introduced in Part Three. Familiarize yourself with them by reading the definitions provided.

@.   The symbol most often seen in e-mail addresses (johnandjane@earthnet.net); in general, the symbol means "located at."

attachment.   A file attached to an e-mail message. The file could be a photo, text, a Web page, or any other type of file. Caution: Do not send files unless you are certain the recipient can find them, view them, and open them. If your e-mail recipients can browse the Internet, then .jpg and .gif graphics files, html files, and simple text files work fine.

bcc.   Abbreviation for blind carbon copy or blind copy; indicates a copy of an e-mail message sent to recipients without their addresses showing on the message. Think of a blind copy as a "secret" copy.

emoticon.   Term coined for emotion icon; a small icon composed of punctuation and other characters, such as colons and parentheses. Emoticons are used to add information visually about a sentiment or tone of voice. For example, :-) is the usual symbol for a smiley face (look at it sideways). If the colon is changed to a semicolon, ;-), the emoticon is winking, indicating jest, humor, or "just kidding."

folder.   An object in a graphical interface, such as Windows®, that can contain multiple documents or other types of files. Folders are useful for organizing or holding

e-mail messages, graphics, scanned photographs, documents created with a word processing or other application, and so forth.

forward.   To send an incoming e-mail message to another recipient or recipients.

listening back.   The art of replying to an e-mail message only after being certain that you have understood and noted ("listened to") every point that the sender made, and then responding completely, point by point.

MAPI.   acronym for Messaging Application Programming Interface, a built-in Microsoft Windows® system that enables different e-mail applications (MAPI-enabled ones) to send and receive messages.

reply, reply all.   To answer an incoming e-mail message. "Reply" sends the response only to the address of the originating message; "reply all" sends the response to the original writer and to everyone who received a copy (cc) of the original message.

signature.   Generally, a statement and a selection of links or images that are automatically attached to the end of outgoing e-mail messages.

spam.   An Internet term for electronic junk mail or junk newsgroup postings. Unsolicited, advertising-oriented e-mail comprises most "e-junk" today.

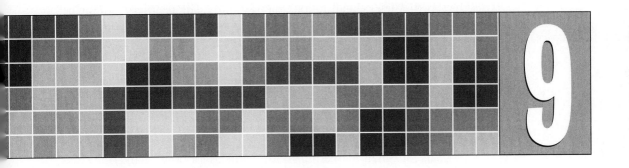

E-mail Marketing

This chapter discusses e-mail marketing to groups. The recipients might be past customers, frequent customers, prospects, or some other identifiable e-mail group. Less desirable, for many reasons, is sending a promotion to a rented or purchased list of e-mail addresses.

Sophisticated merging programs, many of them reasonably priced, now allow *individualized* messages to be sent to thousands of recipients with the same information, promotion, or other material. Marketing by e-mail provides opportunities to place an array of graphics and links before a target audience in an inexpensive way.

The goals for e-mail marketing are the same as for other marketing communications, particularly direct mail—to generate leads, acquire new customers, retain and increase business from existing customers, and revitalize inactive customers. E-mail marketing should be an integral part of a business's overall marketing efforts and, where possible, support and be supported by the firm's other marketing activities.

THE BASICS

E-mail Marketing Goals

The primary goals of e-mail marketing include the following:

- Generate leads and acquire new customers
- Retain existing customers
- Build brand awareness and reinforce positioning
- Increase business from existing customers
- Generate business from inactive customers
- Obtain market research data related to all of the other goals.

Whatever the goal, it must fit into the overall marketing goals for the company, product, or service.

E-mail Marketing Lists

The recipients of e-mail marketing should be identified and grouped or "segmented" just as they are for other types of marketing. The most successful e-mail campaigns are those directed to and designed for specific segments of existing and potential customers or clients. This is why most purchased or rented e-mail address lists are not satisfactory—they are usually not sufficiently focused. Also, marketing recipients change their e-mail addresses easily, so the recency (how recently the list has been updated or corrected) of purchased lists must be an important criterion. That is, older lists have more addresses that do not function or are not accessed. Having said that, some e-mail lists generated from subscriptions to magazines, e-Zines, newsletters, and other sources within a company's area of business may well merit investigation.

Far preferable to rented or purchased lists are lists accumulated from correspondence with customers, product registration cards, order forms (online and off), and e-mail inquiries. A company whose Web site and other communications offer an online subscription to an informative, valuable newsletter or product updates via e-mail has created for itself one of the best opportunities for successful, targeted e-mail marketing. This strategy not only targets certain groups that self-select themselves to receive the e-mails, but also gains the *permission* of the recipients for the e-mailings. Furthermore, this "opt-in" strategy helps firms avoid sending unwanted spam (junk e-mail) to thousands of Internet users who are not interested in what the business has to offer.

E-mail Marketing Content

What should businesses send via their e-mail marketing campaigns? The materials that will help them achieve their overall sales and marketing goals. This differs from industry to industry, company to company, but some of the more common materials include the following:

- Product/service/company announcements and press releases
- Newsletters and infobytes
- Surveys
- Sales/specials
- Web site updates

BEYOND THE BASICS

Goals

Most e-mail marketing goals are related either to acquiring new customers or retaining existing customers. Several studies by large research firms have reported that the dollars spent on e-mail marketing for purposes of retention are as great or greater than dollars spent to acquire new customers. In April 2001, eMarketer reported that spending for retention ranged from 50 to 65.9 percent of all e-mail marketing spending (see Figure 9.1). The primary goals for marketing by e-mail coincide with those for various other marketing communications, particularly direct mail. But the interactive nature of e-mail communications, along with harnessing Web pages and functions, make them different from direct mail and all other media.

E-mail marketing goals and efforts must be part of a business's overall marketing goals and integrated with the company's other marketing work. In this light, the critical goals include:

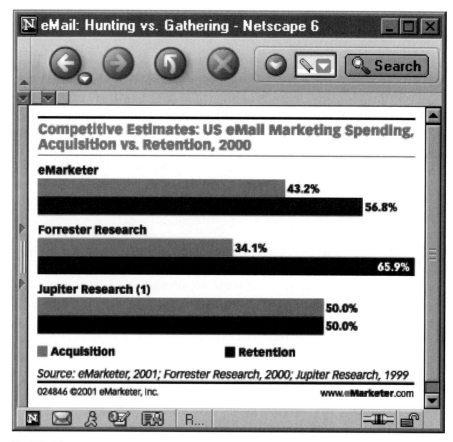

FIGURE 9.1 Comparison of e-mail marketing spending, EMarketer, Inc. 2001. (Screen capture from www.emarketer.com/analysis/images/024846.gif.)

Build brand awareness/recognition

Reinforce positioning

Retain and increase depth in existing customer base (increased sales per customer)

Maintain or build satisfaction and positive interactive relationships with customers

Gather data (market research)

Refine segmentation

Identify prospects (leads)

Increase sales depth in target segment (get new customers)

Specific objectives for an e-mail campaign might include the following:

- Promote new lodging or dining products and send recipients to a Web page that describes these products in detail

- Promote items on sale or free premium items and send people to a Web page about those items (e.g., a greatly reduced room rate at a hotel, available only to those who register online)

- Promote items in a print catalog that recipients received through the U.S. postal service; direct recipients to a Web page order or registration form with their name and address already filled in

Audience

In Chapter 2, you identified your target audience or audiences. Of course, these may vary even within a business according to products or services. For e-mail marketing, the audiences can, and often should be, even more narrowly defined according to the objective of a specific promotion or announcement.

Building E-mail Address Lists

When you know who the audience is, how do you obtain e-mail addresses that will reach them most effectively? The most effective list, the one that will reap the most results, is one that a business assembles for itself from various customer interactions. The following section describes a few of these sources.

Creating Opt-In E-mail Lists

Provide a space for the customer, client, or guest to enter an e-mail address on the following *print* materials:

- Registration cards. Many registration cards do request a customer's e-mail address. This practice is still far more common, however, on registration or warranty cards for software, hardware, peripherals, and other computer-related items. When guests register at a hotel or inn, ask them for their e-mail address. At a restaurant, ask patrons if they'd like to sign up to get new recipes e-mailed to them weekly or monthly.

- Grand-opening or Re-Grand-opening guest books and "free-drawing" forms. Drawings and contests have been used for decades to get contact information. Now that many business cards carry e-mail addresses, drawings that use "drop your business card here" approaches can benefit your firm. Businesses that wish to attract consumers, however, should use forms that specifically ask for e-mail addresses.

- Reception sign-in books. Be sure that the book has a column asking for an e-mail address. Make someone responsible for transferring the new e-mail addresses to the address database on a regular basis.

- Update cards or forms that are printed on physical newsletters.

- Cards for requesting brochures.

- Catalog order forms—and every other order form printed for consumer use—for establishments that sell memorabilia items or products from their onsite shops.

- Customer satisfaction cards for hospitality guests to fill out. If you provide a service, you have a terrific opportunity to gain e-mail addresses of current customers using a short, easy-to-complete satisfaction card. Just put a card in the registration packet, in the rooms, at the tables, by the cash register, or by the exit doors and ask guests to rate your facility on service, selection, cleanliness, or any other factors you'd like feedback on.

- Anything consumers sign and return to you! Rain checks, special orders, catering orders, cake decoration orders, and so forth.

Create many opportunities for visitors to your Web site to give you their e-mail address. Here are a few possibilities:

- Sign-up forms for anything you wish to offer as a free download, product sample, or access to a database

- All online order forms

- Surveys, polls, and daily quizzes

- Memberships to user groups or Web site functions

- Sign-up forms for (daily, weekly, monthly, occasional) tips, newsletters, cartoons, quotations

- Web site guestbook

- Bulletin board

Be sure to *store* the e-mail address of every e-mail sender who writes you.

Gathering e-mail addresses is more effective—more addresses and a higher proportion of correct, current addresses—if you offer some incentive, such as "to receive occasional discount (new product, upgrade) announcements by e-mail, please provide your current e-mail address."

As much as possible, try to make the e-mail addresses you gather fit clear "opt-in" criteria. This means that you give users the choice of receiving information from you or allow them to choose which types of information they are willing to receive by e-mail (e.g., product updates, new product announcements, industry updates, user newsletters). When you have this information and abide by the users' choices, you are marketing to them with their permission.

Permission Marketing

Mass e-mail campaigns that send messages to thousands upon thousands of addresses—"spam" or junk e-mail or our own term, "e-junk"—inevitably provokes hostility. Spam is considered by the vast majority of e-mail users to be an invasion of privacy—worse even than the junk mail that arrives in the physical mailbox because it is so ubiquitous and because it lands in the users' computers in their offices, dens, or family rooms. Marketing by e-mail should be done with permission only.

Does this mean that all e-mail addresses must come from direct contact with the customer, client, or prospect as described earlier? No, but if you rent or purchase a list, try to ensure that it is a highly targeted list, preferably comprised of addresses obtained with permission for mailings. PostMasterDirect (see Figure 9.2) has a database of more than 40 million opt-in e-mail addresses.

If you use a rented or purchased list, give recipients various clear ways to remove themselves from your list ("opt-out"), either by replying to the e-mail with the word "remove" or by providing a link to a page where the user may click on an option to be removed. One reason the latter strategy might be preferable is that many e-mail marketers use the "reply to remove" strategy just to confirm that an e-mail has reached a live person and is active. Rather than removing the person, they send more e-junk. E-mail users have begun to understand this concept and tend to delete the message rather than reply. This will not help you maintain a solid opt-in list. Worse, you may continue to send unwanted e-mails to recipients whose irritation with you will

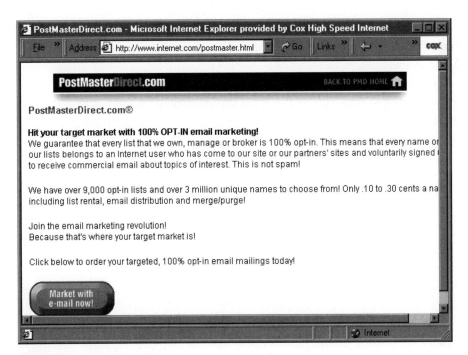

FIGURE 9.2　PostMasterDirect. (Screen capture from www.internet.com/postmaster.html.)

continue to grow. Second, by asking the recipients to go to a Web page, you can give them other choices. This way you not only improve your list, you begin to create qualified or segmented lists for specific purposes.

Publish Your Information Policy

Concerning information policies, Regina Brady, vice president of Strategy and Partnerships, FloNetwork Inc.,[*] says,

> One of the most important steps that a marketer can take to ensure that its e-mail campaigns are implemented responsibly—and thus respect the privacy of Internet users—is to publish an online notice of information practices that is easy to find, read and understand. This notice should cover:
>
> 1. the nature of the personal information that is collected with respect to individual consumers;
> 2. the manner in which such information is collected;
> 3. the nature and purposes of disclosures and the types of persons to whom disclosures may be made; and
> 4. the mechanism by which the individual may limit the disclosure of such information, should they desire to do so.
>
> This careful attention to online etiquette magnifies the power of the medium. Similarly, tapping all of its potential—from its capacity for dynamic, personalized creative to its ability to support instantaneous, detailed response analysis—unleashes that power and focuses it on the market. Indeed, when designed and executed as a comprehensive, integrated strategy, e-mail delivers unprecedented advantages to the marketer. As a consequence, it is now the most exciting and powerful new capability in the direct marketing field."

[*] Strategy and Partnerships, FloNetwork Inc. (http://www.floNetwork.com) manages permission-based direct marketing.
Source: www.thinkdirectmarketing.com/dmlibrary/tutorials/e-mail_market2.html.

Double Opt-in Permission

In most cases, people opt-in for e-mail by registering themselves for some offer (e.g., membership, newsletter, certain types of e-mails, reports) by clicking or un-clicking a box on a Web site or checking a box on a printed form. When opt-in clients or prospects confirm by e-mail or on a Web page that they did, indeed, opt-in, they become "double opt-in" recipients. You know these people want your messages.

TIP   **The Permission Rule**

Never send unsolicited e-mail messages. Always get the permission of a recipient before e-mailing anything.
There is nothing more to know about this rule.

Why bother with *double* opt-in? Many serious marketers (not, however, spammers—they *still* spam) are shifting to double opt-in as their standard. They make sure they can prove that they have users' permission and are complying with their wishes.

Double opt-in provides better protection for your reputation by helping you avoid the possibility of being identified as a spammer. Furthermore, double opt-in procedures can protect you if, under new consumer protection laws regarding spam, recipients claim you sent e-mail to them without their permission. Legal issues remain to be untangled in the courts—but if you want to be on the safe side, opt for the double opt-in.

Refining the Lists: Track E-mail Visitors

Using database technology, you can gather and archive key marketing and behavioral information about every opt-in message recipient. You can tell which customers made reservations online, which ones wanted more information about your hospitality services, which ones wanted to make reservations by telephone, and which made no response at all. For this latter group, you know right away that you need to do something else for them next time.

Once you know all of this, future e-mailings can be tailored for each customer, carrying exactly the kind of message they've historically acted favorably upon and in exactly the format they like best. This process lets you know who your best customers are and lets you send them "hand-tailored" offers.

Try it

1. List eight offline potential sources that your hospitality location could use to gather e-mail addresses for its mail list.
2. List three ways your business could use its Web site to gather e-mail addresses for its mail list.

What to Send

E-mail marketing campaigns must send material that interests the target audience, has value for the recipient, and builds or builds on the positioning of the company, product, or service. The campaigns should be planned to help achieve the overall sales and marketing goals. Random messages sent "shotgun" to a general audience seldom bring the intended results.

Individual messages vary significantly from one product or service to the next. Nonetheless, the most common types of messages include product, service, or company announcements and press releases; short tips or daily (or other periodic) messages; newsletters; surveys; sale and special offers; and Web site updates.

Types of Content

Product, service, and company announcements and press releases.
Announcements of new services or amenities, a new menu or menu item, weekend or holiday special discounts, one-time coupon offerings, and other offers are good candidates for e-mail to your prospective and current customers.

Highlight the features and benefits of whatever you announce that will be most important to each audience. The opening of a new service, such as a special lobster thermador menu item, or perhaps a new culinary or memorabilia product—in case you have a gift shop—also merits its own message, especially if you can target the list to the local area.

Press releases concerning the company's charitable activity, remodeling, new leadership, or recent awards can be of interest to some audiences, especially investors and employees (see Chapter 8 for more on this topic).

Short tips or daily messages with the quotation, puzzle, cartoon, clipart, or other item "of the day."
What would your guests or patrons find interesting? Do tourists routinely take pictures in or of your lobby? Send tips for photography. Do you cater to children? Send parenting tips. Do you sell seafood? Send recipes. Do you have one or more hotels on the seashore? Send out fascinating "oceanography" or "marine biology" newsletters. Then, for each newsletter, create individual pages on your site containing links to more information on that particular newsletter's topic.

Newsletters.
In general, items and subjects that you discuss or offer in your newsletters have more impact than ads you run anywhere on the Internet. Banner ads have terrible click-through rates, but the same banner ad in a newsletter can generate many times the activity. Why? Because the recipients *chose* to receive the newsletter. This self-selection means the recipient's interest level and responsiveness is much greater than that of the general Web-surfing public.

Expect newsletters that talk too much about the company or product and too little about the recipients and their needs and priorities to be ineffective. One key to a successful newsletter is the frequent use of the word "you." Relate as much newsletter content as possible to the reader. Rather than discussing in detail how your brilliant chef's room service kitchen staff created such a terrific Baked Alaska dessert, talk more about how it tastes and smells and looks and tickles the palate and goes down smoothly and how you can get it 24/7 in your room.

Having said that, what topics might work? Besides food product, guest services, and company "news," include laudatory letters from customers, reviews of and links to articles of interest to your readers, calendar notes, some how-to hints, a contest or challenge or puzzle. Pack it with links to pertinent pages on your Web site.

Newsletters may be more effective when they come from an individual rather than a company. Consider having each newsletter be from your manager or president, concierge or chef. In the case of newsletters to past patrons, send the newsletter from the owner of a restaurant or the manager of a hotel or casino and show his or her photo at the start and signature at the end.

Keep e-mail newsletters short—put the details on the Web site. Users who see a long, involved message in their inbox may be all too tempted to hit the delete button.

Surveys and polls.   Many people *like* to respond to surveys or polls. Surveys by e-mail can also engage your target audience. The message could contain the questions and ask the recipient to reply by e-mail or by clicking on a link in the e-mail message itself. This works best if there is only one question. Respondents can give as much or as little information as they wish, so give them some guidance. Tell them to rate something on a scale of 1 to 5, select their favorite something from a list, or answer a more complex question in their own words.

Alternatively, the message could contain a direct link to a survey located on your Web site. This way, users can click in circles or boxes, answer multiple-choice questions, or write some statements of opinion. With either approach, you stand to gain valuable information about your target audience's opinions, needs, and even demographic characteristics. What do they gain? Usually two things: the satisfaction of making their opinion known or helping you understand their needs and statistical information about the other respondents' replies. For example, show all participants the percentage who answered "yes" or "no." If you *promise* to show them this figure only *after* they participate in the poll, it becomes an incentive for many people and can increase audience participation.

Sales and specials.   E-mail "specials" or "Web promotions" can be started and stopped within days—virtually no printing is required. Alert your target audiences to any special or seasonal sales or discounts or other "surprise" promotions. "Two-for-ones," "20 percent off," "children dine free," "second senior over 60 dines free," "buy three nights and get the next one free," and other promotional schemes work just as well or better in cyberspace as in regular space. In fact, "Online Only Specials" work extremely well. Also, mention coupons to print out and take to your facility; any unit in your hotel, restaurant, or casino chain; or to a retailer who may be partnering with you in a promotion.

The marketing opportunity that is most often missed in hospitality e-mail marketing (as well as in other hospitality marketing) is promotions to the local or community market. Such promotions can either be initiated by e-mails sent to an opt-in list or in response to e-mails that you get from being prominent on state, county, and city Web sites where the hospitality industry is now gaining presence.

In regional, or even individual unit promotions, include a coupon that recipients can print out and use at your establishment for a given period of time. Encourage the recipient to forward the valuable coupons to friends and family. The forwarding and re-forwarding process is a technique called "viral" marketing.

Web site updates.   Some Internet users want to know when a particular Web site is changed or updated. They may use an automated service that tells them this information for various sites of interest. Better for the owner of the Web site, however, is the offer to let visitors elect to be updated whenever a change is made on a favorite site. This way you add a user to your mail list and you have an opportunity to build the relationship with that user each time the Web site is updated. What types of updates might be appropriate? Announce the addition of a new Web function, such as a calculator, puzzle, or search function. Send information about the addition of a major travel or dining out "hints section," recipe section, a new discounted local tour obtainable only through your facility.

Autoresponders.   Autoresponders send previously prepared e-mail messages in response to a user's request from a Web site or an e-mail to a particular address. Many companies routinely use an autoresponder to tell e-mail writers they have received an inquiry and will reply with the needed information within a short period of time. If you use this approach, be sure you do get back to the sender within the promised time. Many offices use autoresponders to let people know that they are out of town—at a seminar learning new ways to serve you—and if you need assistance before they return, you are directed to call or e-mail a colleague.

Another use of autoresponders is to send reports or data that have been requested from a Web site. Why not just post the reports on the Web site itself? One reason is that sending them by autoresponder puts your name and e-mail address right into the inbox of the requester. This way, even after they have left your site to pursue other interests, they'll still have your valuable information, e-mail address, and links back to your site waiting for them. Another reason is that you have collected an accurate, active e-mail address, which you can use later to invite the requester to join your opt-in mail list for updates and other material.

Make Each E-mail Count

Various proven ways can make e-mail marketing perform more effectively. Here are key ones cited for us by Regina Brady (www.ftc.gov/acoas/nominations/ bradybio.htm), a leading authority on Internet direct marketing and vice president of Strategy and Partnerships, FloNetwork Inc. (www.floNetwork. com), which manages permission-based direct marketing. The following is from "E-Mail: The Future is Here for Interactive Marketing" (www.thinkdirect marketing.com/dmlibrary/tutorials/e-mail_market2.html). About using e-mail, Brady notes the following:

- Link e-mail with other Web content. Embed hot links (another term for a hypertext link that one can click on to go to another place on the Web) in the message, which will make it easy for the reader to visit its Web site or, even better, the area of the Web site, which provides additional information about the specific offer to which the reader responded.
- Keep its initial mailings short (1 to 2 screens) because people are reading these messages on a computer screen, and the dynamics are different from those of a traditional direct mail letter.
- Employ the one-to-one marketing functionality of the medium to establish real two-way communication with customers.
- Measure the performance of each call to action or link in its mailing so that it knows what works and what doesn't and archives that knowledge in its database for future use.
- Embed multiple calls to action in the e-mail message, offering each recipient several choices or hotlinks based on their specific need or interest. E-mail is not a passive medium; by including a number of exciting offers and live samples, the marketer will encourage the customer to interact with the message, and that involvement, in turn, both increases the probability of a sale and generates valuable new information which can then be appended back to the marketer's database for future use.

Try it

Your boss asks you to design an e-mail campaign that uses daily travel tips, free recipes, how to pack luggage, travel cartoons, or other items that would be appropriate for your patrons. The campaign will send out three messages, two weeks apart. What would you send and why?

The Sending Process: E-mail Merge Programs

As we have grown to expect with Internet developments, e-mail merge programs are far more sophisticated than they were even a few years ago. Today, you can use standalone programs, enhancements to word processing or database products, Web-based e-mail marketing tools, or full-service companies that handle it all for you. Among the current products that support e-mail marketing is E-mail Merge® for the Macintosh, a program for merging database information into messages to create "individualized" messages (see www.sigsoftware.com/e-mailmerge). Word Merge Pro®, also for the Mac, allows you to perform merges that are similar to the built-in mail merge feature of Microsoft Word® without an intermediate export/import stage (see www.wordmergepro.com). For the PDA/Newton, there's Merge®, a mail merge tool for the Works® application (see www.standalone.com). Search www.zdnet.com or www.tucows.com or other software-review Web sites for more.

Advanced Access (www.advancedaccess.com) uses a Web-based e-mail merge program that allows for embedded images, time-specific repeated e-mailings, and other features (see Figure 9.3). The program automatically sends out your preselected campaigns—campaigns that you design and write using "Intellic@rd" tools or campaigns that Advanced Access has created. The program includes online list management, allowing campaigns to specific groups of clients or customers. Find other Web-based e-mail merge programs by searching for "Web-based e-mail merge programs."

The following is a list of some functions that Jumpstart by Responsys (www.responsys.com) offers:

- Lets your customers and prospects register directly on your Web site
- Automatically sends great looking, personalized announcements, promotional offers, and interest-based newsletters
- Manages your target audience, "good customer," and prospect lists
- Grows your customer relationships with every interaction
- Manages your customers' permission preferences, protecting you from sending unsolicited communications or spam
- Tracks your e-mail marketing success with real-time results reporting

If someone fills in your Web site sign-up form, Jumpstart automatically sends them a follow-up confirmation e-mail. Once the recipient clicks on the confirm link, their opt-in status in your contact list changes to "In" and they can be included in other outbound campaigns. Larger firms with huge e-mail volumes may, however, exceed the capabilities of Jumpstart.

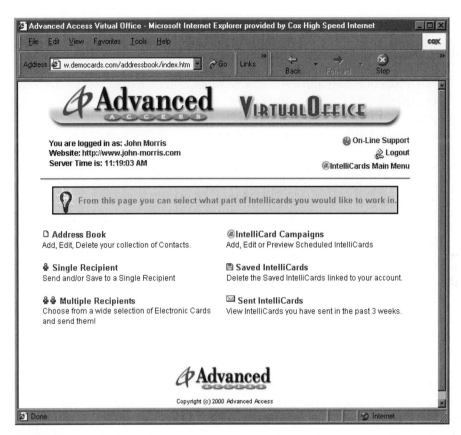

FIGURE 9.3   Intellic@rds. (Screen capture from www.democards.com/addressbook/index. htm.) Copyright © 2000 Advanced Access.

Jumpstart is described as follows (www.responsys.com/interact/demo/ front_page.asp): "Responsys Interact® is a secure, web-hosted application that enables businesses to create, launch and manage permission-based marketing on the Internet. Open architecture, a one-click response option, and unique advanced message personalization capabilities make Responsys Interact the platform of choice for permission marketing on the Internet."

Try it

What would you want an e-mail marketing program to do for your hospitality business? Make a list of the tasks it should perform.

Summary

E-mail marketing should be tailored for specific audience(s) and goals. Although lists of e-mail addresses can be purchased or rented from magazines and other sources, more effective lists are those developed by a business through its customer correspondence, opt-in newsletters and updates, guest book registrations, and so on.

Avoid using spam techniques to reach millions of recipients who may have no interest in your facility or services. Although it may bring short-term sales, it ultimately has huge potential for alienating many people and reflecting poorly on your operation.

Review Questions

1. Name three goals of e-mail marketing.
2. Why should e-mail marketing be directed toward specific groups of customers or potential customers?
3. What is meant by the recency of a list?
4. Name four sources of e-mail addresses that are preferable to buying or renting one from a print magazine subscription list.
5. Why is an opt-in newsletter or product update service offered on a company's Web site a good source of e-mail addresses?
6. Name three types of content that a business might use in e-mail marketing.
7. What is "double opt-in" permission?
8. What is "The Permission Rule"?
9. List three types of information you might wish to store in a database about your opt-in e-mail recipients.
10. What does an autoresponder do?

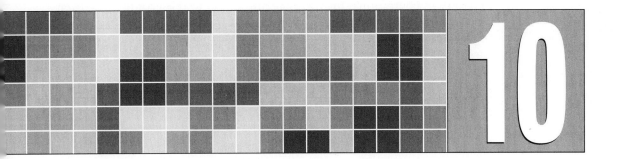

E-mail Mechanics

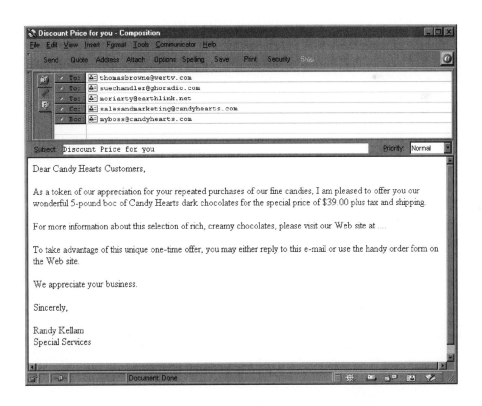

The steps in communicating by e-mail are similar to those for other written communications: addressing it, writing it, and sending it. Likewise, e-mail users can do virtually the same things with e-mail messages they receive as they can with paper letters, memos, reports, and other documents that are delivered to them—read them, discard them, answer them, forward them to someone else, and file them. They can also print them or quote them in other messages.

This chapter covers the basic mechanics of using e-mail. It also addresses a few mechanical issues that are specific to e-mail: links, attachments, and electronic formats. (*If you are experienced with sending basic e-mail messages, you may want to skip to "Beyond the Basics."*)

THE BASICS

E-mail Programs

The e-mail programs used most in the United States include various versions of Qualcomm's *Eudora*®, Netscape's *Communicator*®, Microsoft's *Outlook*® and *Outlook Express*®, and AOL® mail. Many large companies, schools, government offices, and other organizations use their own proprietary programs for their intranet (within the company) and Internet communications.

In addition to these, many Web-based free e-mail programs are available on the Internet, such as those offered by Yahoo!, Hotmail, and others. Users can access their password-protected Web-based e-mail from any computer with an Internet connection and browser. Because Web-based e-mail uses the host's interface, you do not need a separate e-mail application program. This flexible "anywhere, anytime" access, Web-based e-mail also reduces the risk of getting e-mail viruses because moving the messages and any attachments onto your own computer's hard drive involves extra steps.

The four greatest disadvantages to Web-based e-mail are:

1. It can be slow and tedious to use.
2. Some of the applications either do not allow or limit sending attachments and lack other advanced functions.
3. It often carries advertising added by the sponsoring Web site.
4. It conveys a certain implication of thriftiness or even a lack of financial resources because most Web-based e-mail is free.

In short, it is not suitable for business e-mail.

The primary "mechanics" of creating an e-mail message are to open the "New Message" window of your e-mail program, fill in the e-mail address(es) of the person(s) you are writing and a line indicating the subject of the message, and then enter the message text.

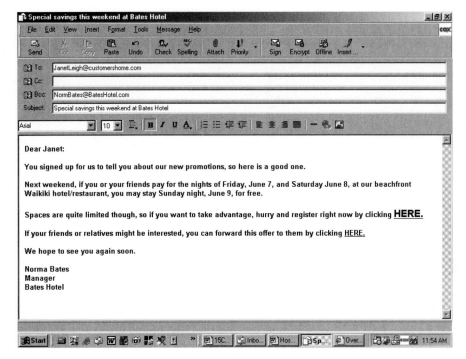

FIGURE 10.1   Outgoing message from Norma to Janet.

Figure 10.1 shows a message that hotel manager Norma Bates is going to send. She has addressed it to JanetLeigh@customershome.com by typing in that e-mail address in the field next to the word "To." She identifies the topic of the message as "Special savings this weekend at Bates Hotel" by typing that text in the field next to the word "Subject." She also sends a blind carbon copy (BCC) to herself to ensure that the e-mail program is working properly.

She types her message in the body of the e-mail. Next, she clicks on the "Send" button to send the message on its way. Note that the recipient was reminded at the very beginning of the message that it was *she* who signed up to get this kind of e-mail from the hotel. Note, too, that the "offer" itself is written in a most explicit manner to avoid confusion.

The recipient is told to click "Here" (a link) in order to go to a Web page and register, which is wise of Norma Bates to do because she very much wants good customers to return to her hotel's Web site. "Viral" marketing aspects come into play when Janet is advised to forward the message to her friends by clicking another link, which will take her to a Web page where she can enter dozens of friends' e-mail addresses if she likes.

Figure 10.2 shows the message that George Manfors, in Customer Service at Smith Stores (the owner of the Market Plaza store inside the Bates Hotel), received from Sharon. In the top left section of George's e-mail screen

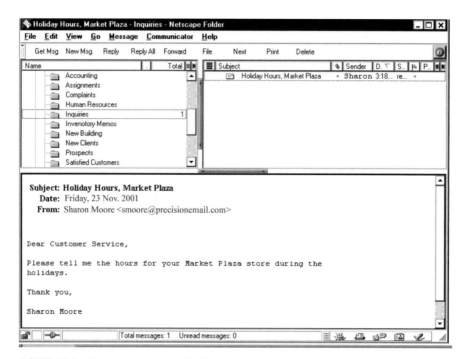

FIGURE 10.2   Sharon's message in George's inbox.

is a list of folders that George has created for storing his messages. On the top right section of George's e-mail screen is a list of messages George has placed in the folder he has open. In the bottom portion of the screen is Sharon's message. Now that George has received Sharon's message, he has several choices. Most of the choices are shown on the buttons just above the list of files and list of messages. These include "Reply," "Reply All," "Forward," "File," "Print," and "Delete." George decides that he will forward Sharon's message to Eddie, and ask him to confirm the information. When he gets the final information, he will reply to Sharon.

Figure 10.3 shows George's message to Eddie. When George clicked on "Forward," several things happened: the screen for creating a message opened; the subject line was automatically included, along with the abbreviation "Fwd" to indicate that the message with that subject was being forwarded; and Sharon's message was automatically included in the message body to be sent to Eddie.

George typed Eddie's e-mail address in the "To" field. Then, he placed his cursor in the body of the message and typed his question to Eddie. George could have just written a new message to Eddie without forwarding Sharon's message, but in this case, he decided that he wanted Eddie to see why he was asking the question.

After Eddie confirmed the hours for George, George went back to Sharon's original message and clicked on the "Reply" button. This time,

FIGURE 10.3 George's outgoing message to Eddie.

Sharon's e-mail address was automatically entered in the "To" field. The subject line was automatically included, along with the abbreviation "Re" to indicate that this was a reply to Sharon's message with that subject. All George had to do was type his message to Sharon in the message body and send it.

George could have quoted Sharon's original message in the body of the message. To do this, he would have clicked on the button that says "Quote," and Sharon's message would have appeared in the message body. This is often useful for short messages. It is also useful for busy business representatives who are helping a client solve a problem that may require a string of several messages—the string of quoted messages helps to ensure that the representative is reminded of earlier questions and comments.

Most e-mail programs allow users to set up their application so that the original message is always quoted. Generally, we do not recommend this option. We prefer having the choice. It's easier to click on a "Quote" button (if available in your application) when you want a message to show, or to copy and paste a sentence or two that you want to quote, than it is to highlight and delete long messages that you don't want to take up space in the e-mail.

One of the choices that did not apply to George's messages is "Reply All." If a message has been sent to two or more addressees, the recipients may reply only to the original sender ("Reply") or to the original sender plus everyone who received the message (Reply All).

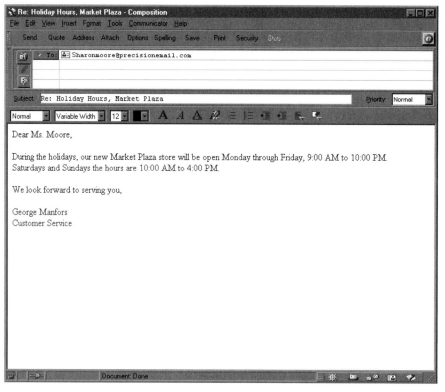

FIGURE 10.4   George's outgoing reply to Sharon.

The following is an example that uses a few more of the options available to e-mail senders. In Figure 10.5, we see a message in which Randy Kellam has sent a special offer to three customers. The e-mail addresses are shown in the fields next to the "To" buttons. He also sent a copy to the Sales and Marketing Department of Candy Hearts, perhaps so they would know about the special offer in case one of the customers should contact them. The e-mail address of the Sales and Marketing Department is shown in the field next to the "Cc" button. Finally, Randy sent a copy to his boss—a blind copy. The boss's e-mail address is shown next to the "Bcc" button. This means that the other recipients of the message—the direct recipients and anyone receiving a Cc copy—cannot see that the message went to Randy's boss. Only Randy and his boss know that he sent the boss a copy.

Try it

As a self-check, describe what each of the following e-mail options does: Send, Reply, Reply All, Forward, To, Cc, Bcc, Subject.

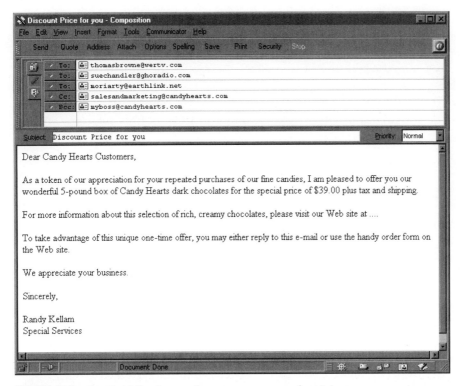

FIGURE 10.5   Randy Kellam's e-mail message to several recipients.

BEYOND THE BASICS

Today's e-mail message applications have much greater capability than they did just a few years ago. At the outset, all e-mail was plain text—just letters and numbers that always appeared in the same typeface. The advantage was that plain text messages do not take up much space. They travel through cyberspace quickly and load quickly into the recipient's e-mail program. Many messages today still use the plain text format, but increasingly, users select formatting options that use specific font characteristics and incorporate links and images. These options use "html" formatting, the same html discussed regarding Web pages in Chapter 2.

Why are e-mails formatted in html preferable to plain text for a marketer? Because html e-mail can generate more responses or interactions than plain text e-mail by as much as 60 percent (see www.travelocity.com). Just as with magazine, newspaper, or television advertising, or brochures and flyers, people pay more attention to things that look interesting and are easy to absorb.

Compare the two e-mail messages shown in Figures 10.6 and 10.7. The formatted text in Figure 10.7 makes important points stand out, and the graphics help the recipients see immediately what the sender is describing.

We are pleased to announce the availability of our ALL YOU CAN EAT Wednesday Lobster Night! ($20) Never again will you hunger on Wednesdays for Maine Lobster. Why? Because we bring you three-pound-plus lobsters just for starters. And as a special introductory offer, the coupon shown below may be redeemed for one free kiddie serving ($14) when you and one other person each buy an ALL YOU CAN EAT lobster dinner.

Eat lobster this Wednesday! You'll be glad you did.

COUPON   COUPON   COUPON   COUPON   COUPON   COUPON

Redeem this special COUPON today.
Buy two, get one kiddie lobster dinner free.
Phoenix Lobster House.

Coupon registration number 1232456789

And don't forget to visit our website at www.PhoenixLobsterHouse.com for more menu offerings, including our awesome SUPERSTEAK Sundays!

FIGURE 10.6   E-mail message Example 1.

Furthermore, the active links allow a user to click straight to the sender's Web site for more information and online ordering.

Sending Links, Attachments, and Web Pages

E-mail offers several options for sending information in addition to a message's text. The most popular options are to put links in the message that connect to webpages with more information, and to insert photos or attach photos and other files for the recipient to download and open.

Analyze it

Examine the following e-mail message. List five ways to enhance the message by using html formatting.

Relieve the stress of today's fast-paced living! Take a moment for just one cup of our delicious soothing herb tea and the cares and tensions of the day will float away. Sip our Oh-So-Soothing Herb Tea, made with delicate chamomile flowers, and let your mind slip off to a peaceful meadow or sun-warmed hillside. You'll find Oh-So-Soothing Herb Teas served exclusively at our Oh-So Coffee Shop or order direct from our Web site.

We are pleased to announce the availability of our new Lobster Feed. . .

ALL YOU CAN EAT LOBSTER on WEDNESDAYS

Never again will you hunger on Wednesdays for Maine Lobster. Why? Because we bring you three–pound-plus lobsters just for starters. As a special introductory offer, the coupon shown below may be redeemed for one free kiddie lobster dinner ($14) when you and one other person each buy an ALL YOU CAN EAT lobster dinner ($20). Eat lobster this Wednesday! You'll be glad you did.

Eat Many Lobsters on Wednesdays! You'll be glad you did!

COUPON   COUPON   COUPON   COUPON   COUPON   COUPON   COUPON

Redeem this special **COUPON** today.

Buy Two Lobster Dinners, Get One Kiddie Dinner Free

See tons more menu choices at our Web site.
Just click on our name:

PHOENIX LOBSTER HOUSE

Coupon registration number 1232456789

FIGURE 10.7 E-mail Message Example 2, with images and formatting. (Screen capture from www.gse.harvard.edu/~nap/gallery/pics/lobster.jpg.)

Messages with Links

Sending links to more information on the Web is very easy and can save a great deal of time—for you and for the recipient. To send a link, just type the entire URL (e.g., www.koelzer.com/marketingtips.htm) into the body of the e-mail. A few older e-mail program versions will not read these as active, clickable links, but most will.

If your team or company has posted detailed product information or the specifics of a special offer, for example, your e-mail message can be brief (e.g., "To See Our Menu, Click <u>HERE</u>"). The recipient can click on the link to access the additional information. Another useful way to serve a customer or prospect is to send helpful, relevant links. Doing this shows that you know something about this person's industry or interests and that you want to be helpful.

Let's say that you have a group of regular guests of your hotel who are interested in converting an old bank building into a restaurant. Some things you could send might include:

- Links to sites containing general information on the pros and cons of using certain types of furniture in certain types of fast-food restaurants
- Links to sites with articles describing state-of-the-art thinking on how to configure restaurant cooking areas for maximum efficiency
- Links to information on the latest cleaning and maintenance techniques for back-bar areas, cooking modules, refrigerators, floors, and walls
- Links that lead to the sites of manufacturers of products that your food distributors nearby carry

---

TIP   **E-mail by Voice**

Can't keyboard (type) well and don't want to learn? Voice-based alternatives are becoming increasingly bug-free, although some still require fairly new and fast computer equipment. See www.dragonsys.com/ for an example. The manufacturers of Dragon's NaturallySpeaking® programs provide ways to "speech enable" many computer tasks.

Voice e-mail is already available on the Web. For information about one such program, go to www.rockettalk.com.

Eudora® products from Qualcomm have integrated voice e-mail right into the regular e-mail program, so Eudora® users have the choice of using character or voice to create messages (see www.eudora.com/).

Attachments

Sending photos, images of charts or graphs, documents, spreadsheets, or other files by attaching them to an e-mail message saves time and delivers critical information quickly. Exercise some caution, however, because some e-mail services will not accept or process attachments. Others allow the user to download the attachment, but inexperienced recipients may not know where to find the material that was downloaded or how to view it. Ask recipients if their program can handle your attachments easily—this helps to avoid frustration and bad feelings.

Avoid attaching large files that significantly increase the time your contact spends downloading the message. How can you be sure you are not sending an attachment that is too large? One way is to send it to yourself first to see how long it takes to retrieve it. (Yes, despite the fact that many people do not know it, you *can* send e-mail messages to yourself.) But remember that the recipient's computer, modem, or connection might not be as fast as yours.

To send an attachment, open a message composition window or click on reply or forward from an existing message. Click on the button that says "Attach" or that has a graphic of a paper clip on it. This opens a directory window on your computer from which you may select the file you wish to attach. Of course, this means you must know what you named the file and where you stored it. Click on the file once to select it and then click on the button that says "Open" or "Attach this file." Note that clicking on the "Open" button will not actually open the file. It will just attach it to the e-mail. You may attach several files to one e-mail, but if you attach too many or files that are too large, the recipient's e-mail service (or yours) might refuse to process the message.

The key to sending attachments is *compatibility between the type of file that is sent and the programs available on the recipient's computer.* If an employee spends two hours creating a handsome report in a format that the recipient cannot open, then valuable time and opportunity have been lost. If you enhance a terrific photograph and save it in a format that the recipient cannot see, you may have wasted your efforts.

Almost all users can see images that are .jpg or .gif files, and these files are compatible with Internet browsers. If you are sending another type of image file, be sure the recipient has a program that will allow it to be displayed.

Similarly, if you wish to send a Microsoft Excel® file, be sure to determine before sending it that the recipient has the Microsoft Excel® program. If not, all is not lost—most spreadsheet programs allow users to export the information to another file format, one that the recipient can open.

Sometimes, a user can open a document, but if his or her computer does not have fonts to match the ones used in the original document, the result can be a document with poor line breaks, poor page breaks, misaligned images, and other visual problems. One solution that the programming whizzes have devised is the use of ".pdf" files. PDF stands for "portable document format," and the program that reads them is Adobe's Acrobat®. Anyone, regardless of the type of computer platform—Mac, PC, UNIX—can download and install the Acrobat® Reader® program for free from www.acrobat.com or www.adobe.com/products/acrobat/main.html. The free program is the *Reader®*. You must purchase the full program (or another Adobe product that includes it) if you want to *create* PDF files. The full Acrobat® program will convert many types of documents complete with images, tables, and so on to PDF files. In most cases, the fonts are embedded inside the PDF file so that when the file opens, the document looks the way its maker intended it to look.

Sending a Web Page by E-mail

This function is probably most useful for small businesses or individual professionals. If you are using a Netscape Navigator® browser (3.0 or newer), try the File/SendPage or File/MailPage function. Sometimes, the choice will be File/SendFrame, depending on the type of site you are visiting.

In Microsoft's Internet Explorer®, the function is "Send Page." What's so great about this function? You can send an entire Web page, graphics included, right from your browser. If you find a particular Web page of interest to one of your customers or prospective customers, just click on "File" and then on "Send Page." Your e-mail program will open and you can enter the person's e-mail address and a note, and then send the page. Or, a similar function, using the following succession—File, Send, then choose "Link by E-mail" or "Send Link"—sends only a link in the e-mail message to direct the recipient to the site you found. You can even add a note above or below the link to explain what it is and why you have sent it.

When you send a page, however, you typically have to enter your message above the top of the captured webpage. If the page has a black background, you may have to change the color of your type face from black to white in order for your message to be seen.

Let's say you are surfing the Web to find new and interesting sites and to stay abreast of what's new on the Internet. You find a railroad history site that looks interesting and remember that, Susan, the travel agent who sends you hotel guests, is a railroad history buff. So, you send her a message about it. When Susan opens her e-mail, there's the railroad history page, or a link to it, waiting for her. She won't even have to type in the site address—another way you can show that you are listening.

Categorizing and Filing E-mail

Where do you file e-mail messages from visitors to your site or from people who have found you by virtue of other marketing? Where do you store your replies? In folders and subfolders that your e-mail software lets you create,

---

Try it

You work for an older hotel that has just upgraded its services to cater to the elderly and individuals with a disability. You've just installed new rails, handles, and ramps throughout the entire complex. Name three types of Web sites that might be useful to the company's customers that you could include (as links) in an informative e-mail to them, encouraging them to come see how easy it is now to get around in your place.

---

and where you can find them later. (Don't get carried away with levels of folders. A good guideline is to create no more than three levels.)

To create a folder in most e-mail programs, open the program's File menu, select "New Folder" from the drop-down menu, then give the folder a name. To create subfolders, go to the folder you want the subfolders to belong to, right click on it and select "New Folder" from the pop-up menu. When the blank box appears, type in the name of the subfolder. Hit the Enter key or click on "OK," and the folder is created for that customer.

Businesses that have proprietary e-mail programs or that have large sales or customer service departments may have already structured the files for team members to use. The organization depends to a certain degree on the type of business and the job of the individual in the company. For example, a sales team responsible for e-mail inquiries about a number of different hotel, restaurant, or casino locations might set up an e-mail filing system that organizes the messages according to the cities being discussed. A marketing team that handles responses to promotions might set up folders by promotion name or date. A very small business or an individual professional might set up folders by clients, prospective patrons, or past customers. Yet another way to categorize e-mail is according to certain characteristics of the senders—low-, medium-, or high-frequency customers, for example. The advantage to the latter classification is that the information is ready to apply to a new promotion, an e-mail announcement enticing low-frequency users to join a rewards program, for example.

To file a message, just drag it from the inbox to the target category.

Figure 10.8 shows an example of subfolders in an Outlook Express® folder called "Clients." From the list of messages, you can see the importance of using a very specific "Subject" on your e-mail messages—a subject that adequately describes the content of the message.

Try it

Make a list of folders and subfolders that make sense for your business and your e-mail communications.

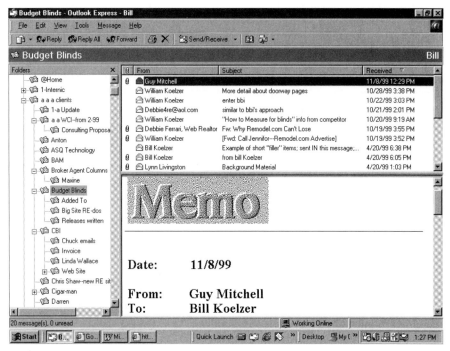

FIGURE 10.8   Bill's inbox.

E-mail Etiquette

The following is a list of guidelines for e-mail communications.

1. Always remember that there's a person on the receiving end of your messages, not just a computer. Write e-mail accordingly.

2. Be sure to put your name, office, phone/fax number, e-mail address, and Web site URL at the end of each message. Many e-mail programs have an automated "signature" to do this for you. Why? It's a good business communication style, and your name won't show on the "from" line unless your program is specifically set up to do that. Don't risk having your reader wonder who sent the message!

Signatures are also used to add links that might be useful to the type of recipient who might do business with your firm. For example, you can add links leading to the most current statistics on your industry.

3. Always enter a topic in the subject field. The readers of your e-mail see only your name and e-mail address and subject line when they retrieve their mail. Make that subject line work for you. It should encourage the recipient to open your mail. It also helps everyone see at a glance a particular e-mail for which they might be searching.

4. Use upper and lowercase when typing in your message. Two reasons: USING ALL CAPS IN AN E-MAIL MESSAGE IS CONSIDERED SHOUTING

and MESSAGES APPEARING IN ALL CAPS ARE MORE DIFFICULT TO READ BECAUSE THE LETTERS ARE ALL THE SAME HEIGHT. Don't make your readers crabby by making your message hard to read! Do use uppercase letters for an occasional word or phrase for EMPHASIS.

5. Read and reread your outgoing messages before sending. If your e-mail program has a spell checker, be sure it is turned on and use that too! If any of your statements can be interpreted two ways, one positive and one negative, inevitably the reader will understand it in the negative! Even if you don't think that's true (although plenty of research shows that it is), don't take the chance.

6. Never send e-mail in anger. You may find it difficult to retrieve your message or take back your angry statements after you've cooled off. If you catch yourself dashing off an angry note, stop. Leave the room, turn off your computer, go eat some ice cream, or, if you just can't stop writing, quickly change the address of the recipient to your own, so the message comes back to you. Then, you'll have a chance to reconsider your statements later, when you're calmer.

7. Do use the common abbreviations and symbols that e-mail users like to include, but *only* if your reader has used them in messages to you first and you're sure your "shorthand" will be understood. But, be very cautious of this because some recipients may consider the use frivolous. Often, though, as in-house service people become more familiar with customers, a good deal of friendly banter ensues. Here are a few examples:

BTW	by the way
TTYL	talk to you later
SYL	see you later
: –)	smiley face (Read it sideways.)
; –)	winking ("Just kidding.")
: – X	Don't tell! (Tape over mouth.)

8. Use great care when selecting who will receive a copy (cc) or blind copy (bcc) of an e-mail.

Enjoy using e-mail. It is a powerful, speedy, easy-to-use communication tool. That's why it's the number one application on the Internet.

Summary

Use e-mail and e-mail tools to their best advantage. Links to additional information on the business's Web site or other pertinent sites on the Internet can be very helpful in getting recipients to interact with your information. Attached images or documents can also be useful, but be sure to send files that the recipients can open and that are not too large for their e-mail service to process.

Review Questions

1. Name two non-Web-based e-mail programs.
2. What is a disadvantage to Web-based e-mail?
3. What are the purposes of the fields next to the "To," "Cc," and "Bcc" labels in an outgoing e-mail message?
4. What is the meaning of "Reply All"?
5. Why might it be better to quote a few lines of a long incoming message rather than quote the whole thing?
6. What is the difference between a plain text message and one formatted in html?
7. How can you include a link to a page on the Web in an e-mail message?
8. How do you send an attachment with an e-mail message? List the steps.
9. Why is organizing and filing e-mail messages important?
10. How do you move a message from one folder to another?

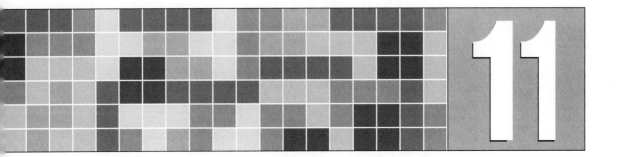

E-Mail Preparation

Think of the Internet as a global conversation. The companies that are going to be successful on the Internet must be part of that conversation. At some point in the probably-not-too-distant future, we'll tune in to the Web and listen to a cacophony of human voices, or just several voices, or just one. You will experience live Web meetings that make you feel as though you are sitting in the same room and at the same table with your colleagues, worldwide sales staff, or clients. Scary? Maybe. Thrilling? Definitely. Before that happens, a lot of e-mail will be entirely e-voice. Meanwhile, however, you have to generate and respond to *written* e-mail.

Not all salespeople or customer service representatives or marketing assistants or independent professionals are great writers. Some are; some aren't. Some people who are great at talking to people on the phone seem reluctant to write an e-mail message longer than a few lines. Is that you?

Many printed and online forms today simply ask for a check mark in a box—but e-mail on a one-to-one customer basis is different. To answer a customer's e-mail inquiry adequately, at least a few short paragraphs are necessary. This may seem difficult to some people, but doing it well is becoming increasingly important. If your business can't communicate well with its clients and prospective clients, another business will.

Sending error-free, well-formulated e-mail messages matters. A single e-mail message may well be all of the information that a recipient has for evaluating the knowledge, attitude, and professionalism of the sender. So, writing skills count!

Some smaller firms assign team members with good writing skills to respond to incoming e-mail, while assigning others to telephones. Other firms outsource the entire customer relationship marketing function or automate it internally by using sophisticated software. Some managers scribble out the gist of a message and then ask a more grammar-wise team member to construct the final version.

If your writing skills are not what you would like them to be, draft your messages and let someone who is better with words help you polish them. Use books or floppy disks of model business letters to start from, changing the facts to suit your intended message. Take a writing class. Meanwhile, review the writing tips in the next section.

This chapter helps you prepare effective e-mail messages related to marketing. "The Basics" sets out a list of tips for writing clear, unambiguous messages. "Beyond the Basics" provides you with a simple process to help ensure that your messages are appropriate for your audience, cover sufficient information, and are as effective as possible in getting your readers to do what you want them to do. Various sample e-mail messages are included to illustrate the key points and provide examples of e-mail message types.

THE BASICS

Communicating by E-mail

Effective e-mail communication doesn't just happen. It requires some thought about the audience, the purpose of the message, and what the message should include to accomplish that purpose.

Following is a short list of steps and tips for writing clear, unambiguous e-mail messages that will not be misunderstood—and that will help you get the results you want:

1. Know your purpose. Are you making a complaint, answering one, or complimenting or thanking someone? Are you trying to stimulate trials of your restaurant or increase its patronage on Tuesday evenings? Are you providing some data in response to an inquiry?
2. Know your audience. The amount of background information or detail you provide should be appropriate for the recipient. Be sure each recipient has sufficient information to do what you want him

or her to do. Too much information, on the other hand, will bore some readers. Worse, providing people with a lot of information that they already know can be interpreted as being condescending. Also, knowing your audience helps you use an appropriate tone or level of formality. Do your guests or patrons tend to be rather formal? Do you know them on a first-name basis? The rule of thumb here is: When in doubt, follow the same business correspondence style that you would use for a letter.

3. Use short sentences. If a sentence is too long, reword it and make two sentences. Use a simple, active subject-verb-object sentence structure when possible—more like Hemingway than Shakespeare. Short sentences are easier for most readers to absorb and remember.

4. Use plain language—clear words that your reader can relate to. Look for terms that might be misunderstood and replace them or give an explanation.

5. Eliminate phrases that could be interpreted as sarcastic, egocentric, critical, and so on. A sentence that sounds fine when spoken may lose its intended effect when read by a recipient.

6. Use short paragraphs and skip a line between paragraphs to make the message easier to read and to emphasize main points.

7. State clearly what you want the recipient to *do!* Answer a question? Visit a Web site? Click *Here?* Give you an opinion? Don't assume that sending someone a list of facts will lead them to do something about them!

8. Avoid long, involved descriptions and explanations. If sending this information is critical, send it as an attachment or post it to a Web site and send the link.

9. Use "you," "your," or the person's name.

10. Read what you write! Always check any e-mail addresses or Web site addresses that you have included. Incorrect Web addresses are "unreachable" and will irritate your contacts. Until you gain experience, read each e-mail message aloud to yourself before you send it. This technique helps you identify statements or phrases that are vague or that could be misinterpreted.

BEYOND THE BASICS

Answer Promptly

When you receive e-mail—or send out your e-mail to a target audience and responses start to come in—what's next? Fast follow-up is what helps make a sale, satisfy a customer need, or move your recipient to whatever action you wanted. Fast follow-up says "good service" to customers.

And *keep* following up. Most sales are not made during the first contact; they are made through follow-up. The importance of following up is made clear by these statistics from the Association of Professional Salesmen and the National Sales Executive Association:

- 2 percent of sales are made on the 1st contact
- 3 percent of sales are made on the 2nd contact
- 5 percent of sales are made on the 3rd contact
- 10 percent of sales are made on the 4th contact
- 80 percent of sales are made on the 5th–12th contacts

You can see from this data that firms who market online using one-time mass emailings might have only limited success. Help prospects reach a decision by presenting a viable, valuable useful possibility that they might not have considered before. Follow up quickly to inquiries—even if you think you answered a question previously! Use every reasonable opportunity to provide information or a service. Do that and your e-mails will produce far better results.

Plan Ahead

For decades, IBM printed the word "THINK" on its employee communications, on notepads, memos, and sales reports—everything that its people read. This watchword applies nowhere better than to planning your communications, especially e-mail. Why especially e-mail? Because we are becoming so accustomed to the speed and conversational style of e-mail that some of the planning we use for letters, reports, proposals, and other communications isn't used.

Basic e-mail planning is very simple. Answer these questions:

1. To whom am I writing and what does he or she already know?
2. Why am I writing?
3. What do I want the reader to do?
4. What information do I have to provide that will improve the likelihood that he or she will take the desired course of action.

A division of DoubleClick Inc. at www.doubleclick.com (targeting technologies, media sales expertise, direct marketing knowledge, and essential research tools) called Abacus (www.abacus-direct.com) is a world leader in targeted marketing solutions. By combining transactional data, advanced statistical modeling, and extensive media reach, Abacus targets the customers most likely to buy your products or services:

The Abacus Alliance database of buyer behavior is the largest in the United States. It contains over 3.5 billion transactions from more than 90 million

U. S. households and includes geographic, demographic, lifestyle, and behavioral data from catalog, retail, business-to-business, e-commerce, and publishing markets. We span multiple channels so you can integrate the most broadly based yet highly targeted campaigns for customer acquisition or retention.

To a great degree, Abacus can predict customer behavior by looking at what customers have done in the past. As a result, you can choose to send e-mail to only the most responsive prospects for your offer. Abacus uses recency, frequency, and monetary value (through summarized transactional data) to predict responsive prospects. Its e-mail names are 100 percent opted-in (see Chapter 9) to receive third-party e-mail messages. All users are given notice and choice when opting in as part of their membership privacy guidelines. Abacus helps larger firms find good e-mail prospects and manages entire programs for some firms. But for the majority of firms, someone has to actually write those outgoing e-mails.

To Whom Am I Writing?

At first thought, sending out an e-mail to a prospect or customer may sound simple. But sometimes, there's more to it than knowing a person's name and e-mail address. Knowing the intended reader of a message may mean understanding his or her business culture, position or rank, decision-making authority, product or service needs, likes, dislikes, priorities, financial resources, time pressures, responsibilities, authority, preferences, and more.

Let's say you work for a United States/Mexico joint venture resort in Puerto Vallarto, Mexico, that has just received government approval for a "swim with the dolphins" attraction to be offered through your hotel. You receive e-mail messages asking for more information about the new attraction. One is from a marine biologist at Scripps Marine Institute (www.sio.ucsd.edu/) who specializes in studying dolphin confinement. She approves of your plan, and she wants you to use only the most animal-friendly training tactics. Another message is from your company's advertising agency that wants to promote and "sell" the joys of swimming with dolphins to consumers. The third message is from an animal rights activist who says she will "stop at nothing until this project is derailed."

Will your response be the same to all three? Probably not—because what you know about the message senders influences what you write and how you write it. To the marine biologist, you might send the detailed steps used by your staff when working with the dolphins—all of which have been approved by eminent marine biologists and dolphin trainers, even some from Scripps Marine Institute. The advertising agency might receive links to hundreds of testimonials and descriptions that people have written about their experience of swimming with dolphins and how the dolphins themselves enjoy the contact; many stories about dolphins saving the lives of humans; and data on dolphin intelligence, language, and almost human-like behavior.

You might direct the animal rights advocate to the latest scientific data about how many resorts today conduct "responsible" encounters with dolphins to the enjoyment of not only the humans, but the dolphins, too. You might even mention that your dolphins are not confined. They could swim away into the open ocean from their encounter areas anytime they wanted—but they actually choose to stay. You point out that well-fed, well-cared-for dolphins really are smart.

If you or your work team has been assigned the task of writing a message or messages for an e-mail marketing campaign, you will likely be writing to the audience you identified in Chapter 2, or some specific segment of that audience. Perhaps, you are targeting just the people who visited your Web site and "opted-in" for product updates, or patrons of your services who are now eligible for a discount on your latest new offering, or customers who have made online purchases from your hotel's Web site at least twice in the past year.

Try it

1. What type of message *readers* do you write to most often? Name three things you know about them that affect their decisions.
2. You work for The Golden Fleece Casino in Reno. Your casino sells dozens of golden and otherwise gilded gambling-related products on its Web site. Your boss has asked you to write a message to your past players advising them of a new line of products that consists of "gold-"plated decks of cards, golden piles of chips, a golden mini roulette wheel, a golden slot machine, and a golden wheel of fortune. None of these items is inexpensive. Name four things that you think might be important for those past customers to know.

Why Am I Writing?

Your purpose for writing a message may be partly determined by your profession, the type of company you work for, or the type of job you do. If you are a product-marketing assistant, for example, perhaps you write surveys to evaluate customer satisfaction, or send updates to the locations of your nationwide chain, or prepare announcements about new campaigns for local sales offices or sales representatives. If you own a vegetarian restaurant that specializes in fresh-only fruits and vegetables, you might write messages describing the foods that are in season at the moment, providing information on how your chef is going to prepare certain special entrees from those items, and urging them to make their reservations while the season lasts.

What Do I Want the Reader to Do?

Isn't this the same question as "Why am I writing?" Sometimes, yes. But, especially for marketing, it serves as a reminder that you want people to do something besides just read a message for information's sake. Maybe you are writing to answer some questions or provide updated information, both valid purposes—but you may *also* want the reader to forward the message to someone else, reply to it, confirm a meeting, send you a fax, print out the message, sign it, fax it somewhere, complete a survey, click on a link for more information or to register for something, or to re-serve or order something.

Asking recipients to take some action has long been a "rule" of direct-response marketing. It applies to e-mail just as much as to direct mail or other media. Indeed, the additional options of linking to the Web to carry out other functions make e-mail the direct-response marketer's dream.

Make sure that your message asks the reader to take a particular action—your e-mail recipients will never wonder, "Now, why did they send me this?"

Try it

Your boss has asked you to review a message she wrote to inform customers about a new e-book on the history of your world famous Bahaman hotel. Her message describes the souvenir e-book in glowing terms and says that it is now available for $19.95. List three actions that the message could ask the recipients of the e-mail to take.

What Information Do I Give?

The general answer to this question is "enough information for the reader to make a decision." Too much information may confuse or bore the reader. It can sometimes be interpreted as "talking down" to a reader. Too little information may lead the reader to believe that you are not well informed. It may just not be convincing. How do you decide? One way is to provide what you believe to be the minimum information to cover the important points and then include links to plenty of additional information on your Web site. You may wish to provide basic information and ask the reader to contact you personally for more details. Or you may wish to write a brief "cover message" with a report or other longer document attached.

Read Actively, Respond by Listening

Begin the process of creating effective e-mail by applying a technique known as "listening back." With e-mail (as with all communication), how well you listen to others is actually more important than what you say to them.

When you receive an e-mail message from a potential customer, read the message actively; that is, absorb it and focus on its details. Then, "listen back," which means respond to *each and every point* that the sender made, leaving nothing out. Listening back ensures that your correspondent knows you understood the entire communication, and you won't miss an opportunity to provide a service.

Why respond to every point? Why not focus on the main point and disregard the others? Because if you make the judgment that a message writer is more concerned about *one* point than another, you may judge incorrectly. You may jump on one issue or question, missing the point that might be the most important to the sender. Remember the cardinal rule: "Never Assume!" Let's take an example. The following is what an e-mail inquiry from a prospect might look like if you were part of a firm that *sells to* restaurants:

Dear (Companyname),

You are no doubt familiar with our firm, HotTime Hamburgers, with its 1,500 units in the Pacific Northwest and northcentral states. We are looking for additional economical sources for our choice of quality stainless steel kitchen fixtures, including griddles, deep fryers, ovens, reefers, and miscellaneous items, for at least 240 units. Work would ideally begin in six weeks.

We are also considering remodeling many of our older units (110) in the motif of the local area, and for this, we are interested in stylized food service booths, chairs, tables, counters, easy-clean salad bar gondolas, and related items. Because you are an area distributor, we know that you supply many of these items, but we are not sure of the number of styles because your Web site may not list all that you can provide. Could you please tell us what you can supply of these items, what the delivery time would be, a bit about your past work in this product area, and your credit and billing practices? If we like what we see, we will send you an itemized list of what we need. Do not call. Please send the information attached to an e-mail.

Thanks,

John Prospect

Wowzers! What do you do now?

Know what Mr. Prospect wants by "listening" for clues and ways to serve him, just as you would in person. From the words used in the example, you can deduce that he probably has the following concerns:

- Your ability to handle large-volume purchases
- Your track record in his region
- Your past ability to serve big order chains
- High quality products
- Your ability to work closely with a chain's interior designers
- Your ability to provide most of all he needs from one source—you
- Your ability to offer him a wide choice of brands, configurations, and materials
- Style and selection
- Custom design capability
- Speed of delivery
- Price, but more importantly, value
- Easy-clean surfaces
- A list of past similar customers
- Your credit practices
- Billing terms and conditions

If you wonder how we could "hear" all of that from the message John Prospect sent, then you should practice your active reading. Try to find the information in the message that inspired us to add each point in the list.

If you had actually received this e-mail message, you could start your listening process by making a list of all of the concerns that you could identify. Then, refer to the "concerns" list—much as you would to an outline—when writing your reply. Because the list is rather long, you should consider writing a short e-mail "cover message" and attaching a longer document with the details.

Do not be afraid to e-mail a prospect to ask for more specifics and then add, "so I can better provide the kind of support that I know you want from us."

At the end of several paragraphs, if it will help the recipient, include a URL for a site or Web page with more information about the topic under discussion. Say, for example, "Besides what I've included here, we've found that the type of chairs that you currently use in your HotTime units in our area can be found in a wide variety at our supplier's site at www. duraformcpi.com/seating.html. But, are these the *same* kind that you are thinking of for the remodeling?" Tactics like these show the prospect that you are doing research, doing your homework.

Try it

Brent is an assistant manager at the Garbonzo Restaurant, which sells its own line of flaming hot salsa. Here's a message that a Canadian restaurant owner sent to the Garbonzo Restaurant asking about a special price if they purchased 10 cases at one time. Read the inquiry and Brent's response. Then, answer these questions: Which points did Brent make that address the customer's concerns? Which points could have been omitted? What did Brent miss?

Dear Garbonzo Restaurant,

Is the offer that you advertised Sunday still available? Is the salsa still on sale for 30 percent off if I buy 10 cases? In the picture on your site, it looks like it could be a thin kind of picante sauce with just a few chunks. Is it? Please tell me more about it. Can you send me a sample overnight?

I want the 10 cases for our big Cinco de Mayo celebration, so they would have to arrive in Canada by Friday. Can you ship it to arrive here at least two days before May 5?

I can pay for the sample and shipping through PayPal.com if you like.

Thanks,

Jerry Garcia, owner

Grateful Restaurant
Toronto, Canada

The reply:

Dear Jerry,

Yes, you remembered our offer correctly. We are still giving 30 percent off when you buy 10 cases (on the same order) of our world famous Zapata salsa, as advertised on Sunday. The discount ends on Tuesday at midnight, so you should place an order with me within the next 5 days.

The salsa is thick and chunky. And there's a big difference between our salsa and what you can buy at the grocery store: Our salsa has what most people think is an incredibly fresh taste. You can taste the difference! That's because we use only the freshest vegetables. You can see a list of the ingredients we use at www.GarbonzoBigSalsa.com/BackDoor/salsa.

I have already sent a Garbonzo salsa sample overnight to your office. The package is sent to your attention so you should have the sample by 10 AM tomorrow.

As far as delivering the 10 cases by Friday, that is easy and I have already had the 10 cases readied on our shipping dock and pre-addressed to you. Just e-mail me back after trying the sample, and I will have the 10 cases shipped (if you get back to me tomorrow) so you get them by Tuesday afternoon. The shipment would arrive five days ahead of Cinco de Mayo.

Yes, you can pay us by using PayPal. You would have to do that before we shipped the salsa because you are a first-time customer. At Paypal, just use the e-mail address payments@GarbanzoSalsa.com.

If you get a chance, perhaps you could take a digital photo of you holding up a jar of our salsa with the celebration going on behind you. We could add such a photo to our testimonials from happy customers. You can e-mail the photo to me at Brent@GarbanzoSalsa.com.

Thank you very much for inquiring about featuring our salsa at your Cinco de Mayo celebration.

Brent Lector
Consumer Service Manager
Garbanzo Restaurants and Markets
Headquarters: 15 E. MickeyHart St.
Phillest, CA 00000
e-mail: Brent@GarbanzoSalsa.com
Web site: www.GarbanzoSalsa.com

Try it

You have received an e-mail asking if you have beach-front rooms with wheelchair access. You have two such rooms. List three pieces of information that you would include in your reply.

Sample Messages

The sample e-mail messages provided in this section are intended to serve as examples of answers to the most common kinds of e-mail messages that businesses receive. Modify these to fit your own needs and style.

Remember, the most important things about responding to customer, client, prospect, and other e-mails are: respond as soon as possible; write so that your recipients feel that you listened to what they said; and convey to them that you or your product or service can do the job, that you care, and that you know how to help.

The "Do's" of Effective E-mail

1. If you do not have an e-mail account, get one *now*. Select an address that people can remember easily and type without making errors. GiantGourmetMealsandHotelChef@ GiantGourmetMealsandHotel.com is *not* a good e-mail address; Chef@GiantMeals.com *is*.

Set up different e-mail accounts for different people, divisions, or departments rather than have all e-mail come to one address, requiring someone's time to sort and forward it. Many smaller firms use "generic" e-mail addresses for different purposes:

info@companyname.com to answer general consumer or trade questions about the firm

press@companyname.com for responding to queries from the media

sales@companyname.com for use by the centralized sales department in a small firm

tech@companyname.com or support@companyname.com often used by technical staff in providing customer service

Avoid using free e-mail accounts, such as those from Hotmail and Yahoo!, or even low-cost ones, such as BlueLight e-mail ($8.95/mo.) from K-Mart, and others. These do not help secure your identity and build recognition. Also, recipients may wonder why a successful firm or its personnel is using a free e-mail program. Furthermore, many of these programs limit the size of attachments, which customers (and you) can find extremely annoying. Worse yet, most free e-mail providers display annoying ads on the e-mail screen, and may attach them to the bottom of messages you send. Don't risk having a competitor's ad appear at the bottom of *your* e-mail message.

2. Check your e-mail regularly—six times a day, at least, because timing could be critical. Rapid responses to requests for information or assistance could make the difference in someone's decision about choosing a firm. Timely responses to questions can relieve anxiety and help a transaction go smoothly.

3. Respond to e-mail inquiries immediately—even if only to say, "I'll check into that and get back to you." If you promise to send something by a certain time, be sure you do.

4. Write clearly. Avoid sarcasm.

5. When writing responses to e-mail inquiries, send useful, helpful information. Listen to what the sender's message said and repeat his or her list of needs or questions in your own words. This shows that you are paying attention and addressing the particular needs or situation.

6. When drafting e-mail messages to people who have signed your Web site's guestbook, lobby registration card, or requested more information at a travel show or on a reader response card ("bingo card") from a magazine, base your message on two assumptions: that they went there to get information about your services and that you have something of value to write them about.

Tell them about new or useful Web pages that the company has added to its site. Tell them the firm has a newsletter they can receive by e-mail. Tell them about your upcoming entertainment; the schedule for conventions, expos, corporate meetings, trade shows, retreats (if not secret), or perhaps new sightseeing tours or new exotic entrees to be served.

Give prospects the addresses of sites where they can get more information on your community and what interests *them*. Select links that you think are related to what *they* want to know.

Likewise, take good care of your vendors via e-mail. Keep them updated on inventory to avoid last minute orders that place a burden on them. Send them the URLS to sites they might find useful in their work. Doing this is similar to clipping a story from a newspaper and sending it to a friend.

In short, give everyone who deals in any way with your firm something that they will perceive as useful. It is similar to giving people a gift. They like it.

Speed counts. Make sure that all of your Web site *forms* work or download quickly. Consumers who have to wait too long for a function to complete—such as approval of a credit card when making a hotel or restaurant reservation—are inclined to quit the transaction, suspecting that something is "wrong."

7.   Use the "signature" function of your e-mail program effectively. Use it to list Web sites (usually these can be active links) that direct the e-mail recipient to certain of your pages or other pages that you would like them to see.

8.   Save the e-mail you receive and that which you send. Save everything, including e-mails to or from any party involved with your transactions. Some correspondence may be subject to business or SEC statutes pertaining to required records retention. Also, a complete "paper" trail is critical to dispute resolution should a problem arise later. Even the seemingly insignificant items you consider not worth saving now may later prove to be the key that makes a huge difference to you or your customer or your attorney.

9.   Promote your e-mail address. Rule of thumb: If your phone number is on it, put your e-mail address on it too. And, be sure to have a short, easy to remember e-mail address. If you do, you should mention it in your outgoing voice mail recording. The easiest ones for recipients to remember are ones including your name (if it is simple to spell) and "@firmname-dot-com." Spoken, it is "Thomas at firm name dot com." Enunciate. Repeat. Speak slowly. Pronounce each syllable clearly.

If your last name is a tongue twister, use your first name and an initial in e-mail addresses and voice messages. Instead of Sam Braunschweiger, become SamB@firmname.com. Also, avoid using underscores as in Sam_B@firmname.com. Once the address is underlined, Sam_B@firmname.com, the underscore cannot easily be discerned, creating confusion.

The most powerful Internet marketing tool for a firm is neither its Web site nor directory advertising; it's e-mail. Your Web site might be graphically impressive and loaded with information, but ultimately, what counts is the direct communication between you and your customers or prospective customers.

Advise buyers to visit your Web site for additional information. Even if your page contains only links to *outside* Web sites that offer related information, your contact will feel that *you* provided all of this wonderful input. This makes you a real "know-how" company when it comes to serving your contacts by e-mail.

Read through the following sample e-mail messages. As you do so, make notes about why each bit of information was included or how you might modify it to suit your own purposes.

Sample 1. Miscellaneous Request—Duplicate Documents

Dear Companyname,

About two weeks ago, I requested a duplicate copy of my check-out form (I lost the original), and it has not yet arrived. Was my original request lost? Can you check and see if everything is okay? Did it get sent yet? Please advise. I need this for my taxes ASAP!

Scully

23456 Round Avenue

Portland, Michigan 48875

Answer.

Dear Scully,

Your check-out form hasn't been lost. We checked the status and here's what we found.

(Then give appropriate explanation. See samples.)

The check-out form was sent last Wednesday. However, in rechecking your fax number, we find that we sent the fax to the wrong number, and that is why you never got it. Because you need the form immediately, I am sending it out to the address that you gave as your registry address, and we are re-faxing the form to the correct fax number. In addition, it is attached to this e-mail. If you do not get the form by tomorrow noon through one of these methods, please call me toll free at 800–555–5555.

We are sorry this happened. We have taken steps in our staff training to ensure that this does not happen again.

Thank you for your patronage. We look forward to your next visit.

Regards,
Fox Mulder
Manager

OR

The duplicate copy of your check-out form was delayed because of our recent computer failure (or give the reason here) and we expect that it will now be sent to you on _____. (Or, it was already sent on _____.)

If you would like to have us fax or e-mail another copy of the form to you today, just reply here and say so, or call me toll free at 800–555–5555 and tell me where you'd like the form sent.

The fax or e-mail approach will probably serve you best. We would have already used that method, but your registration form did not include a fax number.

To apologize for our delay, we have reserved a coupon in your name at (give URL). The coupon is worth $10 off your next stay.

Sincerely,

Penelope Suavely
Customer Service Manager

Comments.

1. Penelope addresses the problem first, head on—Scully's form was not *lost*.
2. She gave Scully information and assurances that the item would get to him. She even offered an alternative faster than U. S. mail.
3. She gave him the power to choose alternate delivery methods.
4. She gave him an incentive to revisit a Web site, which also promoted goodwill.

Sample 2. Service Complaint

Dear (Hotel Company),

What's the deal with my reservation? I made that reservation on-line over a week ago and it was supposed to be for this Friday through Tuesday, and now I go to check on it and your reservation person, Billy Bob, says on the phone that I don't have any reservation at all and he couldn't find that I had one. My confirmation number is BN2627.

What can you do? My family is already packed to go.

Disappointed,

Clem

Answer.

Dear Clem,

By using the confirmation number that you included in your e-mail message, we easily located your original reservation. You do indeed have a reservation for a "family first" room, with your family arriving Friday, August 7 and departing Tuesday, August 12.

We are so sorry that Billy Bob made a mistake on the phone with you. We are upgrading our reservation system and sadly, the computers are not all perfect in delivering the data we seek.

When you check in, the registrar will give you a free pass to something that I am sure your family will enjoy.

OR

We are sorry to inform you that your reservation was not confirmed because the bank did not accept your credit card.

Fortunately, we have a light weekend coming up and if you go on-line today before 7 PM and make a new reservation using a different credit card, you should have no problem. I have also called your home number and left a voice message similar to what you are read-ing here.

When you arrive this weekend, we will have a surprise waiting for your family in your room. We know that you will enjoy it.

Cordially,

Max Plowman
Assistant Manager
Easy As Pie Hotels

Comments.

1. The manager repeated the specific wants of the guest so he would know that the manager fully understood what was requested.
2. The manager provided specific information to address the problem.
3. The manager told the guest exactly what to do.
4. The manager worked to improve relations with the potential guest by promising a surprise.

Sample 3. Regarding Special Meals

(To a Muslim customer who visited the menu section of your restaurant site and asked for more information.)

Dear Mrs. Abou Ben Adhem,

In your message to me today, you asked for more details on our meals that are appropriate for Muslims. As you can see from the attached PDF file, Muslims can safely enjoy more than 15 entrees here in keeping with their practices. The link on our home page that says "Muslim Dishes" leads to a Web site that offers even more data on our preparation steps and on every ingredient used in these entrees.

Here's something that you may find appealing: If you give us two days notice, we can usually prepare a selection of specialty foods for a group of six or more Muslim guests.

From what you said, (quote here), it seemed that you may be bringing a group of that size or larger. If this appeals to you, please let me know the following information:

1. How many people (adults and children) will be in your dinner party?
2. What day and time would you like us to reserve your seating?

I've highlighted our most popular dishes for Muslims:

Menu Item	Price
Menu Item	Price
Menu Item	Price
Menu Item	Price

Please follow this link to www.whatever444.com for a detailed discussion of these four menu items. If the people in your group of six or more select at least three meals from those listed above, we will offer each of them a choice of some very special desserts.

Thanks for contacting me. Let me know if I can be of further assistance.

Cordially,

Claude Hammer
All-Nations Dine Restaurant

You'll find us at AllNations Dining, 224 College Blvd., Billings, Montana, Zip. Phone: 000–000–0000. Web site: http://www.AllNations.com. E-mail: Smudley@AllNations.com.

Comments.

1. Claude referred specifically to the customer's needs.
2. He directed Mrs. Ben Adhem to click on a link for further information.
3. He knows from experience that Muslims and other guests who avoid certain foods like to see the ingredients before deciding, so he provided a link to a page where this data could be found.
4. He provides additional helpful information that the customer might find most appealing, plus an incentive to choose from *the restaurant's* choice of menu items.

Sample Outgoing Marketing E-Mails

Sample 1. Past Restaurant Patrons

Dear Mr. and Mrs. Blake,

I trust that your recent visit to our Fisherman's Boat Restaurant was an enjoyable one.

If so, perhaps you might be good enough to comment on your experience so that we can be better for you next time. Just click on the circle that most closely represents how you felt about your visit:

○ Excellent (If excellent, please <u>click here</u> and write a few words why.)
○ Good
○ Typical
○ Substandard
○ Poor (If poor, please <u>click here</u> and write a few words why.)

If we could carry two more items on our menu, what would you want them to be? To answer, go <u>here</u>.

Here's something that you may want to explore every two weeks. It's our new Italian home cooking newsletter. Not only does it contain recipes from our restaurant's chef, but award-winning ones from the best Italian restaurants in the world. The current newsletter features "Italian Home Cooking Recipes from Rome."

You can pick the newsletter up at our restaurant, or, we'll gladly e-mail you a copy every two weeks. To sign up for it, click <u>here</u>. You will find a form for inviting all of your friends to subscribe to the newsletter, too. (Or, just forward a copy of this e-mail to them and they can go to the newsletter site right from the links above.)

Come back soon. We are eager to make your each visit a joy.

Don Coral
Manager

[Add full contact info here: e-mail and Web site addresses, phone, fax, address.]

Comments.

1. The message begins by using "your," a derivative of "you," the word that people love to hear most, second only to their name.
2. The attitude of the writer, Don, is one of cordiality. Even the requests are positioned as a service to the customer.
3. Something of value is offered—a chance to get a valuable newsletter of Italian recipes. It will also contain many links to the restaurant's Web site, ensuring that newsletter subscribers will return often to the webpage. Doing so promotes quick recall of the restaurant, and helps the customer place the restaurant higher among the places he could dine.
4. A viral marketing message is included, both in the newsletter and repeated on the webpage that the "friends" will visit.

Sample 2. Inviting Organizations

Often service clubs like Kiwanis, Lions, Rotary, and Junior League, meet for years at the same venue. Is this because other venues like yours simply *assume* that the organization is happy where it is? How often do you ask local service groups to hold their regular monthly or weekly meetings at *your* place?

Investigate what they are getting at the present venue, so you know how to make your offer irresistible. Sometimes, having a certain group, especially a large, well-heeled one, may be worth having even if you only break even serving it. Why? Because the opinion makers in many leading community groups will recommend your facility to others and because they will return to patronize your business.

Dear Robert,

We have met several times at various functions over the years, and I enjoyed your talk at the kick-off dinner for the annual tourist season last month. I have followed your extensive participation in the community and often wonder when you find time to sleep.

Your Rotary International Club of Hilo, District 5000, has set and achieved extremely high goals for years. Our community is a far better place to live in thanks to the work that you and your club have done. Maybe I can help a bit.

Your club has met for three years in the Vintage Inn private room, and I know that they offer both good service and good food for your lunch meetings and for a number of your committee meetings. We also understand that your contract with them expires this summer. We think that we can offer your club more than the Vintage or any other venue in town. This is because with our large staff and kitchen, we can *tailor menu items* specifically to your desires and offer you the during-meeting benefits of the dramatic remodeling and equipment modernizations that we have recently concluded.

[Insert image of restaurant]

For example, we will prepare for you each week a lunch menu that is specifically designed to match the tastes of a majority of your members. You can vote to have certain dishes for lunch, well ahead of time. For example, I know that several of your members love the dish known as cioppino, an Italian fish soup. We make the best cioppino in the state.

This same group also loves our delicate and delicious dessert, Tiramisu (click on www.goodcooking.com/tmissu.htm), and we'd like to make an extra special one for your group as often as you'd like it. The same goes for other dishes that you might vote on to have us prepare from time to time. Your wish is our command!

Tiramisu melts in your mouth.

I understand that the room you are now using at the Vintage costs your club between $200 and $300 per month. If you agree to use our facility for two years, with meetings in our newly remodeled "World Business Leaders" meeting room, we can give you the room for free.

If this interests you, let's have lunch here on Tuesday or Thursday of this coming week in the "World Business Leaders" meeting room.

Once you see our brand new A/V, sound, Internet, and excellent conferencing systems, we think you'll be impressed. Over lunch, we can explore the many advantages of meeting here at the Kanapali-Downtown Hotel/Restaurant.

Please let me know if we should expect you and a half dozen members of your Rotary International Club on Tuesday or Thursday of this week.

Cordially,

Bart Nelson
General Manager
Kanapali-Downtown Hotel/Restaurant
Honolulu, Hawaii

Comments.

1. Leaders of clubs and community organizations seldom do their work for money, often out of a sense of contribution and for the appreciation. The praise lavished at the start of this message will likely be well received and once flattered, the recipient should be more receptive to hearing the offer being made by the sender.

2. The tone of the message is confident. The writer does not beg. The writer's attitude is "Well, of course, you want the best for your club, and here is what we'll do."

3. A comparison is being made between what the competitor, Vintage, lacks and what the newly remodeled meeting room can offer.

4. Many specifics about the Kanapali's service are mentioned instead of merely a list of general offerings. The Kanapali is telling the club president that the club, to their own members' liking, can specify meals. Several examples are given to make this clear.

5. The meeting room amenities and equipment are mentioned in a way that could be most appealing to the Rotary president. He wants the best for his club and if gaining it is his find, he becomes a better leader for providing it.

Sample 3. Prospective Guests—Family

Dear Parents,

Here's the south Miami Beach Family Hotel that you've dreamed about finding.

[Insert photo montage of kids and parents together.]

In response to your recent request for information on family vacations, I'd like to tell you about our on-the-beach resort at south Miami Beach.

I'm Blake Andrews, and I am general manager of our 300-room Nakitome Plaza Beach Hotel where every room faces the ocean. Let me tell you why our hotel is great for families:

1. We have dozens of activities to keep kids busy. (Cite some here.)
2. There are plenty of parent–child activities for the entire family. (Give example here.)
3. There are area tours and excursions appropriate for everyone in the family. (Give example here.)
4. We have an on-site restaurant with healthy food for all. (List a few menu choices here.)
5. Within a block, we have a quick-service hamburger place, a four-plex theatre, a video game palace, and an Internet café! Plus, the widest beach you've ever seen begins just outside our door.

We're offering a special until May 10th—make your reservations now for a week and for every seven days you book, we'll give you an extra day for the whole family for free (up to two rooms).

To see 360-degree views and a short movie showing our rooms, restaurant, pool, and the beach, click HERE.

E-mail a reply to me right now, this minute, and upon your arrival, I'll give each one of your children a disk containing 22 *Family Kid Magazine*-approved games that they can play on the indestructible computers located in our recreation room.

I look forward to seeing you later this year. Meanwhile, just e-mail me anytime with any questions.

Forward this message to your friends and relatives just by clicking HERE.

Cordially,

Blake Andrews, General Manager
Nakitome Plaza Beach Hotel

Comments.

1. The e-mail begins by mentioning that the person had opted-in to receive information about Miami Beach vacations.
2. General statements about activities are backed up by giving specific examples.
3. Incentives are offered to motivate the recipient to act now.

4. The promise of more information is offered in the form of a link to see more about the hotel. This also encourages the recipient to visit the hotel's Web site, which is designed to convince a person to make a reservation.

Sample 4. Business Travelers

Dear Human Resources Manager

HugeWorldWideFirm Inc.

Saving Your Firm Travel Money
Is Never Easy—So THIS You'll Like

[Insert image of semi-serious political-type cartoon of a human resources manager balancing airplanes, hotels, diners, etc. with money dropping out of each item, or similar illustration.]

Your task of holding down travel costs for a large firm is difficult. So here's something that might help from World Wide Upscale Hotels.

[Insert image of flagship World Wide Upscale Hotel.]

Sign your company up now for our "Premier Business Travel" service before the 20th of June, and we will provide these upgrades and amenities to executives from your firm who stay at one of our 700 hotels.

See the example below of how much money you will save if only 200 of your executives stay two days at our hotels next month under the Premier plan:

[Show simple chart here and big dollar saving.]

Sound good? There's even more!

To learn how to improve these already impressive

savings while absolutely thrilling your executives, click HERE.

S. William Warren
Vice President – Business Travel
World Wide Upscale Hotels Inc.

Comments.

1. Headlines work best in getting a recipient to see quickly what benefit you're offering.
2. Empathy works; you understand the recipient, thus you might *really* have something he can use.

3. A deadline-intensive incentive is offered to instill urgency on part of recipient.

4. A chart or graph often can make a difficult concept suddenly easy to understand. Just make the graphic a "no-brainer" to grasp.

Sample 5. Group Travel Organizers

**We Cater to Your Groups
Like We Do To Our Own Family
And Make You a Star While Doing So**

[Show image of huge group dining.]

Last year [your firm] brought ten groups of 100 to 140 passengers each—nearly 1,200 passengers—to Orlando. Congratulations on your success as a group travel organizer. Perhaps we can help you succeed even more.

For 15 years, we have specialized in lunches and dinners for large groups such as yours. In fact, we've **become famous** for our group dining service, having been written up in Time, Business Week, USA Today, Travel Holiday, Hospitality, the Orlando Sentinel, CNN TV, NBC Evening News, and **dozens more**.

Because of our fame, which these news organizations say we have earned, it is easy for group organizers to convince their clients that we are a terrific place to take a group for a meal while in Orlando.

Take a look at our **extensive Web site** and see for yourself how we serve large groups. We deliver not only fantastic menu items like **Chateaubriand**, Steak Diane, **Baked Alaska**, and **Cherries Jubilee**, but also traditional "down home" favorites like **pot roast**, **chicken pot pie**, and **apple cobbler**. Whatever you and your group want, we can provide.

Cherries Jubilee

To see some of our menu selections, click **HERE**.

You are cordially invited to come and visit us on your next trip to **Orlando**. I would love to show you around and have you see us serve one or two large groups while you are here.

You should also know that the prices we extend to you are extremely competitive due to our volume, which leaves considerable room for your service-added markups. Plus, we are accustomed to large groups and can facilitate serving them in a timeframe that fits your day's itinerary.

Naturally, your meals are entirely complimentary as would be your stay at our sister Hotel, the **BigHotel** nearby. Moreover, we are located near almost everything in Orlando, including Sea World.

Please e-mail me back and let me know when we might meet here at the Garden Delight and I will set that date aside for you. Meanwhile, see our other services for groups at **www.gardendelightgroups.com.**

Cordially,

Antonia Schwartz
Founder, Garden Delight Restaurant

Comments.

1. Group travel and incentive travel firms often look for places where groups are actually welcome. Not all group food places also serve great food, so variety and quality are emphasized in this e-mail.

2. Group travel firms often need to justify to their clients why they are choosing one hotel or restaurant over another. This message cites media names that have publicized the restaurant. This helps build credibility for clients.

3. The restaurant's central location and proximity to Sea World is stated so that the group travel executive knows that it could be a good choice for en route dining during a day's schedule and itinerary stops.

4. The recipient is encouraged to click on a link (highlighted and underlined above) to visit a page of the restaurant's Web site. The page should directly relate solely to whatever was the subject of the link. If the subject was menu items, the link should go to a menu items page and not just to the home page, where the person will have to figure out where to go next to find menu information.

Sample 6. Local Travel Agents

Dear Jean _____,

President, Washington, D.C. Travel Inc.

Come Stay With Us and
See First Hand Why Your
Clients Will Love It Here

This message contains a coupon worth a Friday and Saturday night stay for you or someone on your office staff between now and the 15th of June. Just cite your IATA number when making your reservations.

We are doing this because we have received [no, few, seldom, etc.] guests from your firm during the past [month, six months, year, years, etc.] Yet, we are one of the best-visited inns in town and have earned a [whatever it is] rating from [whoever it is, AAA, Exxon/Mobil, etc.]. What's more, we are approved by the [government agency] for [whatever types of travel].

Sometimes travel firms think that, because of our location or our amenities, we are too pricey for certain guests. However, the rates that we can offer you for your clients are desirable, indeed, and still leave considerable room for your value-added markups.

To see 360-degree views of our rooms and suites, click **HERE**.

To take a virtual tour of our entire hotel, click **HERE**.

When you or your colleagues want to make reservation using this free offer, simply give your name and your IATA number. You can register in person of course or on our Web site at www.Local HotelVeryGood.com.

I look forward to meeting you in person when you come in.

Cordially,

Jefferson Smith
Manager
The LocalGoodHotel

Comments.

1. Make yourself known locally if you want to get business from locals.
2. The headline makes clear what the e-mail is about and promises something valuable.

3. The citing of the hotel's awards backs up the claim about being good and makes for increased credibility for *everything* that is said here.

4. The number one way to get people from a travel agency to know about you is through trials. Jean _____, the president, may not come herself, but someone from her firm probably will. That person then would report to the entire office her impressions of the facility and its service. If all goes well, and the price is right, the hotel will be placed on a list of approved local hotels.

5. The e-mail encourages a visit to the Web site for more information.

E-mail Masters

Adding e-mail communication to a list of daily tasks may seem somewhat daunting at first. With practice, the process goes more quickly. One technique for speeding up the process is to create e-mail masters for different circumstances.

Use the sample messages in this chapter as models or create your own and save them as "masters." Once your master e-mail messages are composed, typed, proofread, and spell checked, save each one of them to your documents file with a document name that you will remember. Then, when you answer most e-mails, you can use these e-mail masters.

Add information or edit the text in the master so that you are "listening back," and then send it off. Some e-mail programs, such as Eudora® or EudoraPro®, allow users to save each of these "masters" as "stationery."

Summary

Simple writing that communicates clearly is still an essential business tool. E-mail, like other written communications, should be written from an understanding of the readers' knowledge, needs, and priorities. Writers should be clear about their purpose for writing and about what they want the reader to do.

E-mail should be kept fairly short. Extensive or detailed information can be attached in a separate document or provided on a Web page.

Competent writing counts! A single message may be your only chance to make a positive impression or communicate an important fact or idea.

Sending highly graphic, colorful, and animated HTML e-mail is more effective in gaining a response than text-only messages. The problem is, although most people's programs can read HTML e-mail today, many still cannot. You can, however, send colorful HTML e-mails if your audience has elected to receive them by choosing that format when they signed up to get news from your site or when they did at another site.

Many purchased lists of e-mail addresses are already sorted according to who wants HTML e-mail and who wants plain text. We suggest you develop two e-mail versions of each message or newsletter, one for each segment of your audience.

Review Questions

1. Why is there more of a chance of misunderstanding when communicating by e-mail than face-to-face?
2. How can you avoid ambiguity or misunderstanding in e-mail messages?
3. Name three things to think about when planning to write a message.
4. Why are short sentences better to use?
5. Why should you keep paragraphs short and leave spaces between them?
6. How can reading an e-mail aloud help you improve it?

Appendix

Resources on the Web

Resources on the Internet expand daily. They also change, relocate, are replaced, or are deleted. We warn Internet users to avoid purchasing large books that purport to be Internet directories because change happens so quickly. Nonetheless, we are providing a list of Web sites that were current as of January 2003. Some of these we have used for many months, and we are fairly sure of their stability. Others are relative newcomers. When you use this list, understand that it is neither exhaustive nor permanent. Use it as a guide to get you started. The resources listed here are divided into six sections, some of which have subgroups, as follows:

1. General sites with local information
2. Some city, county, and state Web sites
3. Tools to aid your positioning
4. Tools for building and maintaining your Web site
5. Popular links to add to your site
6. Hospitality education programs and hospitality associations

GENERAL SITES WITH LOCAL INFORMATION

Many valuable sites that have general or national information also provide that material for local areas. Some of this can prove valuable for the services you provide or wish to provide on your site. Weather information, maps, local accommodations for home hunters, demographics, movies, and other information can be found on the Web. Be sure to drill far enough down in a site to find the page that pertains to your area, and then create your link solely to that interior page.

Weather	www.weather.com
Track storms	www.storm98.com
U. S. city information	www.usacitylink.com/
Worldwide cities	www.timeout.com
Travelocity	www.travelocity.com
MapQuest	www.mapquest.com
Yahoo! Maps	http://maps.yahoo.com/py/maps.py
TV schedule	www.tvguide.com
Movie schedule	www.moviefone.com
Grocery coupons	www.valupage.com
Employment	www.monsterboard.com
Gov. recreation lands	www.recreation.gov
Aerial views of anywhere	www.terraserver.microsoft.com
Vacations and your pets	www.vetinfo.com
One stop stock info.	www.stocksheet.com
Seniors	www.senior.com
Worldwide recipes	www.wwrecipes.com/
Official baseball leagues	www.majorleaguebaseball.com/
Visit 20,000 online stores	www.shopguide.com
World travel Web sites	www.leonardsworlds.com/camera.html
City pollution by Zip code	www.scorecard.org
Universities online	www.mit.edu:8001/people/cdemello/univ.html
Farmers almanac	www.almanac.com
U. S. museums	www.museumca.org/usa/state.html
Child care sources	www.careguide.net

SOME CITY, COUNTY, AND STATE WEB SITES

Include links to sites with city, county, and state information. Large cities may have dozens of "city" sites. One is probably a site maintained by the city itself. Others are sometimes built for commercial or other purposes. Some state or regional sites have a page or set of pages for cities that can also be helpful.

Some states use a Web address format that has been set aside for them. This is usually expressed with the standard beginning "http://www.state" followed by the state abbreviation and ".us." For example, Georgia's URL is www.state.ga.us; Washington's is www.state.wa.us; and Massachusetts' is www.state.ma.us. Simply change the abbreviation for the state to see if your state has a Web site using this standard Web address format.

Cities have a variation on the state URL, which they can elect to follow, as in www.ci.boston.ma.us or www.ci.saint-petersburg.fl.us. Following are the URLs of some city and state Web sites. The list is far from exhaustive, but will give you an idea of where to start looking.

Alaska	www.state.ak.us
Anchorage, AK	www.ci.anchorage.ak.us
Juneau, AK	www.juneau.lib.ak.us
Arkansas	www.state.ar.us
Michigan	www.michigan.gov
Portland, MI	www.PortlandMichigan.com
Phoenix, AZ	www.ci.phoenix.az.us
Los Angeles, CA	www.ci.la.ca.us
	www.losangeles.com
San Diego, CA	www.sandiego.com
	www.sandiego.org
Santa Barbara, CA	www.ci.santa-barbara.ca.us
Riverside, CA	www.ci.riverside.ca.us
Denver, CO	www.denver.com
Hartford, CT	http://ci.hartford.ct.us
	http://home.digitalcity.com/hartford
Florida	www.state.fl.us
Tampa, FL	http://888tellnet.com
Atlanta, GA	www.gausa.com

Idaho   www.accessidaho.org

Davenport, IA   www.ci.davenport.ia.us

TOOLS TO AID YOUR POSITIONING

- Your URL and e-mail address on your car's trunk or fender
  www.autoidtags.com

- Make free or nearly free "bridge pages"

  The reason you make a bridge page is to have more of *your* pages available for search engines to find. Once found, the bridge page simply redirects visitors to your main Web site.

  www.switchboard.com
  http://site.yahoo.com
  http://agtr.com/act-main.htm
  http://hometown.aol.com/hmtwn123/index.htm
  http://angelfire.lycos.com
  www.freeyellow.com
  www.webspawner.com
  www.webdiner.com/templates/index.htm
  www.hms.harvard.edu/it/www/templates/index.html

TOOLS FOR BUILDING AND MAINTAINING YOUR WEB SITE

Save yourself considerable time and money in making your site effective by using these sources for a free Web site analysis or valuable marketing information based on *your* input.

- See what keywords are best to use
  http://inventory.overture.com/d/searchinventory/suggestion/
  www.searchspy.com

- Make your keywords count
  www.keywordcount.com
  www.keyworddensity.com
  www.searchengineworld.com/cgi-bin/keyword_suggest.cgi

- See keywords being used this minute
  www.metaspy.com
  http://voyeur.mckinley.com/cgi-bin/voyeur.cgi
  www.search.com/snoop

- Check on how keywords are misspelled
  This keyword research tool searches major search engines for the popular spelling of words. Find the most common misspellings and you might just attract that uncontested traffic.
  www.spellweb.com/

- Make your images load faster
  www.gifworks.com
  http://Web sitegarage.netscape.com

- Check spelling on a webpage
  www.jimtools.com/spell.html

- See how search engines rank you
  www.top-10.com/freevisrprt.html
  www.jimtools.com
  www.topdogg.com

- Web site traffic analyzers
  www.hitbox.com
  www.webtrends.com

- Is your HTML code accurate?
  www.anybrowser.com
  www.Web sitegarage.com

- Detect dead links
  http://Web sitegarage.netscape.com/O=wsg/tuneup_plus/index.
     html
  www.SevenTwentyfour.com
  www.jimtools.com/link.html

- See how many links point to you
  www.linkpopularity.com
  www.linkstoyou.com
  www.searchengineworld.com/cgi-bin/linkage.cgi

- Learn how people find your site
  www.WebTrends.com
  www.HitBox.com

- Check how fast your site displays
  www.netmechanic.com/index.htm

- Buy or sell domain names
  www.buydomains.com
  www.greatdomains.com

www.thedomainexchange.com
www.domainnames.com

- Learn from these free newsletters
  www.dummiesdaily.com
  http://bottomlinesecrets.com
  www.netmechanic.com
  www.webpromote.com
  http://searchenginewatch.internet.com
  www.emarketer.com
  www.zdnet.com
  www.internettrafficreport.com
  www.webposition.com/newsletter.htm
  www.forrester.com
  http://e-newsletters.internet.com
  www.nielsen-netratings.com
  www.britannica.com

- Make free banners
  www.mediabuilder.com

- Free graphics for your site
  www.mediabuilder.com
  Microsoft's Design Gallery: http://dgl.microsoft.com

- Let people recommend your site
  www.recommend-it.com

- Add a free guestbook
  www.guestbook.nu
  http://htmlgear.lycos.com/specs/guest.html

- Add a clock and weather to your site
  www.onyoursite.com

- Add the correct time
  www.time.gov

- Search engine updates—keep current
  searchengineforums.com/bin/Ultimate.cgi
  www.searchenginewatch.com
  www.laisha.com/search

- Make meta tags and learn how to use them
  http://WDVL.com/Authoring/HTML/Head/Meta

http://searchenginewatch.internet.com/webmasters/meta.html
http://hotwired.lycos.com/webmonkey/html/96/51/index2a.html
www.scrubtheweb.com/abs/builder.html
www.ineedhits.com/metatag

- Add surveys and polls

  Many tools are now available for online polls and surveys. Some are appropriate for short, fun polls that engage your visitors. Others are more suited to complex surveys, for example, of customer satisfaction.

  Sawtooth: www.sawtoothsoftware.com/ciwov1.shtml
  Survey Shop: www.surveyshop.com/home.html
  Key Survey javascript popup: www.keysurvey.com
  Snap: www.mercator.co.uk/productsprof.htm
  Apian: http://apian.com/
  Survey Solutions: www.perseusdevelopment.com/
  EZSurvey: www.raosoft.com/
  SurveySaid: www.surveysaid.com/
  WebSurveyor: www.websurveyor.com/home_intro.asp
  InfoPoll: www.infopoll.com/

- Add links to map sites

  Yahoo! Maps, driving directions:
      http://maps.yahoo.com/py/maps.py
  Maps of all kinds: www.mapquest.com
  Zip codes; distances between: http://link-usa.com/zipcode
  How far from (city) to (city): www.indo.com/distance
  National parks:
      www.gorp.com/gorp/resource/us_national_park/main.htm

POPULAR LINKS TO ADD TO YOUR SITE

"Constantly changing content" is a major factor that attracts repeat visitors to your site. Along with local area information, you can add links to popular topics that virtually anyone can enjoy. Here are a few idea builders to help you to get started.

- Best of the Web

  Top-ten lists (725 Categories): www.toptenlinks.com/
  Directory of world's online Web cams: www.earthcam.net/
  Best Web sites on internet: www.webbyawards.com/
  Top 100 sites for kids: www.100hot.com/kids/

Top 100 sites for sports: www.100hot.com/sports/

Top 100 sites for recipes: www.top100recipesites.com/

Top 100 sites for travel: www.100hot.com/travel/

- Kelly Blue Book for autos
  www.kbb.com/

- Home and garden

  All about home care: www.allabouthome.com/

  Handy home uses of common foods: www.wackyuses.com

  Home maintenance and repair from MSU:
      www.msue.msu.edu/msue/imp/mod02/master02.html

  Tim Carter's home maintenance: www.askbuild.com

  What's recyclable; What is not:
      www.obviously.com/recycle/guides/shortest.html

  Fix anything anywhere: www.misterfixit.com

  HouseNet home and garden: www.housenet.com/

  House beautiful: www.housebeautiful.com/

  Basic gardening: www.gardening.com

  All about pianos: www.pianoworld.com

  Do it yourself: http://doityourself.com/

- Food

  Culinaria online recipes galore: www.culinaria.com

  Find recipes for anything: www.lycos.com/search/recipedia.html

  Cake recipes: www.cakerecipe.com

  Cookie recipes: www.cookierecipe.com

  Calzone recipes: www.calendarzone.com/recipes/

  Coffee lovers: www.coffeescience.org

  Garlic facts and fun: www.thegarlicstore.com

  New to wine? Enjoy learning: www.enjoywine.com/

  Fast food facts, calories, hints: www.olen.com/food/

  7,600 recipes for cooking: www.epicurious.com/

  Flying noodle pasta recipes: www.flyingnoodle.com

  Oriental food recipes, hints: www.orientalfood.com

  Recipe exchange: www.recipeXchange.com/

  Wine spectator's for oenophiles: www.winespectator.com/

  Vegetarians: www.vrg.org

- Pets

  How many fish to put in a tank?:
      http://fins.actwin.com/articles/howmanyfish.php

  Dog & cat vet advice: www.vetinfo.com

HOSPITALITY EDUCATION PROGRAMS AND HOSPITALITY ASSOCIATIONS

Many schools throughout the country offer education programs in hospitality. Some have a culinary emphasis, others focus on hotel management or tourism. Various certificates or degrees are offered. We list here a *sample* of these programs. Do not interpret inclusion as an endorsement or recommendation—they are listed because they had the basic information on their Web site. As with other topics, use your favorite search engine to find additional sites or URL corrections.

- Links to many hospitality education programs can be found at
  www.hospitalityonline.com/career-links/education/

- Schools (The following programs are listed alphabetically according to state.)

  Northern Arizona University School of Hotel and Restaurant Management: www.hrm.nau.edu/

  The Collins School of Hospitality Management, Cal Poly Pomona, California: www.csupomona.edu/~cshm/main.html

  City College of San Francisco, Hospitality Programs: www.ccsf.edu/Services/Vocational_Education/hotel/hospitality.html

  San Francisco State University, Hospitality Department: www.sfsu.edu/~hmp/res1.html

  Daniels College of Business, University of Denver, School of Hotel, Restaurant, and Tourism Management: www.dcb.du.edu/hrtm/

  Kapi'olani Community College Food Service & Hospitality Education Programs: http://programs.kcc.hawaii.edu/fshe/

  Cooking & Hospitality Institute of Chicago: www.chicnet.org/home.asp

  Purdue University, Department of Hospitality and Tourism Management: www.cfs.purdue.edu/RHIT

  Maryland Hospitality Education Foundation: www.mhef.org/

  The Michigan Hospitality Education Alliance: www.mihea.org/

  Brown College Culinary Program, Minnesota: www.culinary-bi.com/

  Cornell University, School of Hotel Administration: www.hotelschool.cornell.edu/

  New York University Center for Hospitality, Tourism, & Travel: www.scps.nyu.edu/chtta

  Tennessee Hospitality Education Center in the Department of Hospitality and Tourism at Tennessee State University: www.thehomepage.org

University of Houston, Conrad N. Hilton College of Hotel and Restaurant Management: www.hrm.uh.edu/home.asp

Virginia Tech, Hospitality & Tourism Management: www.cob.vt.edu/htm/index.htm

West Virginia Office of Hospitality Education and Training: http://wvheat.org/

- Associations

  Most states have a hospitality association of some sort. For example, the site for Arkansas Hospitality Association is located at www.arhospitality.org/hosedfound.htm. The site for the Restaurant and Hospitality Association of Indiana is located at www.indianarestaurants.org.

  Check your state Web site or use a search engine to find the one for your particular area.

- Various national (or international) associations are also available to help you:

  American Hotel & Lodging Association (AH&LA): www.ahma.com

  Educational Institute of American Hotel and Lodging Association: www.ei-ahla.org

  Hospitality Sales and Marketing Association International: www.hsmai.org

  National Association of Hospital Hospitality Houses, Inc.: www.nahhh.org

  National Park Hospitality Association: www.nphassn.org

  National Restaurant Association: www.restaurant.org

  National Restaurant Association Educational Foundation: www.nraef.org

Glossary

@. The symbol most often seen in e-mail addresses(johnandjane@earthnet.com); in general, the symbol means "located at."

alternative text. Sometimes called "mouseovers" or "alt tags," this text displays while an image is loading and when the user places the mouse/pointer over an image. Unless the Web site owner or creator changes the alternative text, the name of the graphic file, such as house.gif, shows. However, any text may be used, such as "Sam Brown, Realtor® for first-time home buyers in Bowling Green, Kentucky." Some search engines read this alternative text along with visible text to help determine a site's relevance to specific keywords.

animated .gif. A type of graphic that appears to move. An animated .gif combines several images, each a little different from each other, that automatically appear one after another to give the appearance of motion, much like a motion picture.

attachment. A file attached to an e-mail message. The file could be a photo, text, a webpage, or any other type of file. Caution: Do not send files unless you are certain the recipient can find them, view them, and open them. If your e-mail recipients can browse the Internet, then .jpg and .gif graphics files, html files, and simple text files work fine.

auction. A site that offers items for sale using a bidding process. At a predetermined time, the auction closes and the high bidder "wins" the auction and pays the seller. Many auction variations are now available, but the significant player is eBay at www.ebay.com.

audiobook. Downloadable from the Internet or available on disk, users listen to audiobooks using a computer audio program; they are similar to "books-on-tape."

autoresponder. A function on a computer that sends an automated response to a command from a Web site or to an e-mail with a particular addressee or subject line.

B2B. Business-to-business. B2B sites are constructed to sell business products and services to other businesses.

B2C. Business-to-consumer. B2C sites are constructed by businesses to sell their products and services to consumers.

banner ad. Small rectangular, usually horizontal, ad that appears on Internet pages. Banner ads usually link the visitor to the Web site or page of the banner owner (advertiser).

banner exchange. Reciprocal banner display, characterized by the statement, "I'll put your banner on my site if you'll put my banner on yours." The banners often, but not always, include an active link to the target site, becoming link exchanges.

bcc. Abbreviation for blind carbon copy or blind copy; indicates a copy of an e-mail message sent to recipients without their addresses showing on the message. Think of a blind copy as a "secret" copy.

bridge page. A webpage that leads visitors to another site; hence, a "bridge." Several sites offer free pages—Tripod.com and Geocities.com are among the better known sources. Often, but not always, these pages carry their own metatags and their URLs can be registered with search engines. Because some search engines penalize such pages in their rankings, the Web savvy put at least some new or different information on each bridge page, rather than just a list of links to pages in the target site.

bulletin board. A Web site page that displays messages submitted by users. Most bulletin boards are specific to a particular topic.

C2C. Consumer-to-consumer. C2C sites are constructed by individuals to sell products and services to consumers. C2C selling also occurs on auction sites such as eBay.com.

central reservation office (CRO). An online communication system (also called "central reservation system") between all hotels in a company or chain that maintains up-to-date room pricing and availability information. Also used as an online communication system that acts as a central interactive database between all hotels cooperating in a CRO, sometimes with a marketing or other third-party partner, that maintains up-to-date room pricing and availability information. Today's systems provide online (Internet) booking capability. GDSs and CROs now interact seamlessly, providing Internet users with extensive reservation capabilities.

cgi form. A form on a webpage that Internet users fill in and send to the owner of the Web site or some other designated recipient. Often, when you complete a guest book or a survey on the Internet, you are filling in a CGI form. CGI is an acronym for common gateway interface.

chat room. A Web site function that allows a group of people to type statements in such a way that all of the group can see all of the statements.

community site. A Web site featuring content that is primarily for or about a particular city (this term includes county, regional, and state sites). The term also refers to a Web site that is created and maintained by a community of users, or a group of formally linked Web sites on a common topic.

corporate identity site. A Web site whose purpose is to communicate with a company's employees and investors. A corporate identity site promotes the company's market position and philosophy and provides information about its history, size, leadership, dedications, and so forth.

customer relationship management (CRM). A type of marketing based on the goal of building long-term relationships with customers or clients. Web sites that support CRM goals capture data on visitors who make reservations, join clubs, register for newsletters, and so forth. The sites often provide features to communicate with visitors; engage them in "conversation"; demonstrate that they understand visitors' priorities, preferences, and needs; provide visitor-friendly ways to purchase items; and provide means for fast or real-time communication between customer service or marketing representatives and visitors.

dealership. Display of a graphic and link to an e-commerce site in return for a commission on items sold to visitors using that particular link. Sites with large inventories sold in a catalog format are the most frequent offerors of dealerships.

directory. A list similar to your familiar Yellow Pages®, with links and Web site information organized according to categories. General directories, like Yahoo!, are broad-based and include thousands of topics. Some directories focus on a specific topic and may be considered vertical portals or vortals.

domain name. The main part of an Internet address, including its extension. In the address http://www.disney.com/news/pocahontas.htm, for example, "disney.com" is the domain name. Until late 1999, domain names were limited to 26 characters; now they may include as many as 76 characters.

domain name extensions. Indicate the "top-level domain" (TLD) to which the name belongs. For example: .com indicates a commercial business; .net indicates a company that specializes in networks; .gov is used by government sites (local, state, or national); .org indicates an organization, usually nonprofit; .edu is used by educational institutions, school districts, and schools; .mil stands for military. Some extensions indicate the country where the site is based: .mx for Mexico or .ca for Canada. Early in 2000, .md was added for use by physicians, hospitals, and other medical-related entities. In 2001, more extensions were added, such as .biz, .pers, and .ent.

downloadable. Capable of being copied from a computer connected to the Internet to a user's computer.

e-book. Electronic books, downloadable from the Internet or available on disk, that can be read using various reading devices such as Adobe® Acrobat® eBook Reader™.

emoticon. Term coined for emotion icon; a small icon composed of punctuation and other characters, such as colons and parentheses. Emoticons are used to add information visually about a sentiment or tone of voice. For example, :-) is the usual symbol for a smiley face (look at it sideways). If the colon is changed to a semicolon, ;-), the emoticon is winking, indicating jest, humor, or "just kidding."

folder. An object in a graphical interface, such as Windows®, that can contain multiple documents or other types of files. Folders are useful for organizing or holding e-mail messages, graphics, scanned photographs, documents created with a word processing or other application, and so forth.

forward. To send an incoming e-mail message to another recipient or recipients.

.gif. A file extension indicating a type of compressed file for photos and other graphics used on the Internet. These files are more often used for graphics than photos. GIF stands for graphics interchange format.

global distribution system (GDS). Online communication system maintained by the airlines with up-to-date flight schedules, pricing, and seat availability. GDSs and CROs now interact seamlessly, providing Internet users with extensive reservation capabilities.

hidden text. Text written in the coding of an Internet page that does not display on the site. Common examples are the metatags with title, keywords, site description, and other information that some search engines read and store in their databases.

home page. The front or main page of a Web site. A home page often acts as a starting point and leads to other documents stored on the site. A page that precedes the main, navigation-oriented, traditional home page is often called a "splash" page.

host. To store a customer's Web site on a server, thus making the site available to everyone having Web access; a computer system that stores data, such as a Web site, that is accessed by a user or users from a remote location.

.htm. A file extension indicating a page prepared in hypertext markup language (html); one of the most common types of webpages.

html. Acronym for HyperText Markup Language, an authoring language used to create documents for viewing with an Internet browser.

interactive catalog. A database of items with a "front end" that allows visitors to search for an item and some means of online ordering.

interactive functions. Functions on a Web site that allow visitors to interact with the site; that is, visitors take some action (e.g., clicking on something), and the Web site performs some action in response. Usually, clicking to go to another page, although technically causing the Web site to do something, is not included in this definition because it is so common. Examples include adding items to shopping carts, using an online order form, participating in a chat room, and starting a video stream.

.jpg. A file extension indicating a type of file for photos and other graphics used on the Internet. JPG (pronounced jay-peg) files are usually used for photos, but sometimes are used for graphics. These files are compressed so that photos appear on the user's monitor more quickly. Photos compressed as .jpg files can be reduced to about 5 percent of their normal size, but some detail is lost in the compression. JPG stands for joint photographic experts group, for which the compression technique is named.

keywords. Words people enter into search engines to find information on the Web. Most search engines match the words being searched with webpages that have them. A typical consumer keyword search might be Manhattan, NY real estate. Keywords are also listed in the metatags (hidden text) of Web site pages for reading by search engines.

link. A connection between a location on a page and another location on the same or a different page on the

Internet. When a user clicks on a link with the mouse, the location connected to the link is displayed. Text links are often underlined and often blue. Graphics can also be linked. When the mouse is pointed at a link, the mouse pointer usually changes to a different shape depending on the user's mouse settings.

link exchange. Reciprocal linking between sites, usually without the exchange of any fee or other consideration.

listening back. The art of replying to an e-mail message only after being certain that you have understood and noted ("listened to") every point that the sender made, and then responding completely, point by point.

live chat or live customer service. A Web site function that allows a user to communicate with a customer service representative or other person by typing messages back and forth. Compare with "chat room."

mall. A Web site consisting of many individually owned sections or "store fronts" that sell products and services.

MAPI. Acronym for Messaging Application Programming Interface, a built-in Microsoft Windows® system that enables different e-mail applications (MAPI-enabled ones) to send and receive messages.

metatag. Coding with information about an Internet page or site. These tags explain what the page is about (Meta Title and Meta Description) and provide keywords (Meta Keywords) that should represent the page or site content and more. Many search engines use metatag information to determine the ranking of a site in displayed search results.

online reservations. Ability to make air, room, automobile, and other reservations via the Internet.

portal. A Web site that serves as a gateway to the Internet by providing a directory (or directories) of links, featured links, and a search engine (or engines) to help visitors find what they seek (or what the owner of the portal wishes them to find). Portals offer a very broad range of choices to help visitors locate just about anything imaginable on the Web.

position, positioning. A specific place held in the minds of the public or a specific audience (or "market segment") concerning a product or service. Positioning is similar in many ways to "reputation."

product or service information site. A Web site that provides information on the features and benefits of particular products or services but does not help visitors purchase those products or services.

real-time reservations. Online reservations that are requested and confirmed when the user interacts with the GDS or CRO on the Internet. (Some reservations are requested online, but the user must wait for confirmation via e-mail from the lodging or other facility. These are not "real-time.")

reply, reply all. To answer an incoming e-mail message. "Reply" sends the response only to the address of the originating message; "reply all" sends the response to the original writer and to everyone who received a copy (cc) of the original message.

robot. A program that runs automatically. Some webpages have hidden text telling robots what to do; for example, "return every 7 days" or "do not catalog this page." (See also spider.)

search engine. An Internet site, function, or program that maintains databases of Internet pages, the keywords, and URLs and retrieves the information according to keywords entered by users, displaying a list of Internet sites and pages. Examples include Excite, Infoseek, Google, and Webcrawler.

server. A computer or device on a network that manages that network's resources. Your Internet Service Provider (ISP) and all of the people who belong to it share the use of its servers. Basically, a server "serves" the e-mail and Web browsing needs of those who use it.

screen savers. Programs that display animated graphics on a computer's monitor when the computer is turned on but has not been used for a period of time. Screen savers are small programs that are easily downloaded.

shopping cart. A selecting and ordering mechanism on some sites that sell products and services. A shopping cart usually allows visitors to select items to "put in the shopping cart" or "basket" and later "check out" using a credit card or other payment mechanism.

signature. Generally, a statement and a selection of links or images that are automatically attached to the end of outgoing e-mail messages.

signature link. Text, graphics, and links added automatically to the end of outgoing e-mail messages.

spam. An Internet term for electronic junk mail or junk newsgroup postings. Unsolicited, advertising-oriented e-mail comprises most "e-junk" today.

spider. A program that automatically retrieves webpage information for use by search engines; a type of "robot."

sponsor. Site, individual, or company given highly visible credit for supporting a section of a Web site. For example, Goodyear Tires might sponsor a section in AOL called "Tires & Auto Accessories."

streaming media. Technology that transmits (streams) audio and video from a server to a user's computer. Streaming video is played on the user's computer as it is received from the server.

teleconferencing. Voice conferencing using an Internet connection and a microphone and speakers connected to users' computers instead of telephones

tile ad. Small, usually square ads that appear on Internet pages and usually link the visitor to the Web site of the advertiser.

transaction-oriented site. A Web site that provides some level of online purchasing capability so visitors can buy products or services, make reservations, and so on. Although these sites emphasize the selling of their products or services, they do not provide much visitor-friendly information and communication tools.

UMPS. Acronym for unique marketing positioning statement; a concise statement intended to express the characteristics that combine to make up your position.

URL. Acronym for uniform resource locator, the worldwide address of webpages, Web images, documents, and other Web resources. Each page and image or graphic on the Internet has its own URL.

URL registration. Reservation of a primary Internet site address (domain name). Internic, more recently called Network Solutions, is an entity officially authorized to regulate the assignment of domain names.

user-controlled   catalogs. Catalogs that allow users to custom design or select particular models, colors, pieces, and so forth to suit themselves.

videoconferencing. Similar to teleconferencing via the Internet but allows transmission of video as well. Videoconferencing can be used between two people or can connect several people in different locations at one time.

vortal. A "vertical portal." A Web site that serves as an Internet gateway to pages and sites related to a particular topic or interest.

Webcasting. Internet   broadcasting; transmission of live or prerecorded audio and video to users connected to the Internet.

Web fax, Internet fax. A Web site function that allows visitors to send a document from their computer to another person's fax machine.

webpage. A page of a Web site. Every webpage is identified by a unique address, called a URL (Uniform Resource Locator). Although a page is often considered to be 11 inches long, pages actually can be very long and take up many paper pages when printed.

Web site. An organized, related, interconnected group of webpages. Sites typically include a "home page," which is the first page seen by someone entering the site, and additional pages that are accessed from the home page or using internal links.

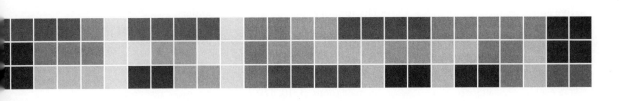

Index